ROUTLEDGE LIBRARY EDITIONS: GERMAN HISTORY

Volume 18

THE EPOCHS OF GERMAN HISTORY

THE EPOCHS OF GERMAN HISTORY

J. HALLER

NEW YORK AND LONDON

First published in 1930 by George Routledge and Sons, Ltd.

This edition first published in 2020
by Routledge
52 Vanderbilt Avenue, New York, NY 10017

and by Routledge
2 Park Square, Milton Park, Abingdon, Oxon OX14 4RN

Routledge is an imprint of the Taylor & Francis Group, an informa business

© 1930 J. Haller

All rights reserved. No part of this book may be reprinted or reproduced or utilised in any form or by any electronic, mechanical, or other means, now known or hereafter invented, including photocopying and recording, or in any information storage or retrieval system, without permission in writing from the publishers.

Trademark notice: Product or corporate names may be trademarks or registered trademarks, and are used only for identification and explanation without intent to infringe.

British Library Cataloguing in Publication Data
A catalogue record for this book is available from the British Library

ISBN: 978-0-367-02813-8 (Set)
ISBN: 978-0-429-27806-8 (Set) (ebk)
ISBN: 978-0-367-24366-1 (Volume 18) (hbk)
ISBN: 978-0-367-24371-5 (Volume 18) (pbk)
ISBN: 978-0-429-28207-2 (Volume 18) (ebk)

Publisher's Note
The publisher has gone to great lengths to ensure the quality of this reprint but points out that some imperfections in the original copies may be apparent.

Disclaimer
The publisher has made every effort to trace copyright holders and would welcome correspondence from those they have been unable to trace.

THE EPOCHS OF GERMAN HISTORY

By
J. HALLER

Ἔσσεται ἦμαρ

LONDON
GEORGE ROUTLEDGE & SONS, LTD.
BROADWAY HOUSE: 68-74 CARTER LANE, E.C.
1930

*Translated from the Second German Edition
(J. G. Cotta'sche Buchhandlung Nachfolger,
Stuttgart and Berlin,* 1928).

PRINTED IN GREAT BRITAIN BY THE DEVONSHIRE PRESS, TORQUAY

CONTENTS

CHAP.		PAGE
I	THE ORIGIN OF THE GERMAN REALM	1
II	THE EXTERNAL TASKS OF THE REALM	13
III	THE STRUGGLE WITH THE CHURCH, AND THE DISSOLUTION OF THE OLD EMPIRE.	29
IV	THE TERRITORIAL STATES	55
V	THE CONQUEST OF THE NORTH-EAST	76
VI	THE TERRITORIAL STATES IN THE FIFTEENTH CENTURY. THE RISE OF THE HABSBURGS.	91
VII	THE REFORMATION	106
VIII	THE THIRTY YEARS' WAR	127
IX	THE LOUIS XIV ERA	145
X	PRUSSIA IN TRIUMPH AND IN ECLIPSE	159
XI	THE GROWTH OF NATIONAL SELF-CONSCIOUSNESS.	183
XII	PRUSSIA'S SHARE IN THE STRUGGLE FOR UNITY	201
	INDEX	241

INTRODUCTION

To many I may seem to be embarking on a remarkable enterprise in proposing, as it might appear, to treat in this small volume of the whole of Germany's history—a subject which might well claim ten times as much space without any fear of excessive prolixity. But to attribute this intention to me would be to misunderstand me. I do not want to write on German history but to talk about its epochs.

What is meant by an epoch is, of course, a period in which some fresh beginning is made, some fresh determining element enters, some event occurs to give a new direction to the course of history. Events of this sort we describe as epoch-making or epochal. By an extension of the sense of the word the whole period dominated by the after-effects of such an event is called an epoch. Anyone who will keep in mind these senses of the word will know what I am aiming at. We are concerned with the critical moments of German history, the turning points in its course. Those are what we want to consider, and also to select as points of vantage from which we may survey the development of the German nation, viewing the panorama section by section.

A simile may help to illustrate my meaning. The course of history is never that of a straight line; it has no resemblance whatever to that of a canal or a railway line, but a great resemblance to the course of a river. As with a river, it is only exceptionally that historical development proceeds directly in the straight line of any path entered on. It proceeds by constant turns and windings, often in bizarre hooks and bends, and not infrequently the original direction is abandoned for a time or even for good and all. The turning points may be evident and conspicuous. In French history, for instance, everyone can see at a glance the significance of the year 1789, or of the entry on the scene of Richelieu; in English history the years 1066 and 1688 are landmarks visible from afar. But this is not necessarily the case; the epochs are not always so plain for all to see. The change may set in gradually, or the development be arrested, it may be concealed for awhile, may continue underground, just as a stream may be held up, may broaden to a lake or a marsh, perhaps ooze away altogether, to reappear at another spot. Thus, any historical survey which aims at a connected view of the whole process must first of all ascertain the critical turning points, must appreciate the moments when the new begins, the old is abandoned, the direction changes.

Every fresh turn has its causes. The river, too, does not abandon the straight lines out of caprice: following the law of its own gravitation, it seeks out the lowest spot. Often in doing so it has to get round an obstacle, sometimes it must pile itself up before it overcomes it; or the influx of a big tributary alters its form and adds to its force, so that it can carve its bed out of a spot that otherwise might have diverted its course.

I need not pursue the comparison further. Anyone who knows anything of history is well aware that the development of a nation is largely determined by outside influences. The emergence of a more powerful neighbour may drive it underground, like a rocky barrier or a ridge of sand; the disappearance of the rival may leave its path clear once more—to say nothing of the growth in power through conquest or annexation, or through the achievements of some great personality, which will give fresh zest and new directives to the ambitions and the efforts of a great nation.

There is bound, it seems to me, to be a peculiar fascination for all who have any historical sense, who feel, that is, the need and have the capacity to bury themselves in the past, in following in this way the course of the history of their own people, discovering the critical turning points and attaining a clear conception of the causes operating at each stage. But this pursuit not only has its fascination, it is a necessary and an indispensable one. In view of the mass of material—incidents and personalities—offered by past history, there is always a danger of failing to see the wood for the trees.

It is not enough to be acquainted with the facts, they have to be understood, their significance rightly gauged in relation to one another, their proportion to the whole story assessed. This is not so easy as it might seem. There are many who possess a rich store of knowledge, but an inspection of it shows something like an untidy drawer, for want of the needed general grasp and ordering of the accumulation. How often one may ask a well primed candidate, familiar with the history, for instance, of Frederick the Great, what was the point in German history at which dualism between Prussia and Austria had its origin, and receive no answer at all or only a hesitating and diffident one ! In this instance the question is a comparatively simple one. It is less to be wondered at if a ready answer is not forthcoming to the question when and how German particularism came into being. That, certainly, is not altogether an easy question to answer, and yet it has reference to a matter of the utmost importance, a peculiarity of the German nation which has seriously handicapped it from the outset in competition with its neighbours, like a racehorse with a heavy rider. And here is one more question, of equal importance, which I should not venture to put to any candidate, since it was put to me once by a fellow-professor of history who was himself unable to supply the answer: whence did the denominational cleavage in the German people originate ? That it dates from 1517 is a fact which everyone knows; but why did it come, what made it possible ? It cannot have been in the natural order of things, since the other European peoples have had no experience of it, or at all events nothing comparable with it in magnitude; in other countries it plays no part of the slightest significance, whereas right down to our own day it has absolutely dominated German history. How comes this ? English, French, Spaniards, all had their share of the religious struggles of the Reformation period, but they healed up the cleavage; the Germans were either unable or unwilling to do so. Why ? Here everyone is familiar with the epochal event, but very few seem to be acquainted with the reasons why it followed its unique course.

This brings us to a line of thought which I cannot leave unexpressed. Past and present are separable only in theory; in reality they are part and parcel of one another. Every conception of the past is lit and coloured by the present. After all we have been through since 1914, and in face of the fearful uncertainty of our future, no one can be blamed if he shrinks from thinking of Germany's past history. It has the appearance to-day of a succession of fruitless endeavours, doomed everlastingly to end in failure. We want consolation for the present, encouragement for the future; do we find it in searching the past? The dark pages in the book of Germany's history, which unhappily occupy the great bulk of the volume, have neither consolation nor encouragement to offer; many of us are driven to say, "We have always been as we are to-day, as if some curse had lain from the beginning on every generation." As for the glorious passages—thank God, these are by no means lacking—is it not precisely to those that that horribly true saying of Dante applies?

"There is no greater grief
Than grief that vanished happiness recalls."

It would not be surprising to find the view advanced that German history is something best not spoken of. Who among us has not been in the thrall of that mood?

But we must not give way to it, to the weakness of indulging it. It is certainly often painful, bitterly painful, to reflect on things that are no more. It is like probing in open wounds. But we must not shirk the pain if it leads to recovery, any more than the surgeon's probing must be shirked. Self-knowledge is the first duty for all, for peoples as for individuals. Our defective self-knowledge was our misfortune and our shortcoming in the recent past. It led us into enterprises which were, perhaps, not in themselves hopeless, but were bound to be beyond our strength at the time, as they would be beyond our present strength. This error needs above all to be avoided if there is to be a better future or indeed any future for us; and a future there must and shall be—to despair of it would be unmanly and unworthy so long as we have a spark of life in our bodies. The German people has been humiliated, but its life is not over unless it pronounces its own sentence of death. If it is now to count on new life, self-knowledge is, after such experiences and lessons, the most indispensable requirement. But how else can a people learn to know itself, save through its history? The nature of a man, his qualities, his line of conduct show themselves in his actions. So also the character of a people, its innate qualities and defects and the limits of its capacity are revealed in the course of its centuries of active life, of achievement and failure.

It may be objected that at a certain age a man's character is definitely formed, but a people's development never ceases; and that our own people especially has quite recently undergone such fundamental change that it would be a waste of time to occupy oneself with its past in order to acquire a knowledge of its present-day character; and that we must therefore abandon "the outworn track of history," ignore it, and make an entirely fresh start. This most modern of wisdoms has an imposing array of adherents. To set one's face against it is to run the risk of being set down as behind the times; it is a popular jibe against historians to dub them prophets with their eyes behind them.

I am not in the least afraid of this jibe; in my view it is quite superficial, not to say unthinking. As for popularity with the crowd, it is not, perhaps, especially nowadays, an unqualified recommendation, and certainly no guarantee of rightness. It is quite true that the historian—anyone who studies the past—resembles the backward-facing seer. But for that very reason he is wiser than the others, whose gaze is always fixed ahead, where, after all, the great majority can see nothing more than the offspring of their own fancy. The backward gazer sees reality, and it is precisely his penetration of the past that enables him to penetrate the future: he sees it in the mirror of the past. It is not to be read plainly and without effort, for the mirror is broken and incomplete. The way to read it has to be learnt, and not everyone can learn it. It is easy, too, to err in deciphering its message. But those who ignore the mirror of the past will never either comprehend the present or foresee the future.

For it is not true that peoples, unlike the individual, change their inmost nature from time to time, and that the Germans of to-day no longer have anything in common with those of a hundred, two hundred, a thousand years ago. Certainly in the course of the centuries many characteristics of a nation are effaced from its features and fresh ones graven in them; certainly radical changes in its environment may modify its character. But can they change the stuff of which it is made, render its experiences and lessons of no avail? Far from it!

And if the nature and character of a people undergo modification, is it not then above all that it becomes an imperative duty for anyone who has to do with the nation as it is to recognize these changes and trace them to their origin? If certain characteristics are not innate but have been acquired, have developed in the course of time, they may disappear again or be effaced, removed. Once the explanation of their origin is known it becomes possible to take the right measures for their maintenance or combating. It will be necessary also to distinguish the natural and perhaps ineffaceable from the acquired and therefore removable, and the causes of the latter. But what else is this but the study of history, its study in the way which we propose in this book—the search for the critical turning-points which have brought changes in the existence of the people and so in its character, so that it has become what it is?

Anyone who admits the rightness of this line of argument will be bound to admit the obligation to form for himself a clear and lucid picture of the history of his own people, in which past and present are organically bound up together and the intrinsic logic of the development of the present out of the past made plain; a picture which teaches us how we became what we are. This is a duty even for those who are content merely to be intelligent, thoughtful, comprehending observers of their own times; but still more for all those who respond to the call to collaborate in working for the future—and the call comes now to all of us, from the oldest to the youngest, and to the young perhaps more than to the old.

In this belief I have found the strength to overcome the intelligible alarm at the mass of material of which I spoke, and to undertake a course of lectures the purpose of which will be achieved if they teach us to see the face of the German nation—the national features of us all—in the mirror of the centuries, and so to create the national self-knowledge that is our first need if we are still to have a future. Self-knowledge should not make us clothe ourselves in sackcloth and ashes and give way in apathy and fatalism to despair of ourselves, because we are just what our history unhappily shows us. Self-knowledge should do the opposite: should lead us to cast off all illusions, to deceive and flatter ourselves in nothing, to open our eyes to our faults and relentlessly declare them, so as to battle with them, to extirpate them like noxious weeds, and in this way to make room for the grain of good qualities and capacities to spring up and thrive. We live still and shall continue to live. But life means development, and development means unfolding, increasing, growing. How we can once more grow aright, how we should develop, what we can become, and not least what we should become, we shall see the better the better we are acquainted with our past growth and development.

With regard to the matter dealt with, I think I owe an explanation. It might be suspected that I have allowed myself to be influenced in my view of Germany's past by the conditions of the present moment. That is not so. The picture which will be found here is the same picture, in all essentials, which I have sought to present to my audiences for more than fifteen years past. Only the conclusion—so much is true—used to have a different ring, since I shared the general confidence that the night had finally been dispelled and the future was ours.

We have had to revise our valuations, and some will think that this has destroyed the significance of Germany's history. May this book be privileged to serve not only by enabling the German people coolly to judge its own character, but by strengthening its faith and its determination that from the misery of the present there shall emerge a better future, and that a new generation with fresh energy will make German history once more significant. That is how I read the motto which I have placed under my title—Day will come!

J. H.

THE EPOCHS OF GERMAN HISTORY

CHAPTER I

THE ORIGIN OF THE GERMAN REALM

For how long has Germany had a history? The true answer is—as long as there have been Germans or a German people. But how far back does that carry us? Very few people seem to ask themselves the question. In most accounts of German origins one is brought up against a gross error. The writers begin German history with the so-called Völkerwanderung (racial migrations), and go more or less fully into the story of Goths, Vandals, Burgundians, and so on, without asking themselves what all this has to do with German history. So great even in science can the force of convention sometimes be, that the confusion of terms involved here goes entirely unnoticed: Germans and Germani (Teutons) are assumed to be one and the same. With what justification? The Scandinavian peoples unquestionably belong to the Teuton group, yet no one has dreamt of including in German history the history of the Scandinavian peoples. The English are also members of the Teuton group, whether they like it or not (and latterly they have not liked it at all, but that does not help them). To be honest one must even admit that the strongest of all representatives of Teutonism and those which have left the deepest mark in history are the English. Yet no one has yet dreamt of presenting English history or even that of the Anglo-Saxons as a section of German history. This is clearly illogical; if the Goths and the Lombards have a place in German history, why not the Danes and Anglo-Saxons?

The truth is that neither the one nor the other has any place in the story. Teutons and Germans are not the same. All Germans are Teutons but not all Teutons are

Germans. Among the Teuton peoples the Germans form a special group, and—an important point for us—not originally an assembled group. They were not associated together from the first; quite on the contrary, they only came together and grew into a community in the course of time. In a word, the German people is not a natural group but the product of an historic process.

Not a little effort has been expended on the attempt to determine the degree of relationship between the various Teuton peoples, in the hope of establishing that some of them stood in a closer natural relationship to one another than the rest; especially has it been sought to show that the races out of whose union the German people proceeded had formed a naturally connected group, a special family. These efforts can only be dismissed as completely unsuccessful. There may have been closer and more distant degrees of relationship between the various stocks of the Teutons, but it is quite impossible to maintain that there was any natural relationship between the later German races as they appear in historic times—we are not concerned with prehistory. A very simple observation may make this clear to all. Anyone who has had the opportunity to compare the people of Hanover, Hamburg, or Bremen, with English people is aware that they are closely akin to them, extraordinarily similar in many respects, almost indistinguishable. Even Englishmen will admit it. I doubt if the same degree of kinship could be discovered from observations of appearance and manner of speech between men of Hamburg and Upper Swabia or of Oldenburg and Upper Bavaria. We may therefore lay it down that the German stocks did not coalesce into the German people because they were naturally akin but because they were brought together by the circumstances of their existence, that is by history.

Everyone knows which are the German stocks: they are with us still, in the flesh and very plainly recognizable: Franks, Swabians, Bavarians, Thuringians, Saxons, Frisians. Their common destinies and deeds are the substance of German history. Consequently, German history can only be regarded as beginning with the union of the six races into a single whole. This occurred in a relatively late period, and not all at once. The union was the work of one race, the Frankish. Frankish kings brought the other peoples successively under their domination.

THE ORIGIN OF THE GERMAN REALM

Chlodwig and his sons conquered the Swabians—then still called Alemanni—the Thuringians, and the Bavarians in the first half of the sixth century. That was the first stage. In the seventh century there was actually a reversion to the earlier conditions, the subjected peoples regaining their independence. Not until the eighth century did the new Frankish dynasty succeed in completing the interrupted task. Charles Martel subdued the Swabians, Thuringians, and Frisians; Charlemagne the Bavarians (788), and finally, after thirty years of struggle, the Saxons. In 804 the process of unification was completed.

Even in the ninth century, however, it is too early to speak of German history. The German stocks were united under a single overlordship, and thus shared a common fate, but they did not yet form a separate unit, they were only parts of the Frankish world dominion, which embraced also Burgundians, Goths, Lombards, and especially very large numbers of Romans. German history can thus only begin from the time when the united German stocks freed themselves from the Frankish empire and formed a separate unit.

This again, as everyone knows, only happened gradually. The repeated partitioning of their territories which the Frankish kings carried out from 840 onwards gradually liberated one part after another, so that first one territory, then a second, and then a third broke away from the empire and began an independent existence. The death or deposition of a ruler would be followed by a break with the Carolingian dynasty and the adoption of a territorial lord as an independent ruler. The last of all to do this were the German tribes who in 911, after the death of Louis the Child, refused to bow to the West Frankish—one might say French—Carolingian monarchy, and made Duke Conrad their king. This finally snapped the long slackened bond which had until then united the German peoples to the Empire. Germany had become a separate realm. Conrad I. is thus the first of the German kings, and one may count the first epoch in German history as beginning with the year 911— the year, if one asks for a definite figure (a method which, indeed, is bound to have something superficial about it), of the coming into existence of the German state.

No one at the time had any clear realization of the event. It was for a long time the general belief that this new

German state was a Frankish state. For another century official language still spoke of a *regnum Francorum*, a kingdom of the Franks, and in constitutional theory this form was maintained right down to the twelfth and thirteenth centuries. At first the citizens of the new separate kingdom were entirely without a name for it. In the course of the ninth century men began to talk of a *regnum theutonicum*, referring to the eastern half of the kingdom. But this never became an official title, and, indeed, the word *theutonicum*, a pedantic refinement of *theotiscum*, the old German *thiutisk*, means no more than "indigenous," that is, non-Roman, the part of the kingdom which spoke the native tongue and not Latin. The name lasted a very long time, until the generally accepted name of the *Deutsches Reich* could be formed from it; this name, moreover, as not everyone realizes, only acquired official and constitutional validity in 1870. The old Reich, formed in 911 and dissolved in 1806, never bore this name, but later, of course, took the title of a Roman Empire.

For nearly two hundred years after it came into existence the young German empire was an unnamed realm—a fact that gives to think. Its citizens and contemporaries, the people of 911 to about 1100, had no word by which to describe the new kingdom, no word to apply in common to its six peoples. We shall return to this point shortly. But first we must guard against an error which might creep in.

It might be very tempting to assume that it was the difference of language and popular tradition which had broken up the Frankish empire, with its greatly diversified national structure. Germans on the one side, it might be assumed, Romans and French on the other, were unable to go on living together under a single roof. So the result might be supposed to have come, following present-day ideas. The common German character of the six branches of the race would then have shown itself at least negatively, in the rejection of what all alike regarded as alien, and some such influence as a quite primitive, not even actually realized racial or national feeling could be assumed to have been operative in the first emergence of the German Reich.

But it was not so. It is demonstrable that differences of race or "nationality"—if we choose to apply this modern word to this early period—played no part in the disintegration of the Frankish empire. This is shown by various considerations into which it is not necessary to enter here. Suffice it to point to the fact which is decisive in itself, that the frontier line between the eastern and western, the German and French territories of the Frankish empire entirely ignored all questions of the speech, race or nationality of the population. The boundary line adhered to was drawn in 843 in order to mark off the territories ruled by the sons of Louis the Pious: it ran more or less parallel to the Scheldt, Meuse, Argonne and Saône and brought Romance speaking peoples in Lotharingia and Burgundy into the German realm and the Frankish-speaking Flemings into the French. Still more unmistakable evidence is the fact that in 911, when the Germans seceded from the Carolingians, the population of the left bank of the Rhine, the so-called Lotharingia, did not join in the movement. These Lotharingians were largely Franks—Trier, Cologne, Aachen had, of course, long been Frankish capitals—and these Franks of the left bank, though they were at least as undeniably German as the Swabians and Bavarians, had not the slightest objection to association with the French under a common ruler They remained loyal to the hereditary line and only later joined the German kingdom, in 925, when the Carolingians were deposed and driven out of France also.

Here we have the most tangible proof that, so far as Germany is concerned, differences of nationality can have had no part in the break-up of the empire. Personal, dynastic considerations, enmities between ruling families, local vested interests of the dominant aristocracy, a growing tendency, after so long a succession of "partitions," to pay more attention to matters closer home and less to the general affairs of the state, or on the other side devotion to the royal house and loyalty to traditions with a long past—these were the real influences at work in the final separation between east and west and the forming of a German realm.

We seem, therefore, to arrive at the very paradoxical fact—which, for all that, is not in the least startling to those who can see with the historic eye and do not carry modern preconceptions into the past—that the German Reich was brought into existence mainly through external influences, almost one might say chance events, as an incidental product of the conquests and partitions of the Frankish Empire. The German races were brought together by no inner necessity, no want felt by themselves, but by the external pressure of conquest and subjection. And they were equally free from any impulse to break away from their association with aliens. Here again the determining elements were external—it was the hereditary system of the royal house, which tended to partition, and the weakness of its representatives that loosened the bonds of union and finally snapped them.

Nor was there yet any impulse towards close association ; far from it—the facts speak plainly in the opposite sense. Scarcely had the German Reich come into existence when it was on the point of dissolving into its component parts, its racial groups.

We must picture the races as very different in speech, customs, and character. The differences remain to this day very considerable ; and they will certainly not have been less originally—apart from speech, for the dialectical differences have increased with the passage of time. In customs and character the races of old even had their thoroughly realized and recognized peculiarities : each of them had its own law, differing sometimes markedly from the laws of the others. Account was also taken where needed of differences in other respects : in the king's army they fought in separate groups, Saxons, Franks, and so on The territories of the various races were themselves actually described as kingdoms, *regna.*

Under the later Carolingians these racial " kingdoms " grew fast in independence and importance. Certain great lords, helped by various external circumstances, came to their head, strong and respected leaders who took the title of Duke, a title implying nothing less than full vice-royalty. The dukes of Bavaria, Swabia, Saxony—the Saxon had brought the Thuringian under his dominion—stood over against the real king as kings uncrowned. They claimed unrestricted authority in ruling their own stock, they conducted their own foreign policy, and the proudest of them, the Bavarian, even called himself duke " by the grace of God," which was nothing less than a claim to sovereignty.

The test had to come which would show which of the two, duke or king, would in the long run be the stronger. Conrad I. failed to establish his authority. All his efforts came to nought, although he enjoyed the support of the Church. King and bishops united were not strong enough to break the independence of the dukes. At Conrad's death (918) it looked as if the realm were already in dissolution. His successor, Henry I, formerly Duke of Saxony, was elevated to the throne by Saxony and Franconia alone. Only gradually did he gain recognition in Swabia and Bavaria, and even then only by capitulating before his rivals. He allowed the authority of the dukes to continue undiminished, thus abandoning all claim to the direct exercise of sovereign rule and contenting himself with simple overlordship, temporal and spiritual. Thus he was king in reality only in north Germany, and no more than a sort of titular king in the south. Only the big successes which he won abroad added something to his power in the course of time, through his increased prestige, and enabled him to leave to his son, Otto I, who succeeded him in 936, the inheritance of a recognition of his supremacy throughout the realm as a settled fact challenged by no one.

But the racial dukedoms were still there, as strong as ever. It was out of the question for Otto I to think of attempting to remove the dukes, even when they openly rose against him. He contented himself with making use of them by bringing them into close relationship with the royal house. Through an adroit policy of royal marriages he procured the dukedom of Bavaria for his brother, of Swabia for his son, and of Lotharingia for his son-in-law. Even this did not serve him : his son and son-in-law rose against him in 953-4 and were within very little of deposing him. Even after this experience the king made no attempt to suppress the dangerous institution of vice-royalty in the various parts of the realm. He has often been blamed for this, but one can scarcely say with justice. If a German king, even in the hour of victory, contented himself with the removal of the guilty duke and allowed the dukedom to continue, one must probably attribute his action to the pressure of necessity. It must have been impossible to rule the Germany of that period without the dukes, or Otto I would have been only too glad to do so.

This leads us to an observation of wide application : the sense of close solidarity, the sense of the state or the nation, was absent or existed only in embryo. The tribes were older than the nation, the dukedom and the duke more firmly established than the realm and the king. The former were the primordial element, the latter the new element which had still to be incorporated. German history begins under the aegis of particularism.

It was a different sort of particularism from to-day's; it was based entirely on racial individuality, whereas present-day particularism has little to do with racial feeling and much more to do with regional dynastic traditions. But both have the common element of the exaltation of the particular at the expense of the general. Here we have to deal with a fundamental trait in the nature of the German people, which has to be reckoned with whether one likes it or not.

Beyond question the kingdom could neither have come into being nor continued in being under such circumstances had not a factor been present which worked against the particularism of the tribal dukes. This was the Church.

The Church in the earliest German nation was a state church, as it had been in the Frankish Empire. It was used to serving the king with its own forces, placing itself at the head of them even if it was not absolute master of them. It felt itself to be in alliance with the ruler, and found this association in harmony with its interests: it enabled it to exercise mastery over the people while serving the king. It stood, therefore, everywhere in opposition to the transition to a tribal state and to subordination to a duke. Bishops and abbots were determined to be the king's bishops, national bishops, abbots of the realm, and to allow no one to intervene between themselves and the supreme authority. Their position, their rank, their influence, their independence would have suffered by the change, and they would also certainly have suffered material loss. For large parts of their property lay outside the racial areas, since the piety of founders was unconfined within the racial boundaries. Thus bishops and abbots were the natural representatives of the idea of the realm and of unification.

They were thoroughly imbued with political ways of thinking, for such education as existed was mainly to be found in their ranks. They were able to apprehend the idea of the state and to be guided by it in their policy. Thus everything, interests and ideals alike, tended to bring them over to the king's side in the struggle between kingdom and dukedom; and, conversely, the king had to rely on their support if he was to win through at all. All that the king could expect from the layman was loyalty

THE ORIGIN OF THE GERMAN REALM

to his person ; from the prelates he could count on more—on a belief in the idea of the realm. He was able especially to rely on them since he had the opportunity of choosing them individually for their qualities, their ability, their known views, and their character. Secular titles and offices were more or less hereditary ; a bishop's see or a great abbey was in the king's gift whenever it fell vacant, the chosen successor received his office from the king's own hands, and often there was not even an election, but a direct appointment by the king. Thus there was the most natural of ties between throne and altar in the old German state.

The tie stood the test of time. The first big success achieved by Otto I was in the wresting from the dukes, in the first years of his rule, of the disposal of all the churches of the realm, and securing it in his own hands. From that time onward the church was the main support of the kingdom. It was the bishops who formed the most effective counterweight to the particularism of the ducal powers. In 953 the dukes conspired to overthrow Otto ; the bishops ranged themselves almost without exception on the king's side, and it was they whom he had to thank for his preservation. The bond was finally riveted by this event ; the bishops became once for all the adherents of the realm.

The Church brought to the service of king and country the great possessions in its hands, possessions which the kings themselves lavishly increased, and the intellectual supremacy of its leaders. Bishops and abbots were the permanent advisers of the ruler, were his ministers and diplomats, at times his leading statesmen ; bishops formed and maintained the traditional policy of the realm ; bishops and prelates administered and organized the forces of the crown, and frequently even led the king's armies in the field. The church was the backbone which held the realm upright, the bond which maintained its unity. Without the church it would have fallen asunder and separated into the natural multiplicity of its parts in the moment of its formation.

The significance of the church in the old German state becomes very clear if we consider the elements of the king's power. The old German king was constitutionally anything but an absolute ruler. He was the supreme judge and army leader ; apart from this, however, in all that we define as policy, he was subject to the consent of his nobles, that is the aristocracy. In war and peace he could only negotiate "with the advice and consent of the nobles." He must be regarded much less as sole ruler than as leader and representative of the ruling aristocracy. All the more importance attaches, therefore, to the question what material force the king could throw into the scale of the deliberations when he intended to impose his will. All power in the state lies in the last resort in the voluntary obedience of its subjects and in the possibility of using force against the refractory, that is of the resort to arms. The importance of the church in relation to voluntary obedience needs no emphasizing. It ruled men's minds a hundred times more securely and exclusively than in the most priest-ridden country of our own day. Even in the sphere of armed resources its services to the king were scarcely less.

To form a picture of the character of the armed forces of the state it is necessary to clear one's mind of all familiar conceptions. In no other point is the olden time more sharply differentiated from the present. There was not a vestige of general liability to military service. All that existed was a sort of territorial reserve for the protection of the homeland, with no particular practical significance as a defence force even along the frontiers. This national reserve was never called up against external enemies. It was only called into action for internal protection, against robber bands and occasionally in civil war.

Fighting was from the beginning, in the old German state, the life's calling of a particular caste—the knights. This system, like so much else, was an inheritance from the Frankish state, in which the body of knights, composed of the king's vassals and his nobles, formed the nucleus and the principal arm of his forces. The great achievement of the first Saxon kings, Henry I and Otto I, was the building up of this king's army of professional soldiers—the knights —on an increased scale on the Frankish model. It was by this means that Henry I added to his prestige in the course of his reign, and that Otto I became master of the whole realm and the first lord of the west of Europe. The king had at call in every part of his kingdom a large body of mailed horsemen, furnished with landed property— knight's estates (*Rittergüter*) as they are still called in Germany—and trained to arms from their youth up, from

THE ORIGIN OF THE GERMAN REALM

father to son and from generation to generation; a class who regarded combat and warfare as their profession and were ready at any moment to hasten to the fray when the king summoned them and pay and booty beckoned.

The landed resources for the maintenance of this hereditary soldiery came from the very extensive domains, the so-called king's domains (*Königsgut*), which comprised the properties of the royal house, including lands inherited from earlier royal lines and all the territory acquired in war and peace from the realm and for the realm by conquest, confiscation, and reversion—an enormous mass of arable and forest land, the yield of which met the national expenditure, part of it going to maintain the knights in the active service of the king.

The burden of the support of these armed forces did not fall entirely on the king's shoulders; a substantial part of it was met by the nobles. They too were under the obligation to maintain knightly vassals, and to place them when required at the service of the king. Pride of place among the nobles belonged to the prelates, the ecclesiastical princes, bishops and abbots. They were enabled to take the lead by their enormous wealth. In the period of German conversion to Christianity, the time of Boniface and Charlemagne, and the succeeding century, all classes, high and low, had competed in endowing church and monastery with lands and servants. This pious zeal had since abated considerably, but the treasures of the church had gone on increasing, especially through the liberality of the kings. The possessions especially of some of the bigger abbeys, such as Lorsch, Fulda, Hersfeld, Reichenau, Weissenburg and St. Gallen, were almost beyond count. They had immensely more than they could make use of; for the monks were few and their rule of life required holiness, that is simplicity of life, with few wants. The superfluous possessions were appropriated by the king, as lord and warden of the abbey, for the service of the realm; he settled knights on bishops' and abbots' lands. Bishopric and abbey were, in modern parlance, the principal contributors to the army budget.

A fortunate accident has preserved for us a few figures which shed light on all this. We have the table of a call to arms issued in 982 by the Emperor Otto II to the Franks, Swabians, and Bavarians for war in Lower Italy against the Moors. The table shows that the bishops and abbots supplied more than twice as many men in armour as all the secular lords together. The biggest of the lay lords, the " Duke " of Alsace—Alsace was for a time a separate duchy in the Swabian line—came at the head of seventy men; the bishops of Mainz, Cologne, Strassburg and Augsburg led 100 men each. And so everywhere. The next biggest lay contingents after the Alsatian were contingents of 40 and 30, whereas Reichenau and Fulda sent 60 knights each, Lorsch and Weissenburg 50 each.

If one considers the moral and material resources which the church brought to the service of the crown, it is not too much to say that the power of the crown rested on the church, and the crown lands and the church were the two pillars of the king's power.

CHAPTER II

THE EXTERNAL TASKS OF THE REALM

WHEN first a German king succeeded in gaining the mastery over the whole country, with the support of the church, the power which he held in his hands was, for those days, enormous. Nowhere beyond the frontiers was there a realm which could have measured swords with the German realm. In the west the Frankish kingdom had sunk into impotence; in the south, in Italy, the divisions which the dissolution of the Frankish Empire had left behind it were not yet overcome. Germany was then, in modern parlance, the only Great Power in the west, and what were its tasks?

People often unconsciously or half consciously assume that states, empires, kings, are able to pick and choose their tasks, and that the policy of a country is an emanation of its ruler's will. There can be no greater error. A temporary divergence may occasionally be observed, always in the very limited sense of an existing possibility having been over-estimated owing to the ruler's personal inclination or a demand having been regarded as more urgent than it was in fact. In general the tasks of every state are imposed on it from without, and its ruler can have no other function than to recognize them and rightly to assess their relative urgency. The tasks of a country are set by geography, by its situation and physical character. On the situation and physical character of a country depend the needs it may have in regard to defence and the prospects it may have of growth. Thus the constant fact which has principally determined political history in all ages is geography.

Germany's history was from the beginning determined by her geographical situation. Her situation involved a problem which has faced her from her first days through all the centuries to the present time and must be visible to-day to the blindest, the problem of the double front. And battle along two fronts has been the constantly recurring theme of German history. This is due to Germany's situation between great neighbouring peoples that differ from her in character, and from whom she is separated only by weak natural lines of demarcation or by none at all.

This element showed itself at the very outset in the old German state, and resulted at once in simultaneous fighting on east and west. In the west Germany had at her first beginning in 911 an apparently admirable frontier: it reached to the Rhine and the Vosges. The territory on the left bank of the Rhine, the former Kingdom of Lotharingia, then reduced to a duchy (it comprised the modern Lorraine, Palatinate, Rhine Province, Holland, and Belgium up to the Scheldt), had not joined in the secession from the Carolingian kings, and had accordingly become "French." Had it remained so, Germany would have purchased a militarily good frontier with a sacrifice in another respect which would have been equivalent to a permanent mutilation. Not only did this country contain a considerable section of the German people, but its territories were among the most thickly populated, the best tilled, the richest and the most civilized lands north of the Alps, greatly in advance of the rest of the German Empire. It must always be borne in mind that the greater part of the territory then included in the Empire was of only recent civilization. For all the lands outside the boundaries of the old Roman Empire—including broadly the German lands on the right bank of the Rhine southwards to the Neckar and Danube—the start along the road to civilization came only under Charlemagne; for the territories which formerly were Roman it came under Augustus. That is a distance of 800 years, as long as from our own day back to the first Crusade. The significance of this must not be underestimated. Besides this, the formerly Roman territories on the right bank of the Rhine —Baden, Württemberg, old Bavaria—were abandoned by the Romans earlier and were more profoundly affected by the Teuton invasion, while on the left bank civilization did not suffer anything like an entire eclipse.

For these reasons if for no others the renunciation of Lotharingia would have been for the German Empire a sort of suicide, a voluntary acceptance of insignificance. Conrad I nevertheless made the renunciation—a proof of his weakness: he was not in a position to establish himself

THE EXTERNAL TASKS OF THE REALM 15

as sovereign in Lotharingia. Henry I seized an opportunity of reversing his policy. In 923 the Carolingians were temporarily dispossessed in the west, and the Lotharingians seceded from France. Henry made rapid and shrewd use of the occasion, and obtained recognition as their sovereign. Lotharingia was thus won for the German Empire, the frontiers of which were pushed to the Scheldt, the Meuse, and the Argonne; the principal nucleus of the Frankish Empire was united with Germany, and Aachen, Charlemagne's capital, became the titular capital of the German Empire—for an actual capital could not exist in the conditions of those times, when the whole country was mainly of a rural character.

The new possession had to be defended, for France had no intention of voluntarily renouncing it. She made three efforts in the tenth century, and at least one in the eleventh, to recover Lorraine, in other words to get back the Rhine frontier. All these attempts failed owing to her impotence, a condition in which the German kings took care to keep her. It is not as well known as it should be how Otto I succeeded in playing off against one another the French king and the Pretender and leader of the nobles, both of them his brothers-in-law, so that neither party had any definite ascendancy over the other and the German king maintained an ascendancy over both. Otto's successors did much the same after him, and France continued to offer no menace to Germany.

The task in the east was not so simple. Here there were at first redoubtable enemies in the Hungarians. They had been settled since the last years of the ninth century in the land which still bears their name and in Lower Austria. Thence they overran the country to the west, robbing, pillaging, destroying, and carrying off the inhabitants. Conrad I went under in battle with them. Henry I succeeded in protecting North Germany if no more. The great victory which first brought him fame was won over the Hungarians, who until then had been unconquerable, in 933. But that was purely defensive warfare, and a troublesome and always precarious defensive. The plague in the land was only finally overcome when the Hungarians, who had returned to the attack, were decimated near Augsburg by Otto I in 955. It was now possible to enter on a counter-offensive, and to drive the hated interlopers out of the former Bavarian lands in Lower Austria. The victory at arms was followed by a stream of German settlement from Bavaria. German colonization of the southern portion of the Eastern Marches (Ostmark) was pushed as far as the Leitha, and beyond it: German Austria was born.

The other eastern neighbours were the Slavs, or, as they were then called, the Wends, in the lands beyond the Elbe, the Saale, and the Bohemian forest. They presented less difficulty: they were without political organization and were not militarily dangerous—a collection of small peoples, weak alike in war and peace. Henry I had subjugated their northerly members, along the Elbe and Havel. His conquests were lost again in 983, when the Wends united in a rising against German rule; only the country between the Saale and the Elbe was held, with the country of Bohemia, the duke of which (later king) had owned allegiance since 929 to the German king and in the course of time had become the foremost among the lay princes of the German Empire. No one who knows the significance of the situation of Bohemia—Bismarck called it the citadel of Europe—will fail to realize the importance of the retention of that country. It formed the principal fortress along the eastern frontier of the Empire. The fortress showed its value during the generation after the year 1000, when the short-lived Greater Polish State arose under Boleslav the Brave and began to grow at the expense of Germany. Henry II and Conrad II made great efforts to ward off this peril. They had little success until in 1031, after Boleslav's death, the disunion among his heirs and the support of the Grand Duke of Kiev enabled the Greater Polish State to be destroyed and an end made for two and a half centuries of the Kingdom of Poland.

In this way, through the weakness of her neighbours, were Germany's natural tasks accomplished in west and east, and her frontiers secured. The German people seemed to have the choice before it, if it desired to grow and spread through conquest, of taking either the westward or the eastward direction or both at once. It did neither. Colonization and conquest in the south-east had come to an end at an early date along the borders of the country actually inhabited by Magyars. There was never any thought of conquering Poland. In both cases a more or less nominal recognition of German overlordship was accepted. Nor was any attempt made after the secession of the Wends in 983 to repeat the advance to the Baltic which Henry I had made in Brandenburg and Mecklenburg. It was considered sufficient if the neighbours were kept under control, if they respected the frontiers and paid tribute. More than this was not attempted. Nor was there as yet any idea of attempts at annexation in the west. Attention was fixed instead, from the middle of the tenth century, on the south. It was towards Italy that German foreign policy looked in pursuit of Germany's growth of power, of her expansion.

We are brought now to a new epoch: The rise of the German imperial power. This fills the whole of the earlier history of Germany, and is the dominating feature of three centuries; later, when in reality it had long disappeared, its memory still worked powerfully and even increasingly. This element therefore needs to be thoroughly probed, clearly visualized, and its causes recognized, in order properly to understand old German history and the forefathers of the Germans of to-day.

The first attempt to subjugate Upper Italy was made in 951. Otto I, called in by the Langobard opposition against the king, Berengar II, crossed the Alps, overcame the adversary, and compelled him to recognize German overlordship. Otto assured himself free access to the country: Berengar was made to cede the Alpine passes and the whole of the country east of the Etsch (Adige), and this territory was added to Bavaria.

These acquisitions were lost as a result of the rising of the dukes in Germany in 953-4 and the war with Hungary in 955. Berengar recovered his independence and regained the ceded territory; at the same time he endeavoured to extend his realm southwards at the expense of the Papal State, and even, it might be, conquer Rome. The Pope called Otto to his side, and in 961 Otto launched the second Italian war. This quickly ended in the conquest of the whole kingdom of Langobardia. Berengar ended his days in German captivity, and Otto himself assumed the title of King of Langobardia. In January, 962, he was crowned Emperor in Rome: which meant that he assumed sovereignty in Rome and in the Papal territory.

The years that followed were filled with fighting and negotiating with the Emperor of Constantinople in order to make secure the newly acquired possessions. In the end Constantinople found it convenient to recognize the new

C

Empire in Rome, and also accepted the fact of the German overlordship over the Langobardian duchies of Lower Italy, Benevento, Capua, and Salerno; in consideration of which Otto refrained from annexing the coastal towns which had remained Greek.

This fixed the constitutional boundaries of the Empire for a long time. Only once subsequently does Otto II seem to have tried to extend Germany's influence over the whole of Lower Italy. This was in fighting the Arabs who were pushing north from Sicily. The attempt, if it was seriously made, which is by no means certain, brought defeat in 982 to the German army and ended in the following year with the death of the young Emperor.

German rule was maintained in Langobardia without difficulty. Only once, after the death of Otto III (1002), was the attempt ventured on to recover independence from Germany. At least a part of the country recognized a Langobard noble, Hartwin of Ivrea, as its king for twelve years. The remainder continued to be loyal to its German rulers, and on Hartwin's death Emperor Henry II was recognized throughout the country. After Henry's death in 1024 the effort for emancipation wilted in the bud, no one being prepared to accept the crown of a free Lombardy. It was offered to French nobles, but they declined the more than precarious honour. From then on Lombardy was definitely united with Germany, no one dreaming of dissolving the tie.

In Lombardy as in Germany the main support of the German rule came from the church. The bishops in Lombardy were natural partisans of the king, as it was through him alone that they could enjoy direct dependence on the imperial authority and so guarantee their own power against the secular dynasties, who were struggling in Italy for dominion over the churches as the dukes had done in Germany. It was thus the bishops who took the part of Henry II against Hartwin and helped Henry to victory. Thereafter it gradually became the settled practice of the German emperors to use every opportunity to fill vacant sees with German bishops. By the middle of the eleventh century the majority of the bishops in the eastern half of Upper Italy were Germans, installed by the king in order to advance German interests in Italy.

Rome presented a more difficult problem. Even Otto I had to cope with risings and secessions. He was compelled to depose the Pope who had called for his aid, and a second secession made a number of executions necessary. Similar trouble came frequently in subsequent years, and during the childhood of Otto III and after his death in 1002 the German imperial rule was actually set aside more than once for years at a time. It was always restored in the end, and from the time of Conrad II (1027) onwards the German king was regarded as unquestioned King of Lombardy and Emperor of the Romans. Rome, Italy, and Germany formed a solidly unified realm, and the king elected in Germany was also ruler of the whole realm, which came to be called a Roman Empire. This conception of the German Empire as a Roman Empire and of Rome as its capital first won general adhesion in the twelfth century, but it existed as early as 1040, when we find the German king, although not yet invested with the imperial crown in Rome, already given the title of a Roman king, *rex Romanorum*, even in official parlance. The German Empire and the German kings had thus at last found their title of Roman Empire and Emperors.

It is doubtful whether it would have been possible for Italy to be permanently held without the annexation of another formally independent kingdom, that of Burgundy. This kingdom comprised the present west of Switzerland (west of the Aare), Franche-Comté, Savoy, Dauphiné, and Provence. It was conquered by Conrad II in 1034 after the Burgundian dynasty had died out. This new domain scarcely brought actual increase of power; its value lay in the increased ease of communication between Germany and Italy which it brought. Until then it had only been possible to use the Brenner and Septimer passes, the latter of which was of little use for military purposes, so that Verona formed the only convenient means of access, and a road very easy to block. There were now in addition to this the excellent roads over the Great St. Bernard, Mont Cenis, and Mont Genèvre (there is no evidence of the Gotthard pass being used before the thirteenth century), so that in the event of war it was now possible to advance simultaneously at two points, in the Veronese and the Milanese. And it cannot have meant little if in peace time communications between Germany and Italy could take five or four routes without hindrance instead of only two.

There must have been Italian interest too in the new

condition; why else should the Italian bishops have assisted in the conquest of Burgundy? Led by the Archbishops of Ravenna and Milan, they invaded the country from the south, while the Germans under Emperor Conrad marched in from the north, from Basle. It was like the cutting of a tunnel: a simultaneous boring from the two ends. This new tunnel between Germany and Italy came into operation at once. The classic period of German rule in Italy begins with Conrad II, and its full prosperity came under his son and successor Henry III.

Such is the aspect of the old German Empire if it is regarded from the point of view of the practical purpose of its formation: the Empire regarded pragmatically. The picture may cause surprise and disillusionment: another picture is more familiar. The Empire of the Ottos, the Salians and the Staufen is usually presented by historians in very different guise. They write of a world dominion with a religious, ecclesiastical nimbus, a " Holy " Roman Empire of the German nation which is imagined as aiming at a renewal, consecrated by the church, of the old Roman *imperium orbis universi*. They talk of the incessant endeavour of the German rulers to acquire the highest dignity of Christendom, with the blessing of the church, a dignity connoting pre-eminence over all other kings and therewith a title to dominion over all the countries of the earth. In a word, a sort of secular theocracy, the practical purpose of which it must be confessed would not be easy to discover. For the German emperors in actual fact never exercised any sort of dominion over the neighbouring states; in this respect their quality of Emperor remained a title and nothing more.

This would be something very strange in modern eyes. Had this been the real idea inspiring the imperial policy it would have to be admitted that the old rulers of Germany let their external policy be guided by motives which could scarcely be regarded as political. The admission would be a very severe condemnation of their activities; for a policy directed from non-political points of view is a bad policy under all circumstances. Such a policy was at times attempted, but never with success or advantage.

There has been no lack of condemnation of the old German emperors on such grounds. Distinguished historians have allowed themselves to suppose that the continual effort of the German kings to conquer Italy was a mistake which revenged itself bitterly on the German people. Blinded by the mystical splendour of the imperial crown, the German kings, these writers suppose, neglected the more modest but more immediate and therefore more important task of the steady consolidation of their power in Germany, either by getting rid of the tribal dukes or by extending the frontiers of the realm and colonizing the east, which might have led to the unification of the nation in a single state at that early period. These critics are able, to all appearances, to appeal to the judgment of history. The imperial policy came to grief in the end, and, as Heinrich von Sybel, the most brilliant and important representative of this view, puts it, the nation had to pay for the dream of a theocratic world Empire which its rulers dreamed by centuries of impotence and disunity.

Such is the current popular judgment, and if I am not mistaken is the judgment usual even in scientific treatises. The majority of students are inclined to-day to regard the Italian policy of the German kings as a misguided one. inasmuch as it lacked a definite goal offering lasting benefits, and was after all one which the Empire had not the strength to pursue to final success.

I do not think that this view does justice to the men or the circumstances or the time. To begin with, I do not find myself able to suppose that whole generations in a past age were politically blinded or out of their senses For that is what it amounts to : not merely that a single ruler, say Otto I, made a mistake, but that all of his successors followed in it. In the long line of German kings from Otto I to Otto IV, lasting two and a half centuries, there was not one who did not want to be Emperor. For all of them without exception the imperial crown was the goal of their endeavours. The German realm was, moreover, as we know, not by any means an absolute monarchy ; its policy was guided by the princes, and no king would have been in a position to embark on military enterprises against the will of the nation. It is thus impossible to suppose that a policy maintained through two hundred and fifty years had not the support of the nation. If it was a mistake, then eight generations of Germans were politically senseless. It is true that we are familiar nowadays with the notion that whole peoples—not only the German people—may temporarily be victims of political insanity. But that the trouble should have lasted 250 years is difficult to believe

Moreover, the period which we are considering was not one in which the politically ignorant and therefore easily infected mass of the people determined policy, as they do to-day. In the early middle ages the masses were entirely without influence. Policy was determined by the princes, a small group of persons who may fairly be described as true statesmen (one must especially have the bishops in mind in this connexion), men at home in political affairs, pursuing them with knowledge and after reflection, men alive to realities, men with accumulated experience and a developed political tradition. Before condemning such men, the wisest heads in the nation during two and a half centuries, as one and all unintelligent or misguided, it is certainly necessary to search for the motives which may have inspired the German Empire, in extending its power, not to look eastwards or westwards, where the way lay open, but to look southwards, where to all appearance the frontier was outlined as sharply as could be by the national contrasts of German and Latin, and by a great geographical obstacle, the high Alps.

There is more reason for considering the question of motives since it has strangely been neglected hitherto. Instead of searching for the motives they have been assumed to be known. One school sees no further motive than the mystical splendour of the imperial crown; the other sees also the old and incurable longing of the Germans for the land *wo die Zitronen blühen*, the call of the southern sun. A closer examination shows that both suppositions are mistaken.

The romantic longing for the land of the sun was something very far from the minds of the Germans of the tenth and eleventh centuries. Where they had occasion to speak of the subject at all they show a plain aversion alike to land and people. Italy and the " Welsch " are distasteful to them; the climate murderous, the people false and faithless. In the whole of this period very few attempts indeed were made at settlement in Italy, apart from the bishops sent thither by Emperor Otto III, son of a Greek princess, who regarded himself as Greek and Roman and despised his German blood. Otto made Rome his capital and home, but that lost him the love of the Germans. The imperial policy had no trace of the romantic feeling for Italy of the modern tourist.

Nor is there any more substance in the myth of an

ecclesiastical romanticism, of the lure of the world Empire. The contemporaries of Otto I, the founder of this line of emperors, show no trace of it, and there is no vestige of it to be found in the succeeding 200 years, again with the exception of Otto III, that entirely un-German ruler. Otto III. liked to pose as the ruler of a Roman world Empire, and wanted to command church and country as servant of Christ and His apostles. But it was for this very reason that the Germans turned away from him ; had he lived longer he would scarcely have kept his German throne.

This imagined " Holy " Roman Empire, supposedly dating from Otto I, is in reality a figment of much later imaginations, a theory which only gained acceptance when the Empire no longer had any real existence. At the birth of the Empire there is not the slightest trace to be found of religious or ecclesiastical romanticism. The matter was one of the plainest practical common sense, a question of power and nothing more. We must try to comprehend it in that light.

Certainly the ecclesiastical point of view must not be left out of account entirely. For a king like the German, mainly relying on the support of the church, it was obviously essential that his foreign policy should be in harmony with the interests of the church. Beyond any question it was so. It is easy to realize, moreover, that the protection of the Roman Church, which had always been a function of the emperors, added not a little to the prestige of the German ruler. That would be entirely in accord psychologically with the fashion of the time, just as when Governments in our day seek to make capital by figuring, with less sincerity, as protagonists of world peace and of the League of Nations.

One may go further and suppose that the German king, whose dominion rested on domination of the German church, had an interest in commanding also in Rome, the see of the spiritual overlord of the German bishops. This consideration too may have played its part.

Above all, however, the German imperial system in the tenth century was true to tradition. It was less than a hundred years since the Frankish Empire had fallen ; its memory still lived in men's minds—the memory of how the West had formed a single unit under the sceptre of a Frankish king and Emperor, in the good old times behind which the mighty figure of Charlemagne loomed up in increasing splendour and glory as time carried it into the distance. The separate kingdoms which had been instituted on the territory of the old Frankish Empire still seemed to men to form parts of a whole, and the closely-knit organization of the Roman Catholic Church worked to keep this conception alive. Otto I, too, unquestionably the mightiest of all, was a Frankish king : he had exercised controlling influence beyond his own borders, in France, in Burgundy, in Lombardy. Was it not entirely natural to want to see restored to life in his realm and his person the greatest and finest memories in the minds of the men of that day ? It must not be forgotten that Otto was offered supremacy both in the Lombard kingdom and in Rome. How could he have declined either without reducing his own stature ?

Let us picture the results which would have followed if Otto I had done as his modern critics think he should have done, and declined the dominance offered him in Italy. An Italian Empire, a united Italy, was in process of formation under the Lombard king Berengar ; but for the intervention of the Germans it would have been completed. South of the Alps there would have arisen a second western power, with which the northern power would soon have had to reckon. Inevitably a united Italy would soon have become perceptibly the predominant power, and have exercised pressure on Germany from without and even within her borders. Picture what that might have meant—the German king relying on the bishops and the Pope dependent on an Italian Emperor ! Any disunity in the German Empire, any rising of the dukes would then have delivered over the German kingdom to the Italians ; the Italian ruler would have been the overlord in fact and might have become so in form.

A united Italy would also have weighed upon Germany in another direction. She would have been in a position to cut the Germans off at will from communication with the world. In this matter we must entirely rid ourselves of certain geographical conceptions which normally govern our thoughts to-day but are altogether inapplicable to the early middle ages. For us Germany lies in the centre of Europe, in the centre of main lines of communication. The Germany of those days lay in many respects in the backwaters of Europe ; she was backward in civilization ; beyond her eastern border was savage

THE EXTERNAL TASKS OF THE REALM 25

territory, the civilized world ended there ; and she lay off the great highway of world trade, the main artery of which passed from Asia Minor and Constantinople through the Mediterranean to Italy and from there across the western Alps to France. That highway passed by Germany, whose only means of communication with Italy in the tenth century were, as we know already, the Brenner and Septimer passes. Thus, the more the need was felt in Germany for participation in world trade, and for the assimilation of the apparatus of higher civilization which the east furnished to the west through Italy, the keener must have been the desire to safeguard its connexion with the east, with Constantinople. The point at which this connexion must be looked for was Venice, the Free State which still nominally belonged to the Byzantine Empire and formed in actual fact that Empire's bridgehead and the principal bastion of its trade in the west.

Consider, then, the situation in which Germany would have found herself if a strong and united Italian kingdom had pushed itself between her frontiers and Venice ! Germany would have been cut off from world trade whenever it suited the Italians ; or, to put it another way, she would have had literally to pay tribute to the Italian kingdom for her traffic with Venice, for everything that she drew from the east. For this if for no other reason a German king was bound to intervene in Italy to prevent the formation of a unified Italian State. The most effective way of doing this, in the long run perhaps the only effective way, was to get sovereign power into his own hands. Here as so often in history, conquest proceeded from a defensive need.

The course which Otto followed shows that this is not merely an explanation evolved after the event. He was far from throwing himself at once against the Roman imperial throne. For most of the time Rome lay quite in the background. Interest centred at first in the Lombard kingdom. Nor was this at once "annexed," but at first (952) allowed to exist and merely compelled to recognize German overlordship and to cede the Venetian hinterland with the roads leading to it. This shows plainly what the Germans were concerned with : direct communication with Venice. But this policy proved to be ineffectual ; at the first opportunity the territory won was lost again. Then (962) the decision was made to go the whole length and to subjugate the entire Lombard kingdom. It is significant that but a short time then elapsed before a trade treaty was concluded with Venice, under which the Venetians were accorded complete freedom to trade within Otto's frontiers.

His successors made no change in this policy. Their attention too was concentrated mainly on Upper Italy, and especially on the north-east. They sought to keep this part of the country above all else firmly in their hold. Aquileia and Verona were united as firmly as could be with Germany, as parts of Bavaria and Carinthia, and German priests installed at every opportunity in the sees of those provinces. In comparison with this territory, Rome and the imperial authority over Italy were but flank protection. As such they were indispensable if the Lombard kingdom was to be securely held, since a rising in Upper Italy could easily be engineered from Rome, especially in view of the dependence on Rome of its Italian bishops, some of whom were direct suffragans of the Pope. Consequently it was essential to be sure of Rome and the Pope in order to maintain hold of Upper Italy. For this, however, it was sufficient if a ruling party friendly to Germany were in power in Rome and a Pope friendly to Germany in the Holy See. The German emperors saw to this, but went no further. Rome and the Papal State remained autonomous, and their internal affairs were interfered with as little as possible. Otto III wanted to change all this, but his policy found neither approval nor support in Germany; he had mistaken his part. On the whole, Germany had made no very serious effort during the first century of the Empire to acquire and maintain dominance in Italy. There had been frequent and costly campaigns against Hungary and Poland, but in Italy in the whole of this period, down to the middle of the eleventh century, only one considerable battle, involving serious losses, is recorded—the defeat of Otto II in 982; and this engagement was not fought within the natural limits of imperial interests or over the imperial crown, but in the course of an adventure beyond the boundaries which Otto I had set to his Empire. All other enterprises were successful at little cost, so great was Germany's superiority in power.

It can safely be assumed that this policy paid; there is scarcely more room for doubt of this than of the advantages

THE EXTERNAL TASKS OF THE REALM 27

for modern Britain of dominance in India. At that period Italy was in every respect the richest country in the world, foremost in industry and in civilization. There can be no question that Germany's progress was greatly assisted by the continual intercourse with Italy which resulted from the German overlordship. The crossing of the Alps must also have been profitable in the most material sense. Italy was the land of minted money, which was still rare and costly in the north. Here, quite apart from rights of conquest, the king had for ages past enjoyed valuable rights of taxation. Duties and tolls belonged to him, and with the high degree of development of trade brought in large revenues. He even exacted a direct tax for the army, a thing unthinkable in Germany. There can be no doubt that Otto I and his successors took full advantage of these sources of revenue; Germany's dominance in Italy, in a word, enriched her. The gains of the German subjects who went beyond the Alps in the king's train or were installed in Italian bishoprics, are impossible to estimate. Where, in those days, could a substitute have been found for all that Italy offered?

The critics of the old German emperors point to the east, to the wide stretches of Wendish territory awaiting colonization. They forget to ask what was the value of the Wendish lands in those days. There was no wealth to be drawn from the marshland beyond the Elbe; the art of reclaiming it had yet to be learnt; it belonged to the more advanced technical resources of a later age. And the sandbox of the marches of Brandenburg remained for centuries the most meagrely endowed territory of the Empire; even in our own day it is no jewel. It was only through infinite effort that this land was tamed to the service of the German nation. In the tenth and eleventh centuries the primary requirement for this was lacking—the men. The Germany of Otto I had no surplus population, and there was still a sufficiency of good land awaiting clearing within its own borders. The Wends had already been subjugated along the Havel and in Mecklenburg, but this dominion was abandoned after 983. It was clearly not worth maintaining because there was no possibility of colonizing the Wendish lands.

Thus it is of no use to produce this argument of failure to colonize the east in order to pick holes in the policy of the first German emperors. Had anyone tried to advise them to leave alone the Lombard and Roman crowns and all the wealth of Italy, and to go to the conquest of the marshes and sandhills of the Wend country, they would have laughed at him, and all their world would have joined in the laughter. Adventure had to be sought in some direction: a warrior state like the old German Empire had to go forth and conquer if it was to maintain its character and its virtue. Imperialism was the guiding principle of these early times in every country. It was the lode-star of the English and the French; there came a time when the English possessed more than half of France, and for three centuries they held to their policy of conquest; and the French marched forth under the banner of the cross to found dominions and dukedoms in the east. But if Germany was to embark on conquests it was Italy that beckoned to her in the conditions of those days. The direction of expansion lies naturally along the line of least resistance and greatest advantage—as naturally as the river flows downhill. The two directives coincided in Italy: the resistance was as feeble as the reward was great. Thus, under the given conditions, the subjection of Italy and the foundation of the German-Roman Empire was the right policy.

We have spent some time over this point, but I do not think that I need defend our doing so. We have been concerned with a factor which governed the whole course of early German history, and which it is therefore necessary to understand if the beginnings of the organized life of the German state are to be understood. It is also a factor which, unhappily, represented the most brilliant political accomplishment which the German nation had the good luck to achieve down to our own day. I hope I have succeeded in giving a few indications of a conceivable explanation of the motives which led its ancestors along the course which they pursued, and an explanation which does not require that they shall be set down as less intelligent than later generations.

CHAPTER III

THE STRUGGLE WITH THE CHURCH, AND THE DISSOLUTION OF THE OLD EMPIRE

THE old German state was based on the support of the church; the imperial power, the temporal rule in Italy could not exist without the benevolent support and loyalty of the Pope. So soon as these conditions ceased to exist, so soon as the church renounced allegiance to the monarch, and the Pope became the Emperor's enemy, the very existence of state and sovereignty, kingdom and Empire were threatened.

That day came. Monarch and church fell out shortly after 1070 and fought each other with extreme bitterness for nearly fifty years. And when the struggle was over no real peace had been won, merely an armistice. Church and Empire remained foes. Often they strove to reach agreement, but no lasting agreement was ever attained. The end was, as everyone knows, the downfall of the German Empire and the break up of the German state.

The rupture with the church did not come with one dramatic stroke; the two powers who for so long had been allies and had found profit in the alliance, did not become foes overnight. Slowly and unobserved the issue developed until finally the open breach came, produced by the combination of a disastrous clash of interests with a fundamental change in the conceptions that dominated men's minds.

It cannot be disputed that the state church of the Middle Ages only inadequately fulfilled its religious mission. It served worldly ends and served them in a worldly way. The church was a worldly power and property and was handled accordingly. If its offices and its honours were not regularly bought and sold—even that happened often enough—at all events services were expected of it which were anything rather than of the spiritual order. Its clerics were often indistinguishable from the laity, its bishops and abbots from the knighthood, and the example set in their mode of life by many of the clergy, high and low, was far from edifying.

But in the latter half of the eleventh century a movement of reform began to make itself felt, issuing primarily from eastern France and Lorraine. It reached its flood tide in Germany and Italy when Henry III (1030-1056) took it under his care. Personally he was stirred by the new religious conception; as a ruler he felt it his duty to purify the church. But he was not in the least disposed to sacrifice any part of his own power to secure that end. The very fact of his reforming the church was to show that he was its supreme ruler; the very purpose of the reform was to establish his dominance and to place the church, the whole Catholic Church, with all its great moral and material resources, at the service of the German Emperor. With this idea in his mind he was not content simply with local measures, with the reforms of individual bishoprics or monasteries often witnessed before; he struck straight at the source, Rome. He would reform the Papacy in the spirit of the new age, and the Papacy itself should then reform the entire church.

The conditions in Rome called aloud for intervention. Things had reached such a pass that three pretenders were contesting the Papal chair, and none of them could truly be said to be in possession when in 1046 Henry III appeared in Italy. He promptly set aside all three, and so completely did he control the situation that no one disputed his action. The clergy and the people of Rome actually conferred on him the right, whenever the Papal chair should fall vacant, to nominate the new occupant for their election, as had been done by Otto I and later by Otto III.

In the use which Henry made of this right he clearly revealed his intentions. He nominated a German bishop; on the death of this bishop shortly after he again nominated a German bishop, and again and yet again. Four times in succession on his injunction German bishops were made Popes.

The intention was unmistakable: the Roman Church was to be incorporated in the German Empire as thoroughly as any bishopric north of the Alps. There could be no better guarantee of the German Emperor's mastery of Rome. The system of Otto I had shown its weaknesses. Only too frequently had Roman citizens failed him as Popes, or the German party been defeated in the Papal

THE STRUGGLE WITH THE CHURCH

elections, and then the German Emperor had had to resort to armed intervention. That was now no longer to be feared. The German Pope, who actually owed his elevation to the Emperor, was a good guarantee for the submissiveness of the capital.

Yet more : a German Pope, who felt himself the friend and servant of the Emperor, if not actually his tool, since he was lost without Imperial protection, necessarily worked throughout the world in Germany's interests. If he reformed the western churches and subjected them to Rome's direct control, it could be depended on that German interests would not suffer. Through the Pope as his agent, almost his deputy, the Emperor controlled Italy as never before. Through the Pope he could make his influence left in neighbouring countries, in France, Scandinavia, Poland, Hungary. A German Papacy as the keystone of the German imperial power—that meant the final achievement of German hegemony in the west. It was a clear and well thought out system, as simple as it was effective.

But no long life was granted it. The premature death of the Emperor in 1056, at scarcely forty years of age, wrecked it. The incapable and unscrupulous men who governed during the minority of Henry IV allowed the creation of the great Emperor to fall to pieces and degenerate into its opposite.

The reform of the Roman Church had been embarked on under German Popes, but the largest share in it had been taken by French monks. In Germany it would scarcely have been possible to find men of the required calibre in sufficient numbers ; they had to be summoned from the home of reform, from Lorraine and Burgundy. These men could not be expected to have anything but distaste for the other aspect of their mission, the buttressing of the German imperial power. Their dream was no longer merely of the purification of the church, but of its liberation from all secular domination. The weakness of the imperial regency gave them a welcome opportunity. It was unable even to offer protection against the attempts which the Romans did not fail to make to rid themselves of domineering foreign ecclesiastics. In Rome men soon ceased to trouble about the German king and his guardians ; they looked for help from quarters nearer at hand, from the rulers of Italy.

First and foremost there was the Margrave of Tuscany, Godfrey, born a Duke of Lorraine, who had arrived at his Margraviate through his marriage with the heiress of Tuscany. He had been constantly at issue with Henry III, and since the Emperor's death had been the unchallenged master of Tuscany and the northern slopes of the Apennines as far as Mantua. He, his wife Beatrice, and later their daughter Matilda, placed all their resources at the service of the reformed Roman Church—a development in no way to the profit of the German Emperor. The Emperor's rule had rested on the support of the bishops; with it he had held the secular princes in subjection. Now a secular princely house had risen to be the controlling power in central Italy.

Another force struck in Lombardy at the basis of the German domination, a pietistic popular revolt in the towns against the way of life of the bishops. The town populations arose *en masse*, under the banner of church reform and with religious slogans directed against the immoral priests, but in reality against the domination of Frankish and Lombard nobles and of bishops who served the German king. The revolt had the support and blessing of Rome, and the Lombard bishops, instead of being, as formerly, pillars of the German rule, now called for the king's help in their struggle to maintain their position, which they could not hold unaided.

A rival princely power established in Tuscany, and in Lombardy the bishops who had been the support of the German throne tottering—the outlook was sombre. Yet a third opponent came on the scene, to become in time the most dangerous—the Normans in southern Italy. The Normans had been arriving in Italy since the beginning of the century as mercenaries, they had settled in it, their number had been rapidly increased by camp followers and partisans; they had become invaders and conquerors, and since about 1050 almost the whole of southern Italy had fallen piece by piece into their hands. Already it was clear that the whole south would ere long be definitely in their power. Unconquerable at arms, they were the plague of the land and a permanent menace to their neighbours, including the Papal State. Pope Leo IX, the Alsatian, had tasted their quality when he marched against them with German troops in 1053. He was routed and taken prisoner and had to accept the victors' terms in order to regain his freedom.

THE STRUGGLE WITH THE CHURCH 33

Then came a development of far-reaching significance, clearly indicating the new policy adopted by Rome after Henry III's death. The Pope not merely gave up the struggle against the Normans but allied himself with them. In 1059 the two principal Norman chiefs, Richard of Capua and Robert of Apulia, did homage as vassals to St. Peter, and held as their fiefs from him all their existing and future conquests—Apulia, Calabria, Sicily. The Pope thus became suzerain of the whole of southern Italy, and won for himself a personal bodyguard of the best troops of the time. With these new gains he turned against the German imperial power: he no longer needed it; he was independent. The Normans at his side were a better protection and support than the distant German king; if need were they could even be used against the latter. The new feudal overlordship of St. Peter also fitted ill with the circumstance that since Otto I and Charlemagne the interior of southern Italy, the old Lombard principality of Benevento, had recognized the overlordship of the Emperor. Here the interests and claims of Empire and church, Emperor and Pope, came from 1059 onwards plainly into conflict.

In another respect too the year 1059 marks an epoch in the relations between the two powers. In this year a synod was held in Rome. It was presided over by Pope Nicholas II, a Frenchman and a favourite of Godfrey of Tuscany. The Pope had successfully held his own in face of opposition from the Romans, not without a struggle, but without help from the Germans. Among other things the assembly adopted a resolution on the method of Papal elections, the provisions of which all reflected the change that had come. The assembly did not venture entirely to ignore the inherited right of Henry IV to nominate candidates for the Papacy, but this provision was relegated to a subsidiary clause as a purely formal reservation. It was intended that the controlling influence of the German crown over the Papal election should in actual fact come to an end, and this it did; never after 1059 did a German ruler successfully bring it to bear. The epoch of the German supremacy over Rome and the church was over.

Another resolution of the same synod cast its shadow over the future: it was resolved that it should be forbidden to receive a church from the hands of a layman. This, if it was carried out, meant a fundamental and universal revolution, for it denied the traditional and acknowledged right of the laity to dispose of churches which it had founded and built. So far as the German king was concerned, it struck at the basis of his power. If the king could no longer dispose of the bishoprics and monasteries in his realm, no longer invest his bishops and abbots with their office, he was reduced to the state of a man who has had his right arm and his right leg taken off. That was entirely unacceptable. Against this innovation the German crown could only fight to its last man ; it was fighting for its existence.

The synodal decree of 1059, the first ban on " investiture by laymen," remained at first a dead letter ; nowhere was it acted on. But its shadow lay over the future. Sooner or later there was bound to come open warfare between kingdom and church, Empire and Papacy.

It came when in 1073 Gregory VII was raised to the Papal chair. To the ideas which had obtained sway over the Roman Church before his time, the ideas of reform and liberation, he added a third : the dominion of the church over the world. Earth as well as heaven belonged literally to the apostolic princes. Theirs was the disposal of all earthly ownership and dominion ; they gave and took away according to men's deserts , kings and princes were bound to obey them and their deputy on earth, the Pope, and were at law his vassals and liegemen. Gregory struggled with fierce energy, with passionate eagerness to establish these claims. When he demanded the universal recognition of the ban on investiture, even from the German king, the latent conflict became an open one.

Henry IV had now come to man's estate, and had set to work to restore his royal authority. He had just victoriously quelled a Saxon revolt (1075) when, in the exercise of his traditional right of investiture in the Archbishopric of Milan, he encountered the resistance of the Pope, who reproached him with disobedience and threatened him with the loss of his crown. Over-estimating the strength of his position, the king went so far as to secure the deposition of the Pope by a synod of the German bishops at Worms, at the end of January, 1076. Gregory answered by deposing the king in turn, and excommunicating him. It was soon revealed who was the stronger. Not merely did the Saxon revolt flare up again, but the

THE STRUGGLE WITH THE CHURCH

German dukes saw their opportunity to bring down this monarch who was becoming all too powerful. They leagued themselves with the Pope. More than ever the issue lay with the bishops. A small section of them, imbued with French ideas, had sided with Gregory from the beginning; the majority had remained true to the king. But to fight an open war against the Pope, their ecclesiastical suzerain, was more than even the loyalists could venture on. Henry then decided, in order to split the hostile coalition and so to avert the danger of a rival monarch being declared, to make his submission to the church. At the end of January, 1077, he unexpectedly met the Pope at Canossa on his way to Germany. Here, at the gates of Canossa, Henry did penance in his own person. So he compelled Gregory to absolve him and readmit him to the church. Thus he was again competent to rule. His chief aim he had not realized; in March the rebellious princes produced a rival king. But their faction was sufficiently weakened to enable Henry to embark on the struggle for the crown with fair prospects. One claimant after another failed against him. Finally, in March, 1080, Gregory himself renewed hostilities against him, and for the second time pronounced Henry deposed and excommunicated. The king retorted by inducing the German and Lombard bishops to nominate a rival Pope, to whom he gave armed support. He laid repeated siege to Rome, and in 1084 captured the city and was crowned Emperor. The belated arrival of the Normans compelled him to retreat; but Gregory too failed to hold the city. The Pope went to the south in the train of his liberators, and here in the following year (1085), alone, abandoned, almost forgotten, he died at Salerno. He had failed.

But that was by no means the end. The war continued, and at last the tide turned. Henry was never able to conquer the Pope's allies, and when the second successor of Gregory, the Frenchman Urban II, succeeded in creating a great coalition between the Normans of southern Italy, the Countess Matilda of Tuscany, and the Lombard cities, now united in a league—a coalition to which the rebel princes in South Germany adhered in 1093—Henry's power was broken. Now it was his turn to be confined for years, helpless and forgotten, to a corner of Upper Italy, without power in the peninsula and cut off from Germany. Even when the hostile coalition broke up and he was permitted to return to Germany, he was still unable to recover more than the shadow of his former power. The reformed party in Germany refused to recognize him; the church persisted inexorably in its anathema. He managed, however, to maintain a partial hold of his dominions until in the end, in 1105, his son rose against him and overthrew him. In the following year, at the moment when he was entering on a final struggle to recover his throne, he died, the most luckless of the German kings. The German imperial power, the German mastery of Italy had already ended. Italian rulers, under the leadership of Rome, now held the field.

The succeeding decades only confirmed this situation. There were occasions when Henry V. carried all before him, but he made only a momentary impression, and the way in which under that Emperor the investiture quarrel was ended, set the seal on the withdrawal of the German power from Italy. In the so-called Concordat of Worms (1122) a distinction was made between the churches of Germany and Italy. In Germany the influence of the king on appointments to bishoprics and abbeys was maintained; the election was to take place in the king's presence, and the prelate elected was not to be consecrated in his office until he had been invested by the king and had done homage as vassal. In Italy the election was free and consecration followed at once; the subsequent investiture and rendering of homage, if it took place at all, was thus reduced to a mere formality. This removed the basis on which the influence of the German Emperors in Italy had mainly rested.

The settlement was lasting. Henry V's successor, Lothar, did, it is true, receive the Imperial crown in Rome (1133); and at the end of his reign (1136-7), in agreement with the Pope, who needed his aid, he conducted a brilliant campaign in the peninsula, penetrating into Apulia, a campaign which earned him the distinction of being compared by contemporaries to Charlemagne. But that was only an episode; it had no permanent result. The next ruler, Conrad III (1138-52), the first of the Hohenstaufen, did not once appear in Italy. There was plenty of discussion of a journey to Rome for the imperial coronation, but the intention was never realized; Conrad died just when realization seemed at hand. Italy had become accustomed to independence. The suzerainty of the German king had become an empty form; the imperial power no longer existed.

In Germany too the king's power had been greatly diminished through the conflict with the church. It was in order to save the very foundation of its power in Germany, its control over the church in the German kingdom, that the crown had entered into the Concordat of Worms, renouncing its earlier influence in Italy. The renunciation failed of its purpose, as was seen three years after the death of Henry V (1125). The church insisted that the concessions in the Concordat were purely personal concessions to Henry, lapsing at his death. The new king, Lothar of Saxony, already known as a partisan of the church and raised to the throne largely by its aid, was not in a position to defend the old rights now denied with any energy. Still less could Conrad III, personally dependent on church and clergy and always tied to their leading strings, do so. He even let himself be driven by clerical influence into a crusade which he had had no desire to undertake, and which was a gross error in policy. The German church became "free"; that is, it liberated itself from the influence of the crown, to fall the more thoroughly into the power of Rome.

Conrad's whole reign shows the effect of this new subjection. Even in Germany he was never really supreme. In the great struggle between the two powerful houses of Babenberg and Guelph, he succeeded in maintaining himself only as supporter or leader of the Babenberg party. Robbed of secure dominion over the church, the main pillar of the royal power, he was unable to stand as the king should above the two parties: each of them was more powerful than he himself. The days of the German kingdom seemed numbered; it looked as if the natural course of events was already, in the middle of the twelfth century, to produce the divisions and the impotence which, as we know, were actually produced a century later.

But things had not yet reached that pass. There were still elements in the nation and in the spirit of the age which only awaited the appeal of a strong personality to aid the Empire to re-establishment. Fate ordained that after Conrad's death (1152) the right man should come to the head of the state in Frederick I. With him a new chapter begins. The course of German destiny, which seemed to be going steadily downwards, was stayed, turned, and once more in a swift ascent reached its topmost peak.

In Frederick I we trace for the first time in German history the living breath of a great personality. We have not by any means the material needed for a full knowledge of his personality and character. Such accounts as contemporaries give of him provide no full-length portrait, scarcely a rough sketch. But all that one does know of him, his deeds not less than the judgment of his contemporaries, reveals him as a really great man, a ruler of exceptional capacity and strength of will.

It is worth while to establish that fact. For it establishes the further fact that the epoch which his accession began was his own personal creation. True, he had worthy fellow-workers, Reinald of Dassel, Wichmann of Magdeburg, Philip of Heinsberg, Christian of Mainz, all statesmen of a high type. But they were throughout the servants and he the master. It is the best sign of his personal greatness that at all times he stood out from among them, that he was always able to find new servants of their calibre.

That his deeds are peculiarly his own can be recognized at once by the fact that he drew up immediately on his succession the programme to which he intended to work during his reign; held steadily to it; and carried it through to fulfilment. Its one brief, ambitious clause was: *ut Romani imperii celsitudo in pristinum suae excellentiae robur reformetur*—to restore the glorious Roman Empire to its old power and dignity: in other words, to make the Empire once more a political reality; that is, to restore German supremacy in Italy.

Circumstances were in his favour. In Italy the course of events since the elimination of German rule had been such as to make the Popes themselves anxious for the restoration of the imperial authority. In the struggle over investiture the bishops of Lombardy had shared the fate of the German rulers; the towns had achieved independence and were now the dominant power. Their example was followed in Rome; the Popes themselves were deprived of their authority over their city and its domains and, for a time, expelled from it. In the south of Italy the various Norman dominions had coalesced into a unified state, the Kingdom of Sicily, a Great Power which controlled the sea and bore heavily on its neighbour,

THE STRUGGLE WITH THE CHURCH 39

the Papal state. Gregory VII had dreamed of the Pope as head of a coalition of small states and ruler of Italy; Urban II had seen the dream actually realized for a while. But that was long since; now the Pope, himself in no strong position, was hemmed in between neighbours who were stronger than he, or resisted him. His authority was precarious; he was being squeezed out.

What could be more natural than that in his search for help he should turn to the German king? The restoration of the imperial authority, the armed forces of Germany would relieve the pressure on him, set him free, and furnish him with protection and support in the future. It was with this purpose that Lothar had undertaken his brilliant expedition, but after Lothar's death it had all come to nothing. Conrad III had been unable to help. Now the Papacy rested its hopes on Frederick.

This dependence of the Papacy on him enabled Frederick I once more to place the king's rule in Germany on a firm basis. He was able to regain the crown's former influence over appointments to bishoprics, unhindered by Rome. The German church once more served the king, and served him with the same loyalty and zeal as in the days of Otto I. Through its assistance and with the aid of its resources he was enabled to restore much of the former German dominion over Italy.

He was able to make a first attempt at this in alliance with the Pope, in 1153-4, but failed completely. On this first Italian expedition he failed to compel the Lombard towns to submit to German rule, and failed even to help the Pope to regain possession of his capital. The campaign planned against Sicily was not begun at all. The disillusioned Pope abandoned his alliance with the Germans, threw himself into the arms of the Sicilians, and joined forces with the Lombards. Frederick was now faced with the choice between abandoning his programme and trying to carry it out against the united opposition of all Italy, against the Lombard towns, the Pope, and the King of Sicily. He chose the latter alternative.

In 1158 he began the struggle. He did not win it. At the end of four years' fighting he was master of all Lombardy, but only for a brief period. The tighter the German administrative hold grew in town and country—a frankly bureaucratic regime, far removed from the conventional feudal organization—the stronger grew the passive resistance. When in 1167 Frederick again appeared in person in Italy in order to consolidate his conquests, he was met in many places with open resistance. Finally the Imperial army, which had just taken Rome, was decimated at the high tide of success by an epidemic. The greater part of northern Italy at once flared up in an unquenchable insurrection. No serious move against Sicily was made at any time. The Pope, the chief foe, proved invulnerable. The split in the Papacy at the election of 1159 brought no advantage to the Emperor, rather the contrary; for one of the rival Popes was everywhere regarded as merely the agent of the Emperor, with the result that in almost all of the west of Europe, apart from Germany—in France, in England, in Scandinavia—the church was passionately on the side of his opponent. Everywhere it was feared that if the Emperor's Pope won the Germans would rule the church. The non-Teuton peoples were utterly opposed to German domination; far from attributing any spiritual pre-eminence to the Germans, they regarded them as backward, uncultured, and inferior.

It was thus the support of the other nations, especially that of the French clergy, which enabled the Roman Pope, Alexander III, to win through in the end against the military power of the Emperor. The French king offered him a refuge if he no longer felt safe in Italy, and the French churches supplied the money which he needed for the war. Finally the eastern powers intervened, and the contest became hopeless for Frederick. Venice and Constantinople saw the danger to themselves if Germany and Italy were to trade together to their exclusion, and united to avert it. They came to the support of the Lombards, and the combined forces were too much for the Emperor. His defeat at Legnano (1176) was not in itself a great military event; part of the German army was routed by a surprise attack. But it convinced Frederick that he had no prospect of final success.

He resolved then to give up the game, but at once began again with new pieces. Under the Treaty of Constance (1183) he renounced the direct control of Lombardy, recognized the autonomy of the towns, and contented himself with their recognition of imperial suzerainty. For his loss here he sought and found compensation in Tuscany. The heritage of Countess Matilda, friend and ally of Gregory VII, was to afford him the nucleus of an

THE STRUGGLE WITH THE CHURCH 41

imperial territory of his own. The great countess, the last of her house, had left her wide possessions to St. Peter, but the Popes had never been able to enter into possession of this valuable legacy. The Emperor now got the whole territory into his hands. From Tuscany he controlled Central Italy and held in check both the Pope and the Lombards. He succeeded also in making peace, friendship and a close alliance with the King of Sicily, sealing it with the marriage of the German crown prince, the young King Henry VI, with the Sicilian Princess Constantia.

Frederick had thus managed to follow up a military failure with a political success. His name was in the mouth of all peoples: they praised him as the most heroic figure and the greatest ruler that the world had seen since Charlemagne. Even the Pope had made terms with him, and owed it to the protection of German troops that he could live once more in a Rome that obeyed him only unwillingly. The close of his reign found Frederick the undisputed leader of western Christendom. In 1189 he started on a crusade for the liberation of the Holy Sepulchre, which had fallen into the hands of the infidels two years before. But death overtook him on the way. None the less, he had fulfilled his life's task, he had restored the Empire to its old power and dignity, and, indeed, to glories unknown before. Down to our day when men speak of the old German imperial power it is not of Otto I or Henry III that they think but of Frederick Barbarossa. Song and story have seen in him the personification of the greatest conception of early German history, and history itself cannot deny him this glory.

And yet Frederick did not reach the topmost peak of complete accomplishment. That was reserved for his son Henry VI. When the male line of the royal house of Sicily died out in 1189 he had as husband of Constantia a claim to the southern throne. He established his claim after a prolonged effort, with the aid of rare good fortune When he was crowned in Palermo at Christmas 1194 all Italy owned his rule. The King of England did obeisance to him, the Frenchman owned his superiority. Of even greater importance was the fact that the possession of Sicily made the Empire a seapower. It could dominate the Mediterranean, and its arm reached to the east. That was swiftly proved. When Henry resumed the crusade which had been interrupted by his father's death, Constantinople found it politic to aid him, and the kings of the east hastened to acclaim the star of German supremacy; the rulers of Cyprus and Armenia held their kingdoms as fiefs from the Roman Emperor. Germany's world power had been established, prouder and more widespread even than under Henry III.

Just as swiftly as before and still more completely, more irrevocably, did it collapse when Henry VI died on September 28, 1197, a young man of thirty-two. His death came at the worst possible moment for the Empire. Once more, as in 1056, the heir was a child. The baby Frederick, not yet three years of age, had already been elected German king, though not crowned. The dominant personality had disappeared from the scene at the critical moment, and there was no one to put in his place. But the circumstance that at this moment made the disaster complete was the infamous attitude of some of the German princes. At an hour when everything depended on steady loyalty and unity for the possession of the heritage of the great Staufen, the restored power and prestige of the Empire, they fell into disunion. Against the infant Frederick the Guelphs entered the field with a claim to the throne; foreign nations, England on one side and France on the other, intervened in the quarrel, and the result was the double election of 1198—Philip of Swabia against Otto of Brunswick. This double election sealed the fate of the German imperial power: it provided the opportunity for the re-emergence of the Empire's chief rival and opponent, the rival who had suffered most from its restored pre-eminence—the Papacy.

The Papacy had neither been subdued nor won over; neither Frederick nor Henry, with all their efforts, had succeeded in reaching a final settlement with Rome. The fact of the Emperor's dominance had been accepted, but the Papacy was merely biding its time. The Pope was as much as ever the foe of the Emperor, the church the foe of the state.

This became plain immediately on Henry VI's death. A revolt broke out at once in Tuscany and Sicily; the Pope placed himself at the head of it. His aim was nothing less than the destruction of the imperial power. He realized it, thanks to the disloyalty and the political folly of the German princes on the one hand, and on the other

THE STRUGGLE WITH THE CHURCH

to the great qualities of the man who at this moment became the head of the church—Innocent III. Innocent's accession and the double election in Germany give the year 1198 the character of a turning point in history. Once again the course of events changed. What 1152 had begun and 1194 seemed to have completed, was now reversed. Hard on the restoration of the imperial power had come its downfall and the victory of the church.

Innocent did not live to see the church's victory completed, but so far as was humanly possible he prepared and assured it. His ruling purpose was no other than that of Gregory VII, which we already know—to eliminate Germany's influence in Italy in order to make himself the leader and overlord of the Italian states. He sought accordingly to maintain the disunion in Germany as long as possible, in order to have a free hand in Italy to confirm and extend his own power.

The Papal State was too small for the leading part which its Prince, the Pope, intended it to play. Accordingly Innocent hastened to enlarge it. Under the plea of reassertion of ancient rights, he embarked on a policy of conquest, and annexed from the territory of the now masterless Empire two wide tracts of country, the Duchy of Spoleto and the Marches of Ancona. He would have annexed Tuscany, but the Tuscan towns refused to submit. Even so, however, the enlarged Papal State lay like a broad trench right across Italy, separating the Kingdom of Sicily from the imperial domains in Italy. The future Emperor must give his assent to these gains: only on this condition would he receive Papal recognition and the prospect of coronation. Until it was fulfilled Innocent would withhold his decision. For this was his new claim: the Pope was to decide on the right of an elected German king to reign.

Otto was ready to meet the Papal wishes, but he came to grief in Germany. Innocent soon found himself compelled to negotiate with Philip. Agreement seemed very nearly reached when, in 1208, Philip was murdered in a private quarrel. Otto received the adhesion of the Staufen party and was now the undisputed head of a united Germany. He reiterated his earlier promise, was thereupon invited to an imperial coronation, and came to Italy. Here he was received with general submission, and everywhere recognized as heir of the old imperial power. Now, however, he suddenly forgot all his promises, and treated the newly annexed parts of the Papal State as though they still belonged to the Empire. Then, once he had secured possession of north and central Italy, he took the road trodden by Henry VI, marched southwards, and began the conquest of the Kingdom of Sicily.

This drove Innocent to desperate measures. He excommunicated Otto. But of what avail was an ecclesiastical ban if no secular arm supported him? A secular arm was necessary to put the sentence into execution. There was only one available, and that a dangerous one: Frederick of Sicily. He must be put up as rival king in Germany, so as to fall in Otto's rear; that might save the situation. But what sort of a situation was it if a son of Henry VI again ruled in Germany and Italy, from the North Sea to the coast of Africa? Where would the independence of the church be then? Where the hope of ruling in security an aggrandized Papal State? The remedy seemed as bad as the disease. Innocent nevertheless resolved to use it, and to get Beelzebub to drive out the devil. He calculated rightly that a Staufen reinstalled by the church would never be so dangerous as a Guelph victorious over the church. At his instigation the German princes called Frederick of Sicily to the German throne, in 1211, and Frederick set out at once for Germany to recover the crown of his forefathers.

Otto, too, turned about to defend his position in Germany. In the war between them Frederick obtained the victory, but not by his own strength. For his elevation he had to thank the Roman Church, for his victory French money and French troops.

That is the outstanding feature of this dispute for a crown: it was an incident in an external struggle, and its issue was determined by external forces. Events in Europe at this period were dominated by the fierce struggle in the west between England and France. As the nephew of the English king Otto was England's ally—without English money he would never have secured election—and accordingly France energetically supported the Staufen. The Anglo-French quarrel was fought out on German soil, and the German kings were pieces in a European game which was directed from the Thames, the Seine, and the Tiber. How often has history repeated itself since, how often has Germany become the chessboard of European wars! In 1214 this happened for the first time. When in that year Philip II of France inflicted at Bouvines a smashing defeat on the German imperial army the Anglo-French war was decided in favour of the French. Frederick II profited thereby; the French victory freed him from his rival, and when, four years later (1218), the latter did him the service to die, Frederick was undisputed king in Germany. Two more years and he was able to be crowned Emperor in Rome.

But this was no longer the old German Empire. The Empire's domination was ended. The hegemony of Germany disappeared, and her place as a Great Power was taken by a newcomer—France. It is worthy of note, moreover, that at Bouvines a German and a French army had met in arms on a great battlefield for the first time in history—and the Germans had been defeated. Even in Italy the imperial authority of Frederick II did not amount to much. He had had from the outset—and how could it have been otherwise?—to recognize the Papal conquests, and to surrender to the Pope the heritage of Matilda, and with it the dominating position in Tuscany. In Lombardy he had to be content with a purely formal suzerainty. Primarily—if, indeed, he was anything more—he was King of Sicily. From this position he tried later to restore the lost imperial authority and to rule in all Italy as absolute monarch. But in this effort he encountered the old opponents who had faced his grandfather and his ancestor, Henry IV—the Lombard league and the Roman Church, supported by the clergy of the west, especially of France. He had no more success against them than his predecessors. The issue was still undecided when Frederick died, in 1250, in the midst of the struggle and perhaps on the verge of victory.

No more than a glance at these events was necessary for our purpose: they do not belong to German history, nor can Frederick II be regarded as in any sense a German ruler. He was never more than a stranger in the land of his ancestors; after his departure in 1220 he made only one short visit to it (1235-7). He was the first foreigner to occupy the German throne. He felt himself an Italian and was interested only in Italian conquest. Germany was of value to him as a source of excellent fighting men, but otherwise of little interest. He paid no attention to events in Germany, and let them take their own course.

His death removed an Italian Emperor from the stage, not a German one. The imperial idea had become dissociated from Germany. The Germans, on their side, lost interest in it, and after Frederick's day few concerned themselves with their old supremacy in Italy, though their right to set up a Roman Emperor in the person of their king was not contested. So it came about that the world knew no Emperor for sixty years after the death of Frederick II. The Emperor had become superfluous. The German Empire no longer existed as a political force, and the first great epoch in German history was at an end.

What is the explanation of this inglorious end of an enterprise boldly begun and so long pursued with tenacity? On what rock did the imperial rule of the Staufen disintegrate?.

Before we seek an answer we must make it clear that this Staufen Empire differed already from that of the Ottos and Salians. The former had ruled Italy from Germany through the bishops appointed by them and the Pope. Since the investiture quarrel that had no longer been possible. In its stead Frederick I had established direct rule through an administration composed of his own imperial officials, first in Lombardy and then, when the attempt had failed there, in Tuscany. Henry VI had won the Kingdom of Sicily and from there, largely through his sea power, had dominated the whole peninsula. The imperial power of the Staufen no longer had its fulcrum in Germany. Its interests lay, and its resources were concentrated, in Italy.

But why did it fall so swiftly? The easiest answer, and that which is most usually given, is that the Empire overtaxed its strength. The domination of Italy in the forms which it took under the two great Staufen emperors was more than the Germans could permanently manage; consequently it had to be abandoned. The wise and worthy censors of world history rarely omit to add the criticism that it would have been " more prudent " never to have embarked on so profitless an enterprise. The Staufen emperors have especially been criticized for overstepping the old historic frontiers of the Empire and adding to it the Kingdom of Sicily. This over-expansion, it has been claimed, was ruinous in the end, and the Sicilian marriage of Henry VI has been pointed to as the root of the evil.

This view proceeds from a complete misapprehension

THE STRUGGLE WITH THE CHURCH

of the political situation of Italy in the twelfth century and also of the permanent geographical conditions of her political existence. How could a German Emperor have retained in his control the northern half of the peninsula with a great power in the south controlling the sea, the coasts, and the ports, and in a position at any moment to destroy the overseas trade of the seaports of northern Italy and so of their whole hinterland? To tolerate such a neighbour permanently was as impossible as for ancient Rome to put up with the power of Carthage or for Victor Emmanuel II to permit the existence of the Kingdom of Naples. In the days of the Ottos and the Salians the situation was different; southern Italy was split up and impotent. But the moment a Sicilian Great Power arose the rule of any German Emperor in Italy would have, to be possible at all, to extend to Sicily. The Kingdom of Sicily must either be destroyed or annexed. Any agreement with it such as Frederick I arrived at was but a step in that direction; the annexation of Sicily, so soon as the chance offered, was in the nature of things.

Was this policy really beyond Germany's strength? It may seem so now that we know the result. But was the hopelessness of the undertaking really evident in advance? Neither Frederick I, who was regarded by his contemporaries as the most prudent of monarchs, nor the many able men who surrounded him can have had any doubt of a successful issue; otherwise they would surely have embarked on a different policy. And it is evident that Frederick's policy had the entire approval of the nation. Frederick I and Henry VI had their people behind them when they set out to recover Germany's lost hegemony. The Staufen Emperors' policy enjoyed the same national support. It was also justified by its success.

But it had no permanency. What happened to bring the restored Empire so quickly to its downfall? If we let events speak, there is one that leaps to the eye—the premature death of Henry VI. There can be no doubt that things might have turned out very differently had he lived twenty, nay only ten years longer. Thus an unlucky chance played, to say the least, a very important part.

It may be objected that an edifice which could not survive such blows had no permanence in it; that it is by its ability to survive misfortune that a political creation proves its right to existence; that if the Staufen Empire, the

German-Italian world power had sprung from a rightly-conceived policy the untimely disappearance of a leader would not have caused its downfall. But that is equivalent to demanding that saplings shall have stout trunks or men come fully grown into the world. In its beginnings a state is a tender plant which can easily be broken, trampled down or uprooted. States may have their own infant ailments or delicate youth. What would men say now of Frederick the Great if he had been killed at Kunersdorf? It is very doubtful whether the young Prussian power would have survived him. Prussia was spared that test, the Staufen creation succumbed to it.

What did it lack that would have ensured its survival? What were the opposed forces which were able to destroy it? The answer is plain: the Empire fell because it was left undefended. At the critical moment the princes, the political representatives of the nation, instead of making common front against the enemy without, split into two parties which for ten years (1198–1208) and then for six further years (1212–1218)—in all, with a three years interval, for twenty years—fought passionately against one another. When unity was restored for a short period after the murder of Philip of Swabia it was seen at once that the strength of the Empire was quite sufficient to maintain its dominion in Italy. When Otto IV appeared in Italy in 1209 at the head of an imperial army, he was able without a blow to restore German rule over the whole peninsula. He was setting out to conquer Sicily when for the second time dissension broke out in his rear among the German princes: some of them had revolted from him and had set up Frederick II as his rival. Otto had to return to Germany to defend his crown, and to let Italy go. It was quite clearly the lack of unity among the princes, who quarrelled over the crown instead of defending it when in danger, that caused the Empire's downfall. The double election of 1198 and the twenty years of civil war that followed destroyed it.

The split at the election of 1198 had nothing whatever to do with the question of imperial policy. Otto IV was no sooner universally recognized than he wholeheartedly resumed the Italian policy of the Staufen. His elevation to the throne against his rival (Philip) was thus not an act of political opposition but of dynastic ambition. And so it was later when Frederick II was opposed to the

THE STRUGGLE WITH THE CHURCH

Guelph. Thus the German Empire did not of set purpose reverse the imperial policy of the Staufen, but it neglected it and did not defend its gains when they were in danger, although it would have been an easy task to maintain them. The Empire in Italy and therewith Germany's leadership among the nations could easily have been maintained, even amid the gravest crisis, with a fraction of the strength which was wasted, to the detriment of the nation, in the long wars over the crown in Germany

The German Empire fell owing to the disunity, selfishness, and short-sightedness of the German princes. Who can fail to see that here defects were fatally at work, defects which one finds continually at work in German history—want of thought for the community, obsession with particularist, selfish aims, weakness of the political instinct ? These national faults are responsible for the fact that at the end of the twelfth century Germany gambled away her predominance in the west.

But it will not do simply to say that disunity, as ever, had brought the Germans low. How came it that disunity could produce such disaster round about 1200 although its effects had been fairly well countered up to then ? And why was no attempt at restoration made later on ? Once before, in 1100, all had been lost ; yet the successors of Henry IV continually reverted to the old plans till the task was accomplished under Frederick I. That did not happen after 1220. Germany only half-heartedly supported Frederick II in his struggle for the mastery of Italy, and in the end left him completely in the lurch. When the church deposed him a considerable section of the German princes deserted him and raised up rival kings. The old traditions of the past seemed to have lost their appeal in the thirteenth century. Such changes do not come without reason, and in this instance the reasons are not difficult to discover.

The constitution of the state was already going through a development which gave free rein to forces of disintegration and placed obstacles in the way of the preservation of unity. That was the fatal element which accounts for the collapse of the imperial power. The imperial power was doomed because there was proceeding at this period a change in Germany's constitutional system which was nothing less than the beginning of the dissolution of the state. This is what gives the period 1198–1220 its peculiar significance. It marks the ending of the imperial power, that is of Germany's hegemony in the west, and the beginning of the dissolution of the state.

The dissolution of the German State did not begin with the collapse of the imperial authority and the decline of Germany's power abroad; still less was it a consequence thereof. It is frequently maintained that the imperial rule involved the German kingdom in its fall; that the strength of the kingdom was wasted in a vain struggle for the imperial crown so that the ending of the dreams of Empire was the grave of German unity. That view can only be the result of a very superficial survey of the situation. The truth is that what may be described as the internal dissolution of the state had been in progress for a long time, and had only been held up and concealed from view by the successes achieved abroad under Frederick I and Henry VI. When these were over and Germany's external power collapsed, the true state of things within the country was at once revealed.

What had happened was simply that the king no longer controlled the princes, because he had lost too much of his former personal power. Let us recall to our minds the basis on which the royal power had rested. It had rested primarily on the rich royal domains, the enormous manorial estates in possession of the crown; these had made possible the upkeep of a large feudal army. During the civil wars over the investiture quarrel these estates had melted away. They had been given away outright or in fee, or simply lost to new owners who had appropriated them. This was part cause of the pathetic weakness of Conrad III; he was weaker than such princely houses as the Guelphs and the Babenbergs. Even Frederick I had begun his reign in no position of predominance. He won his predominance partly by his victories in Italy, which brought him especially a great deal of money, and then through systematic acquisition of land by compelling the German churches to hold in fee from the royal house a considerable proportion of their possessions. But the Staufen lost these gains and yet more in their fight for the throne. The royal domains melted away like butter before the fire; their yield under Frederick II was far below what it had formerly been. They had also depreciated through division and through their dispersed situation. On the other hand the power of the princes had grown. Their estates were great aggregates which were steadily rounded off and increased as the royal domains fell to pieces. The crown had been weakened, its rivals strengthened.

The old tribal duchies no longer existed; they remained only in name; their geographical frontiers had disappeared through partitions. The old duchy of Bavaria, which under Otto I had included the entire Bavarian race from the Lech to the Leitha and from the Danube to the southern slopes of the Eastern Alps, had lost Carinthia at the end of the tenth century, Austria in 1156, and Styria in 1180: all three had become independent duchies. In 1180 Saxony was divided between Cologne and Anhalt. Only Swabia, owned by the royal house of Staufen, had remained intact. And when the house of Staufen came to its end and its possessions were divided among its neighbours, the duchy of Swabia also disappeared.

· Everywhere territories had split up or crumbled away. In place of concentration into powerful aggregates there had been partitioning and splitting up. The attempt of Henry the Lion, as Duke of Bavaria and Saxony, to set up a rigidly centralized dual power of great territorial extent in north and south ended in his fall; he was defeated by the alliance of the Emperor and his princely neighbours. His lands were divided up.

This falling to pieces of the realm brought to the princes not weakness but strength. The reduction of territorial area facilitated government and brought greater cohesion. The princes gained in solidity what they lost in the spread of their domains. In the second half of the twelfth century there came into existence real territorial governments, territorial states which deserved the title of state much more than the kingdom did. The kingdom, the king's sovereignty, was no more in reality than an agglomeration of sovereignties; all the real elements of governing power—justice, police, defence, fortifications, customs and coinage, and above all the right of taxation—lay in the hands of the territorial rulers. These rights were summed up in the phrase " territorial sovereignty " (*Landeshoheit*). State sovereignty was exercised by the territorial ruler, and the king, from whom he derived this sovereignty in theory, rarely intervened. His intervention was conditioned by his power and the esteem in which he was held. The territorial rulers resented his intervention and did their utmost to prevent it.

This was the situation that confronted Frederick II when he arrived in Germany. It was a circumstance of vast and permanent influence that he made no attempt to alter it. In his indifference to German affairs he conceded once and for all to the territorial princes full state sovereignty in their domains. First the ecclesiastical princes, in 1220, and then all lords of the manor (*domini terrae*), in 1232, received the exclusive right of fortification, army leadership, justice and coinage. Of his own accord the king withdrew from their territories and confined himself to the rôle of final resort in justice and administration. The monarchical state thus became an abstraction, the territorial rulers concentrating in their persons all real state power.

The royal power had formerly leaned on a second and even stronger pillar—its dominion over the churches of the realm. We know how much it meant when it lost this pillar through the investiture dispute and the complacency of Lothar and Conrad III towards the church, and how much when Frederick I reasserted the ancient rights of his crown. After the death of Henry VI these rights were soon lost again. Their too exacting enforcement produced a very natural reaction among the bishops, part of whom stood out against the king, and rejoiced when Innocent III struck at the root of the German Kingdom. Innocent took advantage of the struggle for the crown to compel the rivals to renounce the exercise of influence of any sort over the election of bishops and abbots. Both Otto IV and Frederick II yielded. The renunciation which Frederick publicly made in the Golden Bull of Eger (1213) gave the German churches their "freedom"—in other words, there was an end to the influence of the crown on appointments. But it sapped the life-blood of the German monarchy.

Here, too, Frederick II accepted the established order of things. In order to retain a solid block of support in the ranks of the princes, he exerted himself to win over the bishops by favours and concessions. It was for this reason that he granted them, as we saw, full territorial sovereignty. But such gifts failed of their purpose, while they completely destroyed the old foundations of the king's power. When the Pope declared war on him the bishops left him in the lurch, took sides against him, and raised up rivals to him. Why should they not? As

THE STRUGGLE WITH THE CHURCH 53

clerics they had to obey the Pope, and as princes of Germany they had become independent rulers like the dukes before them, each ruling a state of his own, with its own cares and interests. The German state no longer mattered greatly to them; they had nothing more to hope for from the crown, and had only to fear that their newly conceded rights might be taken away again.

These are the real causes of the collapse of the power of the monarchy and the dissolution of the German state; they were operative in Germany contemporaneously with the ending of the imperial authority in Italy. They were not in the least due to the failure of the Staufen emperor's Italian policy; on the contrary, the imperial policy became impossible and had to be abandoned because the kings had lost their supremacy in Germany.

But why, it may be asked, did not the Staufen kings first consolidate their power in their own country before undertaking big tasks abroad? Was this not trying to build the upper storey of a house before the foundation was ready? There is an element of truth in that view. It was illogical and dangerous for the kingdom to pursue an imperialistic policy for which its constitution was so little suited. Imperialism, if it is to succeed, requires a rigid unity in the state, giving the power at any time to throw the whole strength of the community into the pursuit of a single aim. That is why French and British imperialism was so successful; both states possessed the complete constitutional unification which allowed them to throw the weight of the whole nation at any moment and continuously, not just for a couple of hot weeks in August, into the scales of destiny. This unity of purpose was lacking in the old German state, and so the imperial policy of the Staufen, which aimed at securing supremacy in Italy, had from the outset a fundamental defect, which showed itself with fatal results after Henry VI's death, when the state split just at the moment when it stood in most urgent need of unity. It would be unjust to charge the Staufen kings, and especially Frederick I, with neglect in not looking first and foremost to a consolidation of their position in Germany and postponing Italian schemes. That was not how matters stood. When Frederick I ascended the throne the state was already only a secondary power, overshadowed by the princes. To ask Frederick to consolidate his power in Germany would have been equivalent to telling a man fast in a bog to pull himself out by the hair. The only means of escaping from the quagmire of impotence was by securing a strong position abroad. In Italy Frederick secured the superior power with which he later overbore the mightiest princes in Germany, and was able, for instance, in the end to bring down his much stronger rival, Henry the Lion. Undeniably there was something unnatural in letting the centre of gravity of the kingdom be outside Germany. But politics can only deal with the possible. Frederick's policy of restoring the imperial power was, in the middle of the twelfth century, the only possible one if the king was not prepared to accept for good and all the subordinate rôle which Conrad III had played.

Permanent success was denied to the efforts of the house of Staufen. But even its transitory success was a gain. The fairest memories of Germany's ancient history go back to it. Imagine what this history would have been like without Barbarossa and Henry VI! Those who realise how much memories count for in the life of a people will not underestimate that success. The German people drew inspiration from the memory of the Staufen emperors through centuries of political short commons. It may be that their memory contributed more than anything else to a later transitory experience of greatness.

CHAPTER IV

THE TERRITORIAL STATES

To the power and prestige, the poetic charm and beauty which invest the earliest times in the eyes of later observers, one must bid farewell in coming to the second great epoch of German history—the age of the territorial states.

It is extremely difficult to form a clear picture of the constitutional situation in which Germany was left by the fall of the house of Staufen. The controlling power of the throne had completely disappeared; at first there was actually no king. The fact that a number of gentlemen simultaneously assumed that title has no significance. Henry Raspe and William of Holland called themselves kings, as did Conrad IV and later Richard of Cornwall and Alfonso of Castile; but they were nothing more than pretenders. How little they counted may be seen from the fact that of the two last, both of them foreigners, the former appeared only two or three times for brief periods in "his" kingdom, and the latter never.

Meanwhile the development of the territorial states proceeded rapidly. Like all states, their first concern was to grow bigger. At the outset they were not solid geographical aggregates, but were composed of various separated areas, rags and tatters of land. They strove naturally to piece these together, to round off their territories. As that was possible only at the expense of other territories, there arose a permanent condition of things which might be described as the war of all against all. Civil war was the order of the day. The extinction of a princely house almost always provoked it at once, but any other motive would bring neighbouring lords into the field against one another. This condition of things was gradually modified as time went on, wars of succession and border feuds grew fewer, but they never ceased so long as the German Empire lasted. The Silesian wars under Frederick the Great and the war of the Bavarian succession under Joseph II were wars of the same character as those which filled the thirteenth and fourteenth centuries.

Things were naturally at their worst at the beginning—in " the time without an emperor, the terrible time." It seemed then as if the unity of the kingdom, the law and the constitution no longer existed, and the simple right of the stronger reigned in its stead. The result was a kaleidoscopic series of changes from decade to decade. Here and there the nucleus of a considerable state would crystallize; it would more or less successfully round off its territory and define its borders. Such were the Duchy of Bavaria, the Landgraviate of Thuringia with the March of Meissen, and above all the Kingdom of Bohemia, which added to itself Austria, Styria and Carinthia under Ottokar II. Between and around these were the great number of smaller states, church and lay, ruled by princes, counts, or barons, and finally the towns, of which many rose to be small independent states.

It is impossible to say whether this state of things might not have been perpetuated, whether the need for security of trade and communications would alone have been strong enough to put an end to it from within. It is conceivable that the kingdom, which the strong did not need and the weak were unable to set up, might have given place to a system of alliances, neighbouring princes co-operating to maintain some sort of order and security within their common frontier and isolating themselves from the outer world in mistrust and hostility. This is what actually happened from the end of the thirteenth century in the most southern part of Swabia—the modern Switzerland—with the result that in time an actual state arose. Something of the sort might have happened elsewhere—perhaps in the Rhineland, in Lower Saxony and Westphalia, Bavaria, Thuringia, Franconia, provincial alliances and confederations leading to the formation of new and particularist states. Tentative moves in this direction were to be observed here and there.

Any such development, however, was scotched by an intervention from without. The church had destroyed Empire and kingdom; the church now restored the kingdom, considering that in its existing situation it had need of an Emperor. It was Gregory X who in 1273 compelled the election of a universally recognized king in Germany; he counted on using him as Emperor in Italy to maintain the balance of power. The choice fell on Rudolf of Habsburg. It is one of the ironies of fate that Rudolf,

THE TERRITORIAL STATES

who was raised up especially in order to be an Emperor, was never able to undertake the expedition over the Alps, constantly looked forward to, frequently actually resolved on, which was to procure him the crown of the Staufens. Thereby his kingdom took on a new significance; it marks the definite end of the Empire of the Germans, the end of their rule in Italy.

It was in vain that repeated attempts were still made to restore the imperial power. The attack which Henry VII (1310–13) made under apparently favourable circumstances —favourable in the sense that the church supported him at the outset—failed owing to the death of the new Emperor in the midst of the conflict. The renewed effort under Louis the Bavarian (1327–29) failed completely. Charles IV made an end of these illusions by contenting himself with a purely formal title of Emperor and nominal suzerainty over the Italian states, which brought him certain financial advantages and the opportunity of more effective diplomatic intervention in Italian affairs. So the matter stood thereafter. The real gain which Germany secured from the fruitless Roman expedition of Louis and the soberer policy of renunciation pursued by Charles was that France was prevented from getting a foothold in Italy. The same danger which had brought Otto I over the Alps—the danger that Italy might consolidate into a single politically powerful and economically self-sufficing unit, such as might cut off Germany from the main stream of world trade—was successfully averted in the fourteenth century. The multiplicity of the states south of the Alps, and their political and economic disunity, served the same purpose which German suzerainty had served earlier; the world trade routes remained open to Germans.

But the changed character of the kingdom of Rudolf I and his successors did not lie merely in the abandonment of the traditions of a great past. It had its positive side: it rested on quite different foundations. The royal domains and the control of the church were no longer its main supports. The former melted away almost entirely in the flames of the Staufen civil war; the latter had long since been abandoned. The new king counted in the kingdom for just so much as was represented by his power as a territorial magnate. As king he had only his personal resources to live on: the kingdom paid him no civil list. The consequence was that each king sought to enlarge his personal possessions. Everyone of them, from Rudolf I to Charles IV, furthered this policy with the same tenacity which their predecessors had displayed in the struggle for the imperial crown. The reason is obvious. Where every princeling sought to add to his power whenever the chance offered, why should not the king do the same? Each successor to the crown stretched forth his hand to add one territory after another to what he already held from his forefathers. Their purpose was unchanging; only the extent of their success varied. Rudolf succeeded in capturing Austria and Styria from Ottokar of Bohemia. The battle on the Marchfeld (1278) was the foundation of the power of the "House of Austria," as the Habsburgers thereafter called themselves. Adolf of Nassau failed in his attempt to secure Thuringia and Meissen. Albert I was engaged in an attempt to add these two provinces to his hereditary possessions (he had already acquired the kingdom of Bohemia and the reversion of Holland) when he was murdered by his nephew (1308). Henry VII made his son King of Bohemia; Louis the Bavarian won Brandenburg, Holland and Tyrol.

Subsequent generations have held the later kings in evil repute on account of this policy of increasing the power of their "house." They have been charged with indifference to the interests of the kingdom and concerned only with those of their house. It would be impossible to be more unfair to them. The king, as he was situated after 1250, could perform no greater service to the kingdom, that is to the nation, than by making the power of his own house as formidable as possible. There was no other way of furthering the unity of the kingdom, counteracting the disunion between the princes, than to make the crown stronger than any one of them, stronger even than a majority of them and finally than the whole lot of them. That end could be attained in no other way than by adding whole territories to the possessions of the royal house. Where the princes of the land ruled everything, the king could only rule Germany if he was the greatest of the princes. The final goal of this development was the sole rule of the king, the creation of a nation-wide state.

At one time it seemed as if that goal had been nearly reached. That was in the ten years (1298–1308) of the reign of Albert I. From his father he had inherited a power unrivalled in South Germany. With his extensive

THE TERRITORIAL STATES

possessions in Alsace, in the southern Black Forest, and in Switzerland he overtopped all his neighbours. To these he added Austria and Styria, broad, wealthy, excellently governed provinces. Albert's talent as statesman and soldier enabled him to break the opposition of the Rhine princes, who had been too strong for his predecessor Adolf. He won the towns to his side by the wise and farsighted step of freeing trade on the Rhine from all the tolls levied by local princes, a measure calculated also to divert the trade between Italy and the north from the French routes to Germany. From the strong position so acquired the king set out to win for his house Bohemia, Meissen, and Thuringia. If he succeeded he would have a position of supremacy in north-eastern Germany which no one would be able to take from him. He would have become master of all Germany. But the task was no light one. It aroused strong resistance. In Bohemia a powerful nationalist opposition arose; in Meissen and Thuringia the nobles would have nothing to do with this south German ruler, who was known to be an excellent prince but a stern and merciless governor. The struggle was still undecided; the issue trembled in the balance. The king was concentrating all his power—troops and money—on it. Amid the final preparations for a decisive campaign he was struck down by the dagger of his nephew: a senseless act of personal hate destroyed the fairest prospects of the German nation. For the opportunity did not come again, and from that time onwards particularism reigned supreme.

These alternating aggregations of territory in the hands of the various dynasties were injurious to Germany in one respect—through the constant dynastical changes. Here again the new age differed from the old. Formerly it had been a generally accepted principle that the ruling house should supply the new king. This arose from the legal conception of the king—the original meaning of the word suggests it—as the noblest among the people; and who could be nobler than he who sprang from kings? There was also in favour of the former system the practical consideration that the concentration of the sources of the royal power was assured from generation to generation if the new king was the natural heir of his predecessor. The resources of the state and of the royal line were thus identified and remained in the possession of the same family.

This principle was abandoned after 1250 and its opposite prevailed. Every change of monarch brought a change in the royal house. This was intentional: to allow the son to succeed his father would make the king too strong. The princes had no interest at all in the mightiest among them being king; on the contrary he must not be too powerful. Since they had become territorial rulers and governed states of their own, they no longer saw in the king the constitutional sovereign, but an unwelcome rival who must be kept down. Every state has a natural tendency towards sovereignty, towards freedom from restraint. The German territories had been states since the time of Frederick II, but they were not sovereign as long as the monarch stood above them. All the more did they strive to be so, if not in law, at least in practice; and they were so if the king had not the power to make his suzerain rights effective. Consequently it was all to their advantage if a king who had made his house powerful were succeeded by one who had to begin again from the beginning. It mattered nothing to them that the newcomer would have to face the bitter hostility of the heirs of his predecessor, and that the last royal house would always be working against the new one. They lost nothing, even though the German Kingdom had become an imitator of Penelope, who undid by night all she had woven by day.

Nevertheless it may be doubted whether this fixed principle of change of dynasty would have been introduced if a new element unknown to earlier times had not become firmly established since 1250—the Electors. In olden times the whole of the princes had elected the king. Now this right had shrunk to the privilege of a narrow circle, largely because the great bulk of the princes had no interest in the royal election. They absented themselves, and the seven princes who had won a position of privilege at the election and coronation of the new king in the Staufen period found themselves with the business left on their hands; they had become the sole voters, the Electors. There was so little general interest in the matter that a small group of a few magnates came once for all into possession of the privilege of giving the state a king whom greater magnates than they must accept. Only one of the electors was a prince of the first rank by virtue of his power— the King of Bohemia. The Palatinate, Saxony, and, Brandenburg were second-rate and Mainz (Mayence),

Cologne, and Trier (Trèves) third-rate powers. It is easy to understand that these minor potentates clung tightly to their elective right, the sole right which raised them out of the ruck of their fellows and gave them significance. But no one will maintain that this was a natural or sound state of things. The electoral college which had grown out of the unhealthy conditions of civil war in Staufen times injected its poison afresh into the state at every royal election. It did more than anything else to prevent the development of a sound and strong royal power.

There was no lack of attempts to find a remedy. Rudolf I had busied himself with plans to make the crown hereditary in his house; Henry VI had made a first approach to the problem. Albert I also was closely interested in it and perhaps would have solved it had longer life and success in his schemes of conquest been granted him. With his death the opportunity was gone, and Charles IV, who was faced with chaotic conditions in every corner of the kingdom, had to accept the situation. He strove to turn it to useful purpose. He increased the privileges of the Electors, and confirmed them by a law of the kingdom—the Golden Bull of 1356—hoping so to create a strong party in the kingdom on which his house as the house regnant could depend for support. On the whole he calculated well. The change of dynasties was now abandoned. The Bohemian Luxemburgers, Charles's sons Wenceslaus and Sigismund, were one after the other elected king, and after the extinction of the house with Sigismund in 1437 the throne passed to the latter's son-in-law, Albert II, and so to the house of the Habsburgs, in whose possession it remained to the end.

The time of which we are writing is no favourite with its students. One cannot blame them. What attracts one in the past is the outstanding personality or event—whether in human interest or in importance to the course of events. The petty and trivial repel, weary, bore. German history after 1250 lacks all broad significance. Where it does possess it for a moment, as for instance in Albert I's reign, it is but a flash followed by yet blacker night. " It all comes to nothing "—that is the impression with which one is left after reading of all these wars and disputes. The picture lacks not only greatness but unity. That is why the history of the whole period is so difficult or impossible to present. The narrator can no more dispense with unity of treatment than can the dramatist. The history of Germany from the thirteenth to the fifteenth century has no unity. What looks like unity if one confines oneself to the history of the kings is illusory. The history of the kings is but a part and not always the most important part of the whole. The history of the various provinces is one of innumerable threads which cross and tangle and not seldom get tied up into veritable Gordian knots. The indifference of posterity to all this busy pettiness is only too comprehensible.

Yet this indifference is very regrettable. For, after all, in these centuries of planless and aimless expenditure of energy, during which all development seems at a standstill, there does emerge something. For the later history of the nation down to our own time these centuries are even of much greater significance than the heroic period of the Empire. It was at this time that the nation found its permanent state-forms, and more than that: it was then that its character received its cast. Whoever studies the past from the viewpoint of its influence on the present must admit that these dark ages after the Interregnum are actually more interesting than all the glory of the Staufens. The deeds of Barbarossa belong entirely to the past; Rudolf of Habsburg and Charles IV live on, so to speak, to this day. Under them—if we take them as representatives of the whole epoch—the German territorial states arose; from then on it is these states which are the backbone of German history; they have even survived the recent revolution.

Moreover, whoever desires to-day to learn something of the German past can find its traces everywhere: churches and town halls, castles and city walls speak directly to him. But how seldom do they take us over the threshold beyond which the old German Empire sleeps the eternal sleep of its finished history ? What can they tell us of Frederick Redbeard and his son, of Henry IV and Otto I ? Only a few scattered remnants, which have to be painfully assembled, survive of these great days. Perhaps there is more than the scholar is inclined to suppose; but it has to be sought out and pieced together, and will never compete with what the fourteenth and fifteenth centuries have left us. These are the times which influence the present; we live and move in their shadow. No less a person than Goethe observed this long ago. He tells in the beginning of "Dichtung und Wahrheit" how in his youth he visited the imperial palace at Frankfurt: "Of Charles the Great we had various legends; but the historically interesting began for us with Rudolf of Habsburg."

The historically interesting—that is, all that still concerns living men, has application to them, influences them. So it seemed to the bright boy of 1756, and so it is to this day. Frederick Redbeard has gone a second time to sleep in the Kyffhäuser; Rudolf of Habsburg and Charles IV stand in our midst. There is thus every reason why we should make every detail of the history of their times clear to ourselves. In spite of the intricacy of the picture it must be possible to recall and retain it. Here, however, there is neither time nor need for this. We must confine ourselves to the main outlines and to discovering what permanent achievement the succession of royal houses after 1250 transmitted to posterity and what were the lasting results of this epoch.

First of all, the fundamental character of the German constitution was settled for all time. It may be asked, how can this be so when such far-reaching revolutionary changes came in Germany, as elsewhere, to destroy and replace the mediæval forms of government? The objection is easily answered. On a broad view in spite of all changes, in spite of 1806 and 1848, of 1870 and 1918, the fundamental lines of the constitutional structure in Germany are to this day substantially those which were laid down for her between the thirteenth and fifteenth centuries. To this day the life of the nation is organized mainly within the framework of the territorial state. The ending of the old regime in 1806 strengthened the provincial state; the founding of the new in 1870 left it untouched; the revolution of 1918 failed to displace it. All of the states which dominate the scene to-day date from those three centuries. Many states of that period have disappeared, but those which stood in the front rank about 1500 have remained the leading states to this day. Austria and Brandenburg-Prussia, Bavaria, Saxony, Württemberg, Baden and Hesse stand still on the foundations which were laid between 1200 and 1500. Even the vanished Brunswick-Lüneburg intends to rise again as the state of Hanover. So firmly fixed are the roots which thrust down into the German soil after 1250.

The old territorial state was in its origin dynastic. It

was the rule of a princely house, founded on its inherited right over land and people. It depended entirely on the rights, the power, the will of a noble house whether a number of domains should be united in a single state or a domain be split up into two or more parts. Inheritance brought together domains which often had nothing in the least in common with one another, not even geographical propinquity. The principality of Mömpelgard in Alsace belonged to Württemberg; the Bavarian Upper Palatinate belonged to the Elector Palatine. Under the law of inheritance provinces were shared out and riven apart: examples were Hesse-Darmstadt and Hesse-Cassel, or the various states of Thuringia. The Palatinate on the left bank of the Rhine is part of the state of Bavaria thanks to the accidents of the law of dynastic inheritance. So strong did the connexion between dynastically united territories become in the course of time that it might outlast the dynasties. Territories which had been ruled for a certain period by the same princely house regarded themselves as a state unit, even though they may have had little in common. Bavaria is inhabited by Bavarians, Swabians, and Franks, who yet feel themselves a united people and intend to remain one. The character of the state embodied in the princely house impressed itself on the people, so that they felt it to be their own ingrained character.

Mention should here be made of an element in the political life of the nation which sharply distinguishes the period after 1200 from earlier times. There had been particularism before, but its character had now changed. The particularism of the beginnings of German history was tribal. That no longer existed. It had been succeeded by a particularism rooted, as to this day, in dynastic and state individuality. This particularism may be regarded as a misfortune, even as irrational, but it is not to be removed with a flourish of the pen. It has been found in the past and will be found again that the sense of individuality and local solidarity of the territorial states, although based only on historic development and on no compelling natural causes, is not to be decreed out of existence by resolutions, however big the majorities behind them. To be blind to this is to show ignorance not only of history—that to-day is considered pardonable—but of life, and so to be revealed as a bad politician. It is not necessary, however,

THE TERRITORIAL STATES

to take strong exception to the "irrationality" of the new particularism. All life is decidedly irrational, and true wisdom lies in recognizing the fact and trying to remove its evil consequences without presuming to attempt more.

Another aspect was, and still is, much more serious. The growth of the territorial states affected the German character adversely because these states were all so small. To realize this it is by no means necessary to measure them by the standard of the world powers of to-day. Even by contemporary standards, compared, for instance, to France and England, the German states were all small states. This was true even of the greatest among them, such as the Kingdom of Bohemia and the Duchy of Austria, Styria, and Carinthia; and these larger states were the exceptions; the great majority were pygmy states like Reuss, Waldeck, or Liechtenstein.

A small state is always in some degree unnatural, irrational, since it cannot fulfil its own mission. The aim of the state is to look after the needs, the desires, the interests of its inhabitants. For this it requires power; it must be able to exercise pressure within and without. Lacking power, it cannot fulfil the purpose of its existence. It will find itself forced into indirect, surreptitious courses to attain its ends, or such of them as it does not abandon from the outset. Under all circumstances it will tend to place its aims as low as possible, to content itself with bare necessities and even with less. A small state can only have small aims and pursue them with small means. But every state influences the character of the citizens, and that not simply by the way it rules them, by constitution and administration. In a state which must dispense with many things because it cannot enforce its rights, the citizens soon become accustomed to suffering injustice which they cannot avert. Where the state can set itself no higher aims, how should the citizens set themselves nobler tasks? They know in advance that they can find neither protection nor support. And, finally, where the state is forced to attain its just ends surreptitiously or by cringing, the individual citizen naturally loses the faculty of marching openly and straightforwardly to his goal. He too will regard the crooked path as the safer and will keep to it. How true that is a study of past and present shows over and over again. The most striking instance of all is supplied where a people is compelled to live without a state like the Jews. Conversely, the free, open and confident approach which not a few nations exhibit in their whole population is only possible through their reliance on a big, closely knit, powerful state. Even the recollection of past power and greatness can produce these characteristics, as the Dutch and Spaniards show.

If we apply all this to the German as we encounter him in the later centuries of the middle ages and since, we find it proved point by point. The German provincial state has only small aims and problems. To secure a few square miles of land, to raze an inconvenient frontier fortress in a neighbour province, or to appropriate it, and above all to squeeze a few more taxes out of their beloved subjects—such were the high politics of its all-serenest lords. Conquests in the grand style, which might have made them lords of the whole realm, none of the kings attempted after Albert I. From the time when Charles IV had based the suzerainty of his house on a system of petty tricks, those great ambitions which increase power and so contribute to development died out in the ranks of the German princes. Duke Leopold of Austria, who fell in 1386 at Sempach, is a possible exception. His conquests, which extended as far as Italy and added Trieste to Austria, his plans to round off to complete unity the Habsburg lands in south Germany had undoubtedly an element of greatness. But he stands out among contemporary Germans like a peacock among hens, and he failed in the end. His enterprise had no solid basis: it was unsuited to the conditions of the Germany of his time.

How narrow and trivial does it all seem when we look at the internal life of these territories! There we see the superior classes—clergy, nobility, burghers—on no particularly friendly terms with one another, each section concerned above all with its own privileges, and all agreed only in the determination to make the task of ruling as difficult as possible for the sovereign and to evade taxation. If the prince had no high ambitions, his subjects had none at all. The clergy thought of their own livings, the barons of their rent, the townsfolk of their trade—no common aim existed to unite and elevate them. Each was an end to himself.

The picture of the average German was entirely in keeping with this. The small state in which he was compelled to live narrowed his horizon. He knew only a tiny world in which one had to move with circumspection and could not go upright for fear of damage to foot, or elbow, or head. He never pursued great ends, for he knew that he could never attain them. He had to get accustomed to putting up with insults and outrages from the outer world, for there was none who could effectively protect him. The circuitous and hidden path was to be preferred to the straight open road; it was safer. Above all he lacked free self-expression and a natural pride in himself. He could not permit himself these luxuries since they are only possible and permissible on condition of belonging to a strong, feared, and respected community.

Who is not familiar with this picture? It has been exhibited to us often enough, and no one will deny that it is a true picture of German life for whole centuries. The Thirty Years' War is usually blamed for it, but wrongly; it is four hundred years older; it dates back to the thirteenth century, and only became more deeply embedded as time passed.

What a poor part the Germans played in European history after the fall of the Empire! If they sought to intervene with the mailed fist in international politics—as, for instance, in the Roman expeditions of Henry VII and Louis of Bavaria—the best they could achieve was an honourable failure after convulsive efforts with an element of irresponsibility in them and almost a comic disparity between exertion and reward. Their diplomacy, too, showed again and again how little they were at home on the great stage of Europe; they moved awkwardly, and as a rule were made use of if they did not get their ears boxed. What a pathetic figure did the ablest and most experienced of the German princes, Charles IV, cut when he ventured in 1365 during a visit to Provence, which officially belonged to "his" Kingdom of Burgundy, to have himself formally crowned in "his" capital of Arles. The ruler of the province, the Queen of Naples, protested; Charles hastened to apologize and to assure her that his coronation meant no invasion of her rights. Yet with his ability Charles IV was a factor who counted in European politics and was taken seriously abroad, unlike his second successor, Rupert of the Palatinate, whom the Venetians and Florentines allowed to set out for Rome at their expense, but sent home again before he got to Brescia because the business was proving too expensive. When Charles's second son, Sigismund, set out on the same expedition, it turned into a quite grotesque and humiliating farce. He was first paid to come by Milan and then left in the lurch, without troops and without money. The city of Siena assisted him; the Florentines almost imprisoned him and set him free only reluctantly, after he had unscrupulously changed sides. He had simply wriggled into possession of the imperial crown through the services which he rendered the Italian powers, which had also had to subsidize him.

If that could happen to the green tree of the kingdom what could one expect from the dry brushwood of the petty territorial rulers? The whole lot of them counted for nothing in the contemporary world, save in so far as they might hire themselves and their subjects as mercenaries in other rulers' wars. In that capacity they were very serviceable when they were paid, and they were always ready to serve if the pay was good. They would serve anyone—to-day the King of France, to-morrow the King of England, the next day the Duke of Milan and the next the Venetian Republic. It even happened—the proof lies in the documents in the Paris archives—that an entire coalition of West German princes, led by King Adolf of Nassau, left the King of England in the lurch, in flagrant violation of a sworn oath and in spite of subsidies received, because the King of France offered better terms.

The grasping venality of these princes became proverbial outside Germany. Everyone knew that since the creation of the Electors the king's elections had become a market in which every vote had its price. So it was that for half a century France could pursue in all seriousness a policy of getting a prince of her own royal house elected in Germany, not because the crown of Germany was so desirable in itself, but because this indirect method offered the simplest way of acquiring the imperial crown and therewith the control of Italy. That the method was practicable, if enough money was spent, no one doubted. In contrast to this pettiness there was almost a tinge of statesmanship in the undertaking which a Duke of Austria gave in 1324 to support the election of a French prince to the German throne on condition that all the important towns on the Upper Rhine and in Switzerland were incorporated in the Habsburg domains.

Such transactions—and examples could be multiplied—showed over and over again that the princes cared only for their own narrowest interests and their personal profit; the nation and its welfare counted for nothing. The king and the realm were for them either means to the attainment of their own ends or enemies whom they must fight. That the king and nation had a claim to service and sacrifice was empty rhetoric which they refused to take seriously.

But nothing would be more mistaken or unjust than to pass this criticism on the princes alone. They even have some excuse in so far as they were rulers of states of their own, to which they were primarily bound and the interests of which they had to consider. But the same excuse cannot be pleaded for the leading citizens of the states when they absolutely refused the princes ways and means to pursue their policy. They had no wide interests to consider, and they cared even less than their rulers for kingdom and nation; neither money nor service were they prepared to give either for prince or emperor.

There was a time when it was supposed that one section of the nation could be excepted from this judgment—the towns. In all seriousness it was supposed that there were times when the king, supported by the towns, could have defeated the egoism of the princes and made himself master of the realm. The burghers were imagined as the upholders of the conception of the unified realm against the princes who represented territorial particularism. A strange notion, which may serve as a warning of the errors into which the historian may fall if he lets himself be influenced by current political ideas. This was in the seventies of the last century, in the days when the liberal middle class of Germany flattered itself that it had created and was to rule the new German Empire founded by Bismarck. What the middle classes did, according to this self-satisfied view of theirs, in the nineteenth century, they might, it was suggested, have done in the thirteenth and fourteenth centuries if only the king had placed himself as a Bismarck at the head of a national league of that day.

In actual fact the burghers of the towns were just as incapable of such action as any other class. What was the German town of those days and what were its ambitions? The rise of the towns to economic and political power coincides with the dissolution of the kingdom and proceeded from the outset in opposition to the landed nobility. At law each town belonged to the owner of its site; it was neither free nor independent. But a number of towns won their freedom from the rule of their landlords, where these were too weak to enforce their legal right. It was the bishops' towns which thus became "free" towns; Augsburg, Strassburg, Basle, and for a time Cologne, Mainz, and others. A second and larger group gained a certain independence because they were built on state lands, former royal domains which the state had lost the power effectively to administer, contenting itself with levying taxes. In this second class were some large towns, Nuremberg, Frankfurt, Ulm, and many smaller ones such as Friedberg, Wetzlar, Reutlingen, Dinkelsbühl, Rothenburg. Both groups had this in common, that they sought to maintain their independence and escape from incorporation in the territory of a neighbouring prince. It was a purely negative policy, betraying an even denser particularism than that of the princes. These towns were for ever appealing to the kingdom and loudly protesting that they belonged to the kingdom and wished to remain so; but this was a mere formula to put the best show possible on their narrow self-regarding policy. These worthy townsmen never dreamed of making sacrifices for the kingdom. If they paid their taxes to the king and on occasion bought his favour with an extra gift, they did so not to serve the state but because their princely neighbour would have demanded more. And how did it help kingdom or nation if Reutlingen remained a royal town instead of becoming a Württemberg town? It was exactly as Schiller in "Wilhelm Tell" says of the first confederates: "They want to have the Emperor as their lord, Wishing to have no lord at all." The patriotism of the towns was merely a cloak for the rankest particularism.

Apart from their independence these towns were interested in only one thing—their trade. They demanded that commerce should have safe and free routes, and as the princes taxed travellers by land and water and the knights played the brigand and made the roads unsafe, they were hostile to both and appealed to king and realm. Where king and realm failed them they banded themselves together for mutual protection. These alliances of towns made their appearance in the first half of the thirteenth century; one, the Rhenish League of 1254, assumed great proportions and a certain significance for a short period. This movement was misunderstood by the middle class liberal historians of the seventies and eighties, entangled in their own preconceptions. The apparently big scale of these leagues—they crossed provincial frontiers and extended to great distances—might create the impression that they contained a germ of national unity, even if only based on selfish interests, a germ that needed only to be developed. A renewal of the movement took place when the Swabian royal towns united in 1376, the free towns of the Upper Rhine in 1381, and the two groups finally joined together, to protect their rights and interests against the princes. It came to actual war in 1388-89, the towns and princes of South Germany measuring their strength against one another in two great coalitions. The towns were defeated in two decisive battles, at Döffingen by Eberhard of Württemberg and at Worms by Rupert, Count Palatine, in August and November, 1388.

These defeats of the towns have been bewailed by some writers, and a fair picture painted of what might have happened had they won and placed themselves at the disposal of the king as victors over the particularism of the princes. It did not occur to these writers to ask whether that was ever really possible and whether the towns would or could have desired it. In point of fact nothing of the sort was conceivable. Had the Swabian and Rhenish towns been the victors in 1389 there would have been no revolutionary change in the constitutional situation. The princes were far too strong in the south, and were complete masters in the north. Even had the towns desired it, they would have been entirely unable to undertake any unification of the realm; and they did not desire it. Their horizon was too narrow altogether for this—narrower even than that of the princes. They were concerned purely and simply with the establishment of their immunity from princely interference and with the restriction of fetters on communications. So much they achieved, on the whole, even without victory; after their defeat things remained as before, and this was all they wanted.

They were, moreover, no longer in the strong situation of the days of Döffingen and Worms. Since the middle of the fifteenth century a considerable number of the free towns had lost their freedom and had had to accept the yoke of the princes. Only a few big cities still remained free—Regensburg, Nuremberg, Augsburg, Ulm, Basle, Strassburg, Frankfurt, Cologne—with the mass of little towns in Swabia and Wetterau, which were of no particular importance. The bulk of Germany had become once more the country of the princes; the towns had not even won equality of standing with them. The towns were occasionally represented in the national diet as early as the fourteenth century; in the fifteenth they appeared in it more and more often and in the end regularly, but they were by no means always asked to give their views, and generally only when Electors and princes were unable to agree among themselves.

There would be no reason for devoting so much time to these questions if all that was involved was the need for combating an error into which past historians have fallen—an error which scientific historians have already corrected, though it still recurs in one place and another. What is involved is more than this. The position held by the cities and their burghers in German history is a thing peculiar to Germany and unknown to other nations. In French history the towns, broadly speaking, did not begin to count until the Revolution of 1789. Paris, with its unique situation as capital, was an occasional exception, but only for quite short periods. Still more so does this apply to England; there, up to the end of the eighteenth century, the towns played no part whatever in national affairs. Even London, which in some ways enjoyed an exceptional position, exerted no independent influence. Both in France and England history was made and dominated entirely, until the threshold of the nineteenth century, by the nobility. Not until 1789 did the bourgeoisie in France gain control and thrust the nobility aside. In England the middle class has for a century or so been steadily increasing its influence, but to this day it still largely marches alongside the nobility if not in its train.

Very different was the development in Italy. There the cities were very early, in the eleventh and twelfth centuries, the strongest element, and increased their advantage from generation to generation. They thrust aside the nobles—and also the prelates—and took over

THE TERRITORIAL STATES

the entire leadership in the life of the nation. The formation of states thus proceeded from the towns. The only exceptions were the Kingdoms of Sicily and Naples in the south and Piedmont in the extreme north. Here the nobles were the ruling element and the state was accordingly feudal and agrarian. In the rest of Italy the town was everywhere the dominating element in the territorial state. It is enough to mention the names of the cities to appreciate this : Milan was Lombardy, Venice was not only a city but a complete state, Florence was Tuscany—the capital gave its name as it had given life to the state. The result was that the bourgeoisie overtopped all else. Ninety-nine per cent. of the Italian nobles of to-day are of bourgeois origin.

In France and England the countryside ruled the town ; in Italy the town ruled the countryside. Germany took a middle path. Here the princes, who represented and led the nobles, failed to incorporate the towns entirely in their territorial states ; still less could the towns dream of subjecting the princely states to themselves. Consequently nobles and bourgeoisie existed alongside one another, not as entire equals in prerogative, not entirely on a level in strength, but each a law to itself, standing apart from one another, and each side jealous of any infringement of its independence by the other.

This condition had the advantage of enriching the internal life of the nation. But it is very doubtful whether there were not more than compensating disadvantages. It was certainly not a fortunate circumstance from the point of view of national unity and concentration of strength that the political divisions produced by the development of the territorial states were added to by the sharp social division between the nobles and a bourgeoisie independent of them and hostile to them.

For nobles and burghers were enemies in Germany in a sense unknown in other countries. They are so to this day. This is an ancient legacy ; it dates from the hostility which sprang up in the late middle ages between town and country, burghers on the one side and princes, barons and knights on the other, growing at times and in various places into bitter hatred. In the sullen spite with which to-day the democratic townsman is filled towards the " baron " there is an echo of the spirit of the countless big and little feuds once fought out between townspeople and barons, of the impotent rage of the defenceless burgher against the knight of the road, who for his part despised the "shopkeeper," and on occasion plundered him and "put him down."

In these old-time fights the forces and weapons of the combatants were too incommensurable for a clear issue to be possible. The barons had all the advantage militarily, but the towns were equally supreme financially. As civilization advanced and economic activities broadened out the towns grew steadily richer. From the end of the thirteenth century Germany became a country studded with towns, an industrial and trading country in which money accumulated in the hands of the townspeople, while the mass of the nobles grew poorer and poorer. A situation developed which it is impossible to call a natural one: political and economic power were dissociated, faced one another as enemies, and neither was in a position to overcome the other and absorb it.

It is probably as well that the townspeople were unable to gain the upper hand. Apart from the question whether and to what extent an urban middle class has the capacity for ruling a state of any importance, the German burgher of the late middle ages was certainly ill-equipped for governing the German nation. As already mentioned, he was farther than his rival from being blessed with any wide vision. The burgher was much more of a villager than a city-dweller. The biggest cities of that period were but small; none of them exceeded some 20,000 inhabitants; and the horizon of men who pass their lives in a community of ten to twenty thousand souls, shut off from the outer world by thick walls, high towers and narrow gateways, all visibly announcing that the basis of the whole life of the community is fear; men sharply differentiated in customs and view of life from the rest of the nation, forming an exception to its general rule—the horizon of such men could only be narrow and their ideas and sympathies the very reverse of bold and broad. Here and there one of them would be engaged in long journeys to trade in distant lands; he would do little, however, to remedy this narrowness— at heart, in all his aims and endeavours, he would remain a petty burgher. Not until a very late period, around 1500, was this narrowness of outlook overcome in isolated cases such as those of the Fuggers and the Welsers, with their world-wide business relations. But it was only their business horizon that had expanded ; their political horizon was little changed. It is, indeed, amazing how petty were the ideas and the judgments of these great merchants of the late fifteenth and early sixteenth century in political questions. None of them could be compared with the Jacques Coeur of Bourges who financed the French war of liberation against England under Charles VII. Their thoughts were for themselves ; at best, for their city. The Emperor was their friend because they did good business with him. The realm, the nation, seemed to have for them no existence. And these were the greatest and best, standing out from the common herd, and for that reason not particularly popular at home.

Such is the general picture. The unhappy tendency ingrained of old in the people to foster selfish, personal, special interests at the expense of those of the general community was exceptionally favoured by the development of the petty state on the ruins of the Empire. It should have been the function of the state to correct it ; instead it fatally encouraged it. Through the pettiness of his environment in public life, the German himself became narrow and petty. The life of the nation had no element of greatness ; the nation had accordingly no great characters or great ideals.

An unedifying picture, this vicious circle, in which the unhappy qualities in the popular character produced a mistaken type of state organization and the defects in the forms of the state reinforced and perpetuated the ingrained defects in the popular character. But the world is full of contradictions. This picture has fortunately another and a very different aspect. The same period of which so far we have had so very little that is encouraging to say, the period which created the German petty state and petty burgher, gave the German people also its widest territorial extension and brought it the acquisitions of a prestige and influence which were to last long and the effects of which were to last down to our own day—acquisitions which were thus of more lasting value and therefore of greater historic significance than the glorious expansion of the imperial period.

CHAPTER V

THE CONQUEST OF THE NORTH-EAST

THE original boundaries of the old German kingdom were formed by the Elbe and the Saale. When Charles IV mounted the throne (1347), the kingdom extended as far as the Narowa and Lake Peipus. There had been expansion in that direction even in the period which is generally described as the period of decline in the history of the Empire, an expansion of astonishing extent and of a degree of importance which led in time to an entire shifting of the centre of interest of the history of Germany.

The centre of interest at the beginning of the thirteenth century was still entirely in the west and south, along the line Cologne-Frankfurt-Augsburg. A time was to come when it would shift to the Elbe and Oder, more or less along the line Hamburg-Breslau, concentrating around Berlin—a territory which in the earliest centuries had not belonged to the Reich at all and had not even been inhabited by Germans. This simple geographical fact speaks more eloquently than a host of words of the significance of the expansion of the Reich north-eastwards. The beginning of this movement marks an epoch which must count among those of the most far-reaching importance in German history.

The German state had always claimed overlordship over its Wendish neighbours beyond the Elbe and Saale. There had been no lack of attempts to draw these peoples into closer union with the Empire. The means for this lay in the Christian mission. But no permanent results of any importance were achieved by this policy or, probably, aimed at. It was conceived essentially as a defensive policy. The neighbours were to be tamed and made no longer dangerous.

A very different element entered about the middle of the twelfth century. From then on there was no more thought of the conversion of the Wends and their transformation into peaceful and submissive neighbours, but of their subjection, generally their extermination, and the seizure of their lands for colonization. The new policy can be clearly traced to two men, virtually contemporaries. They were the first to enter on it with success, and were subsequently copied on a big scale by all concerned. One was Albert the Bear, the Margrave of the northern marches of Saxony. In 1142 he claimed to be heir to a Wendish prince and made himself master of the territory adjoining his own as far as the Havel; thereafter he took the title of Margrave of Brandenburg, and he was the founder of that state. Much less striking was the figure of the other, but his influence was more direct and more powerful. Count Adolf von Holstein, of the house of Schauenburg, was only a petty ruler, but in spite of this he gave a new turn to the history of all Germany by conquering, about 1140, the country of the Wagrians along the east coast of Holstein, exterminating most of its inhabitants, and opening it up to settlement by German peasants. There is a biblical ring about the story told by the contemporary historian, Pastor Helmold of Bosau, by Lake Plön: " Inasmuch as the land was without inhabitants, the Count sent out messengers into all countries, into Flanders and Holland, Utrecht, Westphalia, and Friesland, to the end that all those who had sore need of land should go thither with their households to receive gifts of wide and fruitful soil, abounding in fish and meat and the sweetness of fat pastures. And he spake to the Holsts and Stormars: ' Did ye not invade the land of the Slavs and purchase it with the blood of your brothers and fathers ? Wherefore then are ye the last to come over and take possession thereof ? Be ye rather the first, and come hither into the promised land, and till it and enjoy your portion of the precious fruits thereof; for the best portion is yours, seeing ye have delivered it out of the hand of the enemies.' When he had said this there arose a countless multitude out of many tribes, and they took with them their servants and all that they had, and came into the country of the Wagrians to Count Adolf, to receive the lands which he had promised them." That was the beginning of the German colonization in the north-east.

What Adolf von Schauenburg did in Holstein, Albert the Bear did in Brandenburg. Their example was followed by the Archbishop of Magdeburg, by the Margrave of Meissen, even by the Slav princes themselves in Mecklenburg, Pomerania and Silesia. The Wendish crusade (1147), with its very unchristian slogan: "He who will not be baptized shall die," saw to the provision of land, and the settlers streamed in from all over north Germany.

> "Eastward let us ride forth,
> Eastward let us fare,
> Over the rich green sward,
> Merrily over the sward,
> To the better land out there"—

so they sang in Flanders. The new lands in the east seemed the land of promise to all who had no hope of a homestead in their own country. The result did not fail to show itself. Mecklenburg and Pomerania, Brandenburg, Meissen—the later kingdom of Saxony—Lausitz and Silesia soon became German lands, in which the Slavs were absorbed by the German immigrants save for a few scattered remnants.

At the same time something of greater significance had occurred. With the settlement of eastern Holstein the Germans had for the first time reached the Baltic. The result was not long in showing itself. Let us listen once more to the contemporary chronicler. "Thereafter," writes Helmold, "Count Adolf came to a place called Buku, and found there the wall of a forsaken fortress which Cruto, a chieftain and enemy of God, had built, and a spacious island, bordered by two streams, the Trave and the Wakenitz... There this good man, observing the beneficent character of the place and of its fine harbour, began to build a town, and called it Lübeck." This was in 1143. The first German port on the Baltic had been created—a year before Albert the Bear took possession of Brandenburg. But the little Count of Holstein was not the man to make full use of the opportunities secured. That needed a greater than he, one whose strong arm offered better protection. This was Henry the Lion, the powerful Duke of Saxony. In 1157 he induced the count to cede the town to him, and from then its development really began. After the fall of Henry the Lion in 1180, it became a free town of the Reich, and this greatly assisted its progress. Before long the Germans had begun to dominate the Baltic from Lübeck.

Up to then the Baltic had belonged to other peoples. The Wend had manœuvred his boat along its southern

CONQUEST OF THE NORTH-EAST

shores, fishing and plundering ; in earlier times the Swedes and later the Danes had passed along them. Now there came the German, pushing the others aside, and the first fruit of his labour was the founding of a German colony on the farther shore of the Baltic, in Livonia. Missionaries and traders had already shown the way thither. There followed in 1201, with the founding of the town of Riga, the creation of the strong bridgehead from which the conquest and opening up of the country could proceed. This was the work of the founder of an ecclesiastical state, Albert of Bremen, Bishop of Livonia. As early as 1225 the territory was organized as a separate state.

In this period it seemed as though the colony would lose all connexion with its home country. The Danes in their retreat did their utmost to stem the German influx. They endeavoured to recover their lost ground, and a moment came when it looked as if everything that had been won would be lost again to the envious neighbours. Here, too, Germany's enemies had a winning game in the time of the struggle for the throne between Staufen and Guelph. Waldemar the Victorious made himself master of Holstein, Mecklenburg, and Pomerania ; Lübeck and Hamburg accepted his rule, and he entered into rivalry with the Germans on the far side of the Baltic ; Esthonia had to be abandoned to him, and he built his royal castle in Reval In the end, however, all his German neighbours joined forces against him, and in the battle of Bornhövede (1227) the greatness of Denmark came to a sudden end. For a long time Denmark ceased to be formidable.

A third competitor for the possession of the shores of the Baltic had come on the scene some time before this : the Poles. They already possessed the lower reaches of the Vistula, with the port of Danzig. They reached out for more, and in the end lost everything. Duke Conrad of Masuria, in order to extend his rule over the Lithuanians in Prussia, invited the Teutonic Order into the country. The Order came (1230), secured a footing in Prussia— and drove out the Poles. It secured a grant of the land from Frederick II. Step by step, amid hard and persistent fighting, it conquered Prussia and opened the country to German settlement. Thus the whole of the southern shores of the Baltic became German. The easternmost point, Memel, was reached as early as 1252 ; but Danzig was not wrested from the Poles until 1309. The Order had entered Livonia about 1240 ; in 1346, when it succeeded in purchasing Esthonia from the King of Denmark, German dominion extended unbroken along the whole of the Baltic from the lower Elbe to Lake Peipus and the Narowa.

The value of these new conquests lay not only in the increased room to live that they afforded to the German people, but probably still more in the domination over one of the principal trade routes. It may safely be said that Germany became in the course of the thirteenth century a country of towns, that is, of trade and industry, and the towns in the newly won districts prospered multitudinously as in the homeland, indirectly through the effects of the Baltic trade to which the Germans had gained access at the beginning of the century, and which fell in the course of time entirely into their hands.

The middle ages, that is, the whole period up to the discovery of the new routes over the ocean, had only two main arteries of world trade. One route lay across the Mediterranean, the other through the Baltic into the North Sea. The former brought westwards the wares of the Near East and of India, the latter was the trade route for the wide plains of Russia. This latter route had always existed, but only became a busy one after the beginning of the German conquest of the Baltic shores. Its economic importance must not be measured by the standard of Baltic trade in later times, when the Baltic lost steadily in importance to the great trans-oceanic routes. Before these routes were opened its importance was probably about equal to that of the Mediterranean route. A great quantity of essential raw material was carried westwards over the Baltic either from its coastal territories—Prussia, Poland, Livonia, Sweden—or from the immense Russian hinterland : grain, flax, hemp, wax, honey, butter, hides, fat and tallow, timber, resin, tar, ashes, iron ore, copper, furs, and finally, one of the main articles, fish. Conversely, the Baltic countries were a remunerative market for the industrial goods of the west, especially woven fabrics, and salt and wine and all that came from the east as the result of exchange between the western and southern countries.

The whole of this very extensive barter trade was secured for themselves almost exclusively by the Germans from the thirteenth century onward. It was German merchants and shippers who brought the goods from the east to the great world trade centre in Flanders, and there took over the return freight for which the east was waiting. By close co-operation and loyalty to one another they succeeded in almost monopolizing the Russian market. No other country was able to compete with the German merchant in Novgorod on Lake Ilmen, and his domination of Russian trade assured him predominance and a position of advantage in the western countries. Out of this joint working of the German merchants in foreign markets and common representation of their interests there grew in time an alliance between the German towns engaged in trade in the Baltic—the German Hansa alliance. No one knows when it first came into existence. It was never " founded " or " created by resolution," it just grew. Towards the middle of the fourth century we find it in full working as an alliance embracing most of the towns of north Germany, including the colonies, from Kampen on the Zuider Zee to Reval on the Gulf of Finland—not only the coastal towns but also the inland towns that lived by trading with the coast. The purpose of the alliance was no other than the maintenance of German domination of shipping and trade on the Baltic. It has often been credited with aims beyond this, aims which it did not and could not pursue; it has been imagined as a sort of potential substitute for the waning power of the Empire or the germ of a new order based on the rule of burgesses and municipalities. Such ideas never entered the heads of the Hansa merchants, and lay far beyond their horizon. Their sole and single concern was with their trading interests, and they would have regarded it as an ill-advised suggestion had they been asked to subordinate these interests to national and political aims. Nor were they either so united in view or so closely organized as might appear at this distance; on the contrary they were themselves divided by sectional interests which only too often crippled their operations. In the last resort the Hansa was entirely without means of compulsion of its members; its whole basis was voluntary. The alliance could thus only endure if it did not put too severe a strain on the spirit of sacrifice and subordination of its members. The conditions of its existence set narrow limits to its possible political aims and activities; any ambitious positive policy would have destroyed it.

Only once in its long history did it venture on an important political initiative. This was in the time of King

Waldemar IV of Denmark, the restorer of the kingdom, who laid the axe at the root of Germany's trade in the Baltic by robbing it of its bases in Gothland and Schonen. The loss brought the whole of the Hansa towns together in 1367 into the Confederation of Cologne ; they warred as a single body, and in 1370 reduced Denmark to submission in the Peace of Stralsund. This success not only secured the possession of the Baltic trade to the Germans, but gave them a political dominance, openly exercised, over their Nordic neighbours. In the struggles that followed for the crowns of Denmark, Sweden, and Norway the Hansa everywhere turned the scale, and it was the German princes—Dukes of Mecklenburg and Pomerania, Counts of Oldenburg, even on one occasion a Bavarian—who struggled for mastery, won, held, and lost again, until in 1397 the treaty of Kalmar brought the union of the three kingdoms, another triumph of the policy of the Hansa, effected through its intervention.

It may be well to devote a little more attention to the German colonization along the Baltic and its results. It is too often forgotten that this is the greatest achievement of the German people in all the centuries of its existence, an achievement which would alone assure the Germans a place among the pioneers of civilization. To appreciate this one need do no more than glance at the map of the wide territories from the Elbe to Lake Peipus. They had been a wilderness, and had been converted by the Germans into highly cultivated country. This achievement may be compared to what the Romans had made of the provinces which they had subjugated in ancient times. It is excelled in intrinsic importance by the Anglo-Saxon colonization of new continents, but, measured by contemporary standards, the German achievement in the Baltic countries must rank at least equally high.

The effects of German colonization were by no means confined to the limits of the territory actually won for the Empire. They extended far beyond this, throughout Poland and Galicia and down to the Ukraine and Roumania.

One may well regard Poland as the hereditary enemy of the Germans in the east. The two neighbour countries had been enemies since first the old multiplicity of Polish princedoms was gathered up into a kingdom at the beginning of the fourteenth century. Yet Poland came for a while, in the middle of that century, under German

CONQUEST OF THE NORTH-EAST

influence. King Casimir himself, the only lord of Poland who gained the title Great, lent his hand to the development. In the peace of Kalisch (1343), which he concluded with the Teutonic Order, he brought old disputes to an end for a generation or more, renounced Danzig, and introduced a policy of dependence on Germany. He brought German colonists into the country, encouraged them to found villages and towns, which he allowed to be governed by German law, and so covered his kingdom with a network of German settlements. Later he conquered Eastern Galicia and followed the same policy. At that period the services in the churches of Cracow and Lemberg were said and sung in German, German was the language of the courts, and the University of Cracow was simply a German university in Polish territory. Figures exist which show the extent of this German influence. It has been calculated that the total number of districts in Poland and Galicia which were under German law was some 650, and the majority of these must originally have been German settlements. Polish historians have freely admitted in the past how much the country gained by this. The earliest of them, John Dlugosz, writing about a century after King Casimir's day, considered that the king might have said of himself, as Augustus did, that he had found an empire of wood and left an empire of stone. Other writers recognized, in the sixteenth and seventeenth centuries, that without the work done by the Germans Poland would never have progressed as she did, and up to the last the German settlements were greatly superior to the Polish. Unwilling testimony is given to this down to our own day by the Polish language, in its large use of words borrowed from the German in all that concerns business and municipal life.

The work done by the Germans along the Vistula and in the Carpathians is very simply defined: they introduced into the country, as along the shores of the Baltic, a higher civilization. In the face of this fact, and what became of these countries when the German influence diminished or ceased altogether, one might well say—if it is permissible to speak of a mission in life of whole peoples, specially assigned to them—that history tells us that the German people was called to civilize its eastern neighbours. Around 1400 no one would have contested that the whole north and east of Europe—the Scandinavian countries, Poland and Hungary—were what would to-day be described as a German sphere of influence, and somewhat later the fact actually received formal recognition. At the big ecclesiastical congresses of Constance and Basle the Danes and Swedes, Poles and Hungarians were all counted in as part of the German nation. All these countries were secondary extensions of German civilization.

All this was only possible because the German element represented something more than a superiority of civilized resources. Emperor and Empire had virtually no share in it. Their part was confined, over this whole region, to the intervention of Frederick I in 1163, when he cut Silesia off from Poland and united it more closely with the Empire, so furthering its Germanization. That is all that the Empire did for the growth of the nation. The Bishops of Livonia were made feudal lords of the territories which they conquered in 1207 and 1225, and East Prussia was granted to the Teutonic Order, but these cannot rank as more than simple acts of registration by the Imperial Chancellery. The conquest of the north-east by the German nation was effected with no help from the Empire; for that reason the work outlived the imperial power.

The elements which provided the needed background of force for the German colonization in the neighbouring countries on east and north were the Hansa and the Teutonic Order. The Empire played no part in the creation or support of either of these. This is the astonishing feature of the whole drama of the German colonial movement of the middle ages, that it proceeded so entirely from particularist elements, without any reliance on a strong central power, and yet was filled with a consciously national spirit. The Hansa and the Teutonic Order were German first and foremost. The former had no other purpose than to espouse the common interests of Germans, and Germans alone, in rivalry with foreigners; the Order by its very basis excluded all that was not of German origin; it was the only strictly national spiritual order that the middle ages produced. How strong must the motives have been that gave rise to such a movement, so powerful, so far reaching, so deliberate and concentrated, in spite of the absence of any uniform plan and resolve, a completely spontaneous movement proceeding from the vital needs of locally isolated elements as though by the working of a natural instinct! It is impossible to withhold one's admiration from this movement, but the admiration is mixed with regret for the results that might have been achieved from such efforts had they been unified and ordered by a strong central power. Lacking that, entire success was nowhere achieved. The work was not pushed through with that finality which alone could have given permanence to its results, and the frontiers attained were of an entirely impossible nature. The connexion between Livonia and Prussia depended primarily on sea communication, as the intervening Samogitia (Kovno) was never conquered.

Emperor Charles IV, that shrewd observer and calculator, saw the possibilities offered here in the east, and tried to avail himself of them. In other districts he carelessly abandoned territory and allowed claims long pressed to lapse, but in the east he conceived a far-seeing policy of expansion. His plan was to unite the whole of Bohemia's neighbour countries under the rule of a German princely house. For this purpose he acquired from the house of Wittelsbach the Mark of Brandenburg, concluded a treaty with the Habsburgs under which if either of the two houses died out the whole of the Bohemian and Austrian states should come into one ownership, and arranged the betrothal of his younger son Sigismund to the daughter and heiress of the King of Hungary, who in 1370 had become King of Poland also. Had these plans ripened into achievement, there would have been formed a great empire embracing Brandenburg, Bohemia, Poland and Hungary, and reaching from the Elbe to the Dniester, the lower Danube, and the Balkans; for such was the extent at that time of Hungary's overlordship: it embraced Roumania and Serbia. In this empire the German element would have been in control. Here was a first foreshadowing of the political idea which in later centuries was to be the central idea of the Habsburg state.

It was not then realized. Charles IV died in 1378, four years before the question of the Hungarian and Polish succession arose. Sigismund only maintained his hold of the Hungarian crown with great difficulty, and at the cost of long continued struggles; the Polish crown he lost. And this failure produced a counter-movement which was in the end to destroy German dominance in the east.

The backbone of the German predominance on the continent was the Teutonic Order in Prussia and Livonia.

Its nature has been exaggerated in the same way as that of the Hansa; its successes have misled observers as to its power. It was never a very great organization; its rule, based on military force and often exercised in brutal forms, had no deep root in the country. It was able to maintain its existence so long as it did not stand face to face with a consolidated great power. It had at all times to take into account two opponents, Poland and Lithuania, but these were deeply hostile to one another. So long as their mutual enmity lasted the Order was safe. It came to its end in 1386, when the Poles, in order to get rid of the German heir to the Polish crown, called in Grand Duke Jagiel from Lithuania, gave him the younger daughter of the king in marriage, and invested him with the succession to the throne. Faced with this Polish-Lithuanian union the situation of the Order in Prussia became critical. Ill-fortune and defective political and military leadership completed its downfall; the collapse came in 1410. The united forces of Poland and Lithuania faced the army of the Order at Tannenberg, before the Livonian contingent had been brought up. The Order was routed and its power broken from that day, especially as within the country the nobles and the towns stood aloof from it and eventually revolted. For half a century the Order still tried to defend its position; then, in 1466, faced with the defection of the nobles and the towns, who were making common cause with Poland, it had to capitulate in the Peace of Thorn. The western portion of its territory, with Danzig, was ceded to the Poles; Polish suzerainty was acknowledged over the eastern portion. The Empire had lost Prussia.

About the same time as the heavy blow struck at Germany's power at Tannenberg, she suffered another serious loss—that of Bohemia. The Czech kingdom owed its rise mainly to the stream of German immigration, which had almost always been encouraged by the lords of the country. The German element had thus become predominant. But in the course of time the very work of civilization done by the Germans awakened a nationalist reaction among the Czechs. This found its expression in the vigorous religious and social movement which is associated with the name of John Huss. From the very beginning this movement was also of a nationalist character, directed at the removal of the German predominance in state and church, learning and trade. The struggle began with the expulsion of the Germans in 1409 from the University of Prague, which they had governed until then. Church and state together failed to overcome Bohemian separatism. Ultimately terms had to be come to with the heretics, and a wide measure of ecclesiastical and political autonomy and privilege conceded to them. From then on the period of German dominance in Bohemia was over. In the Hussite wars the Bohemians had come into close relations with the Poles; for a while a Polish prince had played the part of a Bohemian heretic king. After the conclusion of peace Germanism remained the enemy. The régime of George of Podiebrad, first regent and from 1458 on King of Bohemia, was definitely Czech and nationalist. In the very spot which had until then been the centre and mainstay of Germanizing influences in the east, the Slav element had come into power in openly admitted hostility to everything that was German.

Thus from the beginning of the fifteenth century the German predominance in the east had been on the wane on land; German rule of the seas was also to be challenged a little later. The Dutch, who had never allied themselves with the Hansa, came out into opposition to the German monopoly of trade and shipping in the Baltic, and very soon proved most formidable competitors. The Hansa tried force against their rivals, prohibiting them from sailing in the Baltic. But they failed to maintain their supremacy in the two years' war which followed (1438-1440); in the peace the Dutch wrested a temporary permission to trade, and not only were they never again ousted, but from decade to decade they pushed their way more and more into what had been the Germans' exclusive province. Here again the beginning of the end is plainly to be discerned about the middle of the fifteenth century. Germany's eastern front, only a little while before so powerful and formidable, had been forced along the whole line into the defensive, had begun to waver, had already here and there been broken.

Much the same process had been going on about the same time in the west. The geographical problem of the double front, the evil gift placed in Germany's cradle by the fates, the simultaneous threat from east and west, showed its full peril in the fifteenth century and began to dominate the situation of the Empire. At the moment when the old Empire was falling to pieces, a formidable

Great Power had arisen in the west. Philip II, the founder of France's unity, was contemporary with the civil war between Staufen and Guelph. The significance has already been pointed out of the fact that the first victory which the French won over the Germans, at Bouvines in 1214, decided the issue over the German crown. France's new military power meant from the very beginning a threat to the German frontiers: she was out for conquest at the cost of the German Empire. The French-speaking population of the frontier territories of Lorraine and Hennegau were a standing temptation to this. Accordingly there came into French heads at a very early date all sorts of conceptions of natural frontiers which the kingdom had got to have. There was talk in Paris as early as the beginning of the fourteenth century of the necessity for the Rhine to be the dividing line between France and Germany. On top of this came the efforts of French kings to acquire the German throne for themselves or their house. Such ideas found no decided rejection at the hands of the German princes. In 1324 the Habsburgs had seen no harm in helping the French candidate for election to the German kingdom if he would cede to them all the principal towns on the Upper Rhine and in eastern Switzerland. The power of his own house mattered more to the normal German prince than the Empire.

No wonder, then, that the French pressure met only with faint resistance. It was directed first towards Lorraine and the former Burgundian kingdom. The bishoprics and towns along Meuse and Moselle, Toul and Verdun and their environs, were either annexed or came under French protection as early as the thirteenth century. Franche-Comté and Lyons went the same way; in 1343 the Dauphiné followed. Charles IV settled outstanding questions in 1378 by ceding his sovereignty over the kingdom of Burgundy to France, after he had separated Savoy and western Switzerland from it and added them to Germany—thus shaping the frontier which France retained until the middle of the last century.

The only reason why the losses of the Empire were not more severe lay in the situation in which France herself was placed. The unending war which she had to wage with England for her very existence, the so-called Hundred Years' War, had long afforded the best of protection for Germany. Towards the end of the war, when the English

CONQUEST OF THE NORTH-EAST

were coming off badly, that became clear at once. The French army, deprived of its employment by the armistice of 1444, appeared in Lorraine and Alsace, took up winter quarters there, demanded submission from Metz and Strassburg, and made an attack on Basle. Its demands were rejected, and it was finally induced to retire through a combination of negotiations and threats. But Alsace had been within a hair's breadth of there and then becoming French.

These, however, were petty episodes compared with the tasks on which the new Burgundian State was embarking. This state had grown to greatness through the union of the French duchy of Burgundy with the French county of Flanders in 1386. From the first it had pursued a policy of ruthless expansion at the expense either of the French or the German crown. Artois and Picardy fell to it on the one side, and on the other Brabant, Hennegau, Holland, and finally, in 1440, Luxemburg. Nor did the duke admit German overlordship even in respect of the incontestably German territories which he had acquired. All Sigismund's efforts to oppose him (on one occasion he declared war on Burgundy, in alliance with France) failed at the outset.

From 1467 on, this new Great Power had as its ruler Duke Charles the Bold. His ambitions reached out far and wide: he would rule as far as the Alps, even beyond them as far as Genoa; he would found a kingdom extending from sea to sea, would recall to life the old Lotharingian State, and, needless to say, be its king. In 1469 he succeeded in gaining a footing in Alsace. Sigismund of Tirol, a Habsburg in need of money, pledged to Charles his house's possessions and rights in Alsace and the Black Forest in consideration of a money payment. In 1473 Lorraine fell; the duke surrendered the fortresses of the province to Charles. In 1474 there came an attack on Neuss, in the electorate of Cologne. The attack was beaten off, but it showed plainly where the compass of the Burgundian plans pointed: the left bank of the Rhine was in danger.

The danger was averted not by the Empire, not by the Emperor and Diet, but by an alliance of the threatened Upper Rhenish towns and lords with the Swiss; the allies in a determined assault brought to a sudden end all the majesty of the lord of Burgundy, Alsace, and Lorraine. In January 1477, on the battlefield of Nancy, Charles the

Bold lost the day, lost his last army, and lost his own life. Alsace was freed and the left bank of the Rhine saved.

It had been only an episode, but the episode had thrown a vivid light on the situation of the Empire. The Empire was defenceless. And who could say whether with the death of Charles the peril in the west was finally past? Whether another would not soon begin the same adventure with better success? Everything now depended on what became of the Burgundian realm, which Duke Charles had left to his only daughter. If her cousin and feudal lord, the king of France, were to lay hands on her duchy, and after absorbing it to take up the work of her father, the peril which Charles the Bold had represented to the German Empire would have returned in yet more formidable dimensions.

At the same time the clouds were gathering ominously in the east. There had been war with Bohemia since 1468. Matthias Corvinus, King of Hungary, had begun the conquest of Bohemia. Before the issue had been decided George of Podiebrad had died (1471); Poland had come in, and the two conquerors had shared the booty: a Polish prince received the Kingdom of Bohemia itself, and the neighbouring provinces of Moravia, Silesia and Lausitz were incorporated in Hungary. How long would the victorious Magyars rest content with this success? Austria lay in the midst of their territories; she had not ventured to intervene in the struggle for Bohemia as her prince had not felt strong enough to do so. But this prince was no other than the German Emperor, Frederick III. Emperor and Empire no longer had the strength, or no longer the courage, to prevent the loss of imperial territories like Bohemia and Silesia. Would they be able to defend Austria?

Cologne and Strassburg on one side, Vienna on the other in danger—the situation could not be worse. The problem of the double front was pressing on Germany with all its weight. The Empire seemed to be face to face with the destiny which in such situations has sooner or later overtaken many a country—partition between its neighbours. But this did not come. Once more destiny changed her course; the peril was averted, and new prospects opened up, through a capricious concatenation of events which raised the house of Habsburg to a Great Power and a world power, and so furnished Germany for a period with greater influence and better protection.

CHAPTER VI

THE TERRITORIAL STATES IN THE FIFTEENTH CENTURY. THE RISE OF THE HABSBURGS

It should not be assumed that it would have been hopeless for the Empire to engage in a war on two fronts. Its forces might have sufficed for this. Germany was very far from being as thickly populated as to-day: France had, if not more, certainly not much fewer subjects. But Germany had the best of soldiery, a soldiery with which the French king himself was unable to dispense. Germany was in every respect stronger than her eastern neighbours, and with any reasonably well-devised policy could count on allies in the west. Thus the struggle would not have been hopeless. But success would have depended on one essential thing: organic internal unity and the association of the country's forces in a common purpose. In a word, it would have been necessary for the Empire to become a unit.

It was the very opposite of this. The fifteenth century was one of the periods of extreme division of forces, as extreme as the period of the Interregnum. It was the heyday of the territorial states. They had progressed and attained not a little in their own sphere. Most of them had won through out of the anarchy of irresponsible and insubordinate estates; the princes had reduced barons and towns to subservience. The nucleus had been formed of a trained body of officials, a body that felt that it had grown up with the state, lived by it and for it, was its support and defence. An ordered administration and adequate finances had been secured. It is well known how much the first Hohenzollerns achieved in this direction in Brandenburg, how they reduced to submission the insubordinate nobles, the "robber barons," and subjected the towns to their authority. Much the same process had been going on in most of the German territories, if not everywhere in the same dramatic way or with the same entire success. About the middle of the fifteenth century the princes established their authority over the towns also. A number of towns which until then had been " free " were forced into submission to the territorial ruler. The most striking instance was Mainz (1462). The time of the great alliances of towns was over; the princes had triumphed all along the line.

It was on this soil that there sprang up the type of the princely father of his country, who with more or less understanding and self-control took thought for the needs of his people because in doing so he increased his own strength. This type of ruler appeared frequently towards the end of the fifteenth century; one may mention Eberhard of Württemberg or, indeed, Gerhard of Jülich. The type found its best expression in the following century in Frederick the Wise of Saxony.

Among the princely houses a few, owners of wide lands, stood out as the leaders: the Wittelsbacher, the Wettiner, the Guelphs, Habsburgs, Hohenzollerns—the latter in Brandenburg from 1415 on. But these houses were rarely united among themselves; for instance, the Guelphs were weakened by dividing their inheritance, and the Wittelsbacher were split up into two lines, Bavarian and Palatinate, which were continually at issue with one another. There remained as the most powerful, apart from the Habsburgs, the houses of Bavaria, Wettin, and Brandenburg. The last-named house was the least influential as its lands were remote and very poor. It gained importance for a while through its Frankish inheritance of estates around Nuremberg—Ansbach, Bayreuth, Kulmbach. But these were dispersed by division in a succeeding generation. In 1423 the house of Wettin added to its old possessions of Meissen and Thuringia the duchy and electoral title of East Saxony. But from 1485 on the house was divided into the elder (Ernestine) Thuringian and Saxon line and the younger (Albertine) Meissen line, and the two branches were not always on the best of terms. This division among the principal dynasties made it possible for some of the lesser ones at times to play almost an equal part with them. Examples were Württemberg, which was raised in 1495 to a duchy, and Hesse, which gained considerably in importance through such inheritances as Katzenelnbogen and Ziegenhain.

It cannot be said that the increase in the power of the

THE RISE OF HABSBURG

princes brought improved internal order or increased stability to the Empire; rather the reverse. What the princes gained in power the king lost. It would have been easier for him to maintain the royal prestige among a crowd of small and weak territorial states. Actually we find the monarchy sinking from the middle of the fifteenth century into an insignificance which recalls the times of the Interregnum. Nor was internal order within the Empire improved by the change. The territorial rulers, especially the greater ones, used their new power first of all to increase their territories at the expense of their neighbours'. The second half of the fifteenth century especially is filled with frontier feuds and inheritance quarrels: Palatinate against Bavaria, Bavaria against Hohenzollern, and so on. These issues were the things that really mattered to the princely rulers in their own view, and their thoughts and activities centred on them; on them they squandered their personal fortunes, which frequently were of no mean size. The classic type of this society was the Brandenburger Albert Achilles, who had spent half his life in feud or war, and was himself wounded so often that his body was covered with scars. He was extraordinarily shrewd, *vulpes germanica*, the German fox, was the name the Italians gave him; a man of restless activity, enterprising and persistent, a man of resource and a subtle diplomat, in every respect a man of mark; and yet, what is there to show for all his active life? It would be difficult for anyone to say. So with many another of his contemporaries. Their aims were too petty, and one gets from the whole period almost an impression of purposelessness.

Such was the political leadership of the nation at a time when its situation between its neighbour states was becoming daily more precarious. It is easy to conceive that under these circumstances the Empire had no foreign policy of any sort. Whence could it draw the means for a foreign policy? Its means were being eaten up by internal dissension. And whence could the insight, the judgment of world affairs be drawn? Every eye was fixed on the next-door neighbour. The sight was keen as far as the horizon of the petty state, fairly clear even for the surrounding landscape, but for the rest of Germany it grew dimmer and dimmer, and to all that lay beyond it was completely blind. The princes had no conception whatever of a common interest of the nation.. They were completely indifferent to the losses on the western frontier of the Empire, and equally so to the subjection of the Teutonic Order to Poland. The Empire was like an animal that has no central organ of communication between its limbs, so that the suffering of one left the rest unaffected. Its body could even be mutilated without causing pain to it.

The Empire had a King and Emperor; theoretically he should have played the part of a central organ. But nowhere was the gap between theory and reality wider. Sigismund was the last Emperor who made any attempt at pursuing an imperial policy. He rarely succeeded. His successor, Albert II, in the few months of his reign, in 1438-9, did not approach the problem, and his successor, Frederick III (1440-93), did not attempt to do so in all the fifty-three years of his reign.

At the very outset Frederick awakened the most stubborn resistance by his attempt to use foreign forces on the soil of the Empire to further the interests of his house.

From the time of Rudolf I onwards the house of Habsburg had been the strongest of the German princely houses. It had long been in possession of Upper Alsace, central and eastern Switzerland, and the southern part of the Black Forest. Rudolf had added Austria and Styria, and Carinthia and Tirol had been acquired under Charles IV. On the other hand, the Habsburg possessions in Switzerland had gradually been lost to the Eidgenossenschaft, the Swiss Confederacy, which was first formed on Habsburg soil by the Lake of the Four Cantons, had gradually absorbed the whole territory from the Jura to Graubünden, and had grown under the leadership of the towns of Zurich and Berne into a separate federation of States. By the time of Frederick III all that remained to the Habsburgs was a small territory on the left bank of the Upper Rhine. The Emperor's first concern was to recover the lost territory. He was indifferent, in pursuing this aim, alike to the dignity of the king and the security of the Empire. He himself summoned the French army into his country in 1444, to enter his personal service against the Swiss. He denied that he had done so, but the French made public the letter in which he had invited them in, and when they withdrew with nothing accomplished the Emperor had to suffer not only the losses of his unsuccessful enterprise but

THE RISE OF HABSBURG

the disgrace that attached to it. The episode shows how even the king had ceased to take thought for the nation. He had become a mere territorial magnate with the same narrowly personal interests as the rest. Imperial policy, imperial interests no longer counted with him, only the interests and policy of the house of Habsburg, and the imperial crown meant to him no more than a means of more effectively pursuing the interests of his house.

Frederick's unsuccessful attack on the Confederacy had helped it forward to greater military efficiency. Thirty years later, in the war with Charles the Bold, this federation of towns and cantons showed itself far more efficient than all the princes. The Confederates, the " Schwyzer " or Swiss, as they began to be called, became a European power through their victory over the great Duke of Burgundy. They considered themselves an independent power. They no longer took seriously their allegiance to the German Empire ; they pursued their own policy without consulting the Empire, and, as the Habsburg Emperor was their hereditary enemy, in opposition to Emperor and Empire.

Even after this loss the house of Habsburg, *illustris domus Austriæ*, would have been the most powerful in the Empire, but for the fatal divisions at inheritance and the enmities that sprang from them. Emperor Frederick III was at first only duke in Styria and Carinthia. Austria belonged to his nephew Ladislaus, son of Emperor Albert II, for whom he was only regent and guardian. Not until 1458, with the death of the nephew, did it fall to Frederick. In Alsace and the Black Forest his brother was ruler, and after the brother's death a cousin, Duke Sigismund of Tirol. Relations with both were strained. And what a character was Frederick's ! Phlegmatic, apathetic to the point of cowardly indifference to all dignity, yet invincibly persuaded of the future greatness of his house, he was summed up by one of his councillors in the sarcastic remark that " We mean to conquer the world by sitting still." It is difficult to suppose that he ever had a thought for the German Empire. At one time twenty-seven years passed without his ever leaving his hereditary possessions, or showing himself " in his kingdom ; " he was merely represented by envoys at the Diets, like a foreign prince. Such was the man whose duty it should have been to fight the battles of the Empire and protect it from loss. What he actually did was just the opposite : he calculated that the losses which the Empire suffered in his time would serve the advancement of his house.

He never lifted a finger against the plans of conquest of Charles the Bold. He was quite content to see the Burgundian State grow in importance, for he hoped to inherit it. Charles had only one daughter, and the Emperor's son should marry her. Marriage and inheritance were Austria's methods of advance at this period, in east and west alike. Frederick easily consoled himself for the Hungarian conquests since he had a treaty of inheritance with Hungary, dated 1463, under which if either house were to die out the other succeeded it. And Matthias had no children. Thus Frederick stood to gain the Burgundian inheritance in the west and the Hungarian in the east, both without a stroke. With such counting-house calculations was the supreme head of the German nation content.

Sometimes, however, Fate allows herself strange freaks with the careers of men. She exacted in the end a very usurious reckoning from the most incurably lethargic of all rulers. For all his efforts Frederick never secured the betrothal of Maximilian with Maria, the daughter and heiress of Charles of Burgundy, during the Duke's lifetime; Charles knew better than to play this best card in his diplomatic hand. The Netherlands Diet, in order to protect the country from France, who proposed to lay hands on Charles's inheritance, called in the Grand Duke, and gave him the hand of their princess. Maximilian became Maria's consort, and, after her early death in 1482, regent for her son Philip. He had severe struggles in the Netherlands, but maintained his position and assured the continuance of the Burgundian State. Thus was laid the foundation of the new Habsburg power.

The Burgundian marriage of 1477 was also an event of far-reaching consequence in the history of Germany. It brought to the most powerful of the German princely houses an increase of power which lifted it far above all the others. The imperial crown could no longer be taken from it without letting loose civil war. It was bound also to demand it, for only as the reigning imperial house could the Habsburgs knit together in mutual defence and so maintain their hold of their far-spread possessions—on the Lower Rhine and the Scheldt, on the Upper Rhine, in the Eastern Alps, and along the Danube.

THE RISE OF HABSBURG

This newly won power, however, of a German house involved the Empire in foreign complications which it had not known in its earlier history. The Burgundian State had not only been at issue with Germany but almost more acutely so with France. With its territory the Habsburgs inherited its hostility to the French crown, and in increased degree. The King of France had had no alternative but to accept the fact of Maximilian's inheritance ; it had still withheld certain portions of it from him—Bourgogne, Franche-Comté, Picardy, Artois—and had never given up the idea of annexing the rest, especially Flanders. Maximilian, for his part, had no intention of renouncing everything that in his view was due to him as his father-in-law's successor. He secured Franche-Comté and Artois, to the cession of which France reconciled herself in 1493 ; Picardy and Bourgogne he demanded to the last without success. From then on there was no cessation of the hostility between France and Austria, which for centuries grew more and more to be a dominating element in European politics.

Into this dispute Germany was bound to be drawn The French hostility was extended quite as a matter of course to the German Empire, at the head of which the house of Austria stood, and the seed was thus first sown of the hereditary Franco-German enmity. It quickly germinated and struck root, ultimately to cast its malignant shadow over the history of the German nation for all time. No one can say whether even without the marriage of 1477 there would not have come a permanent enmity between the two nations. The geographical conditions and the character of the French people might together have produced it in any case. But the fact remains that the hostility was first called into existence by Austria's succession to the Burgundian-Netherland State. Therein lies the significance of the year 1477 in German history.

While the house of Habsburg was thus laying the ground for its future greatness by acquiring new provinces in the north-west, it had lost its old possessions in the south-east. In 1485 Matthias of Hungary decided that his opportunity had come. He attacked and occupied Lower Austria, and settled down in the Habsburg capital, Vienna. Emperor Frederick had had no other resource than to seek aid from " the Empire." The help he asked for was not given. On the contrary, in his desperate situation he was compelled to agree to the appointment of a co-regent. On February 16, 1486, his son Maximilian I was elected King of Rome.

Maximilian was a remarkable man, one of those who present problems for their contemporaries and posterity to solve. Highly gifted, many-sided, artist and soldier, he stood far above the other princes of the Empire in talents and knowledge ; a man of restless activity, over big and little matters alike, a most brilliant representative of the ruling class ; and yet no ruler, because he lacked the gift of self-rule, the inward balance of spirit and will, fantasy and judgment, lacked steadiness of purpose and a sure sense of realities.

His elevation to be king amounted to the abdication of the old Emperor, for Maximilian at once took over the control of imperial affairs. So soon as circumstances in the Netherlands permitted and opportunity came with the death of Matthias without issue (April 6, 1490), he reconquered Austria. More than this he failed to achieve. The Hungarians were not to be persuaded to recognize the succession treaty of 1463, under which Maximilian should now have become king of Hungary. They elected to the throne Ladislaus, the Polish king of Bohemia. Austria had to make the best of the presence on her eastern frontier of a united Bohemian-Hungarian power, secundogeniture of the Jagellones, dynastically and politically supported by the Polish Empire, which then included not only Poland, Lithuania, and White Russia, but Prussia, Galicia, and the Ukraine, the Greater Poland, stretching from sea to sea, which represents once more the goal and ambition of the Poland of our own day.

Maximilian made no real effort to combat this powerful union of neighbour states, though it represented the most serious threat to Austria, even when the death of his father made him ruler of the hereditary lands. He merely continued his father's policy of alliances and expansion by inheritance. The old inheritance treaty was renewed by Hungary and Bohemia, and reinforced by a double marriage ; Louis, Crown Prince of Hungary and Bohemia, was united with Mary, granddaughter of the Emperor, while his grandson Ferdinand married Anna, daughter of the King of Bohemia.

Maximilian was content with a prudent acceptance of existing conditions in the east because all his thought centred on the western front, on the struggle with France. This he carried on with every possible means, with all the arts of warfare and diplomacy; he declared wars and concluded treaties, broke treaties and started war afresh, always in the effort to prevent France from growing stronger, since a strengthened France would infallibly stretch out her arm to seize the Burgundian heritage of his house. This was the primary reason for his hostilities against the French in 1494 when they set out to subdue Italy.

With this year begins, of course, the period of the constantly renewed warfare over the ownership of the peninsula which commanded the Mediterranean trade and so, at that time, Europe's principal world trade route. There is no need here to follow in detail the course of this involved series of military and diplomatic events. Complicated as the picture is, its outlines are simple so far as Maximilian's share in events is concerned. One day he would unite with the Italian states to drive out the French, and, in consideration of Italian money, send German soldiers to fight the French in Tuscany; the next, he might come to an arrangement with the French at the expense of the Italians. One day he might be speaking eloquently of the restoration of German imperial rule in Rome, and the next, instead of this, opening war on Venice, in order to annex the continental territories of the republic. But through all these contradictory moves and subterfuges there runs one leading motive: to prevent the French from becoming sole masters of Italy, since in that position, with the superior power so won, they would bring to bear an intolerable pressure on the hereditary Austrian possessions in Tirol and Flanders. Only his methods varied. If there seemed to be a chance of driving France right out of Italy, he joined in the war. If that prospect vanished, he sought an understanding with the enemy, in order at least to secure a share of the booty, if possible the lion's share.

With all his efforts, however, he got no farther than to leave the French masters in Milan and Upper Italy, and the Spaniards in Naples and the south. He himself gained nothing, and would have had to say that the reward of his life's work had been reaped by others, had not Fate favoured him in the eleventh hour, enabling his successor ultimately to inherit the lands of the rivals before whose superior power he himself had always had to stand aside.

On January 23, 1516, Ferdinand the Catholic, the first ruler of the whole of the Spanish realms of Aragon and Castile, died. His heir was the Emperor's grandson Charles, who since the death of his father Philip in 1506 had been ruler of the Netherlands. The chances of birth and death had paved the way for the young Habsburg to the throne of a realm which united Spain and Naples with the legendary gold lands across the ocean, as yet scarcely opened up. In addition to this he ruled the Burgundian State and the hereditary Habsburg possessions in Germany, which had been united under one ruler through the dying out of the last of the subsidiary lines (Tirol). It was an empire such as the world had never before seen that the Emperor would be able to leave to his grandson when he himself left the stage.

For that event preparation had to be made in one other thing: Charles must become the German Emperor. This was essential if he was to retain possession of his realms. For if the German Empire were to have any other ruler, then, however powerless he might be in Germany, he could still be extremely dangerous in alliance with the permanent enemy, France. At the least he would interfere with the communication between the scattered territories; perhaps he would attack the Netherlands in the rear, perhaps Austria. The Emperor's office alone formed the unifying bond for the scattered members of the new Habsburg world empire. It had to be secured if the Empire was to last.

Maximilian did not attain this goal. He died in 1519, before the election of Charles was assured. The work had to be completed by his counsellors and his grandsons.

Everyone knows what now happened; we need only deal briefly with the story. Charles's election would mean for France the risk of encirclement by her rival, and the French king and his statesmen decided to press his own candidature. They would win over the Electors with eloquence and gifts. The Electors accepted both; but Charles's envoys not only paid and promised but could threaten, for they had soldiers in readiness to march. Maximilian had secured a strong party in his support in Germany; its kernel was the Swabian Union, the only efficient organization in Germany, the only power in possession of a small but prepared army. The Union had just shown its mettle at this moment by driving out Duke Ulrich from Württemberg. It had annexed his territories and at once ceded them to the Habsburg monarch. Its victorious troops stood ready for further service.

It was under this military pressure that the election was carried out in Frankfurt in June 1519. For a moment it had seemed that the French candidate would win, but this had been illusory; Charles's election had been a foregone conclusion. The only possible way of preventing it would have been through a third, neutral candidacy, but no neutral candidate was discovered. The only possible one, Frederick the Wise of Saxony, refused to stand. He "preferred to be a powerful duke rather than a weak king." He has often been charged with cowardice in this, but his attitude only showed his shrewd insight. What part could he have played between Austria and France? He would at once have become dependent on the French, and the consequence would have been that the struggle between the European powers would have been fought out on German soil, as actually happened a hundred years later. This at least was saved from happening when Charles of Spain was chosen by the Electors as Roman Emperor on June 28, 1519.

But apart from that, there can be no doubt that the election was a grave misfortune for Germany. Everyone knew that it bore within it the seed of a declaration of war from the Empire against France. The programme of the Spanish-Burgundian policy was well known. On the Burgundian side it had the familiar plans of conquest—Artois, Picardy, Bourgogne—in other words, the destruction of the unity of the French state. And even if this aim was renounced there was on the Spanish side the desire to conquer Milan—in other words, to destroy the French predominance in Europe. To acquiesce in the presence of the French in Milan and Genoa was more than could permanently be expected of the Spanish King of Naples, if only because it rendered his hold of his own throne insecure. And as Roman Emperor he gained a legal title to Milan, which was a duchy of the Roman Empire.

Maximilian had tried his best during his lifetime to drag the German Empire into his war with France. He had never succeeded. The German princes and towns alike had no interest in these questions. They had seen only the burdens which the war would entail for themselves in the form of money payments, and had seen no personal gain to be had from it. It would, indeed, have been difficult to demonstrate what the Duke of Saxony or of Bavaria or the city of Frankfurt stood to gain if the Emperor won Picardy or Bourgogne or drove the French out of Milan or gained possession of the Venetian territories. Maximilian, with all the fire of his splendid eloquence, had pointed out again and again that his purpose was to assure to the German nation its proper rank among the peoples, to protect its ancient right which the foreigners wanted to deny it. He was referring in this to the imperial office, which the French were trying to secure. But he had found only lukewarm listeners among the princes. He might win applause among the lower orders of the people, but in political circles, at courts, in municipal council chambers, his appeal had aroused no answering echo.

Modern critics have held divided views. Some have taken the Emperor's part and blamed the princes for attention only to their personal interests and neglect of national considerations. For these critics Maximilian is the embodiment of the national idea in foreign policy. Others agree with his opponents and question the authority of the Emperor to be the mouthpiece of the nation's needs, as the national slogans were in his mouth only a pretext for purely egotistical dynastic aspirations. This latter view is unquestionably right in so far as it is impossible to describe Maximilian I as a ruler with a national way of thinking. He understood very well—what did not this gifted but unbalanced and unstable man understand!— how to be popular in Germany and with the Germans; but he was not a German. In family life he spoke and wrote French alone, and he felt best at ease among the Burgundian and Walloon nobles in the Netherlands; occasionally a contemptuous remark escaped from his lips about these stupid animals of Germans (*questi bestiali Tedeschi*). Nor did his policy take any account of the interests of the German nation when the advantage of the house of Habsburg was in question.

He showed this in the agreement of 1515 with Poland, Hungary and Bohemia. Here he sacrificed the interests of the nation in order to open the way for dynastic advantage. The Emperor and Reich had not yet recognized the Peace of Thorn, under which the Teutonic Order and Prussia made submission to Poland. Without the ratification of the Empire this Peace was open to question. Maximilian ratified it in 1515 in the hope of securing the succession to Hungary and Bohemia for himself and his heirs. Little can be more certain than that the Emperor only waved the flag of the German nation and the Roman Empire when they served him usefully as cover for dynastic interests of his own. The only question is whether the glorification of the imperial house in itself conceivably brought advantage to Empire and nation.

The Estates of the Reich were equally indifferent to the interests of the Empire. And, from their standpoint, with justice. What interest could they have in seeing the Empire grow in power ? They would have had to pay for it with their own resources and at the sacrifice of their own power. For nothing was more certain than that if the Empire grew more powerful the Emperor would gain a predominance over the princes which was in contradiction with constitutional usage and all tradition. It is easy to understand that the princes would not lend a hand in this direction.

We may well ask, however, whether it would really have been of advantage to Germany if Maximilian had attained his aims ; if the Burgundian State had recovered its former territories and the Emperor had even, perhaps, permanently acquired the Venetian lands. If this cosmopolitan house of the Habsburgs, scarcely to be counted any longer among the German princely houses, had acquired yet further non-German lands—French and Italian—would it or could it have given loyal consideration to Germany for her own sake ; would it not have followed the example of Max in 1515, and again and again have subordinated German national interests to its own international schemes and strivings ?

Thus the reluctant, refractory attitude of the Estates in face of the urgency of the Emperor is not only psychologically intelligible but entitled to recognition as more or less justifiable on material grounds.

The election of 1519 had, moreover, effected infinitely more than Max had worked for : the German crown had been delivered over to a ruler who could only regard Germany as a secondary possession, important by virtue of its geographical situation as a connecting link between his dispersed territories and as a field on which to assemble his forces for war against France ; valuable by virtue of its soldiery; but for the rest designed to be merely the servant of the possessions which were of primary import— Spain, the Netherlands, and Italy. This ruler, moreover, had forces at his beck and call which could indeed be a danger. There had been resistance when his grandfather threatened to become too arbitrary; but what was to be done with the grandson, who could bring into Germany in case of need, and play off against her, his Spanish troops and his Netherland wealth? It was no far-fetched apprehension that saw rising on the horizon the peril of a foreign dictatorship in the German Empire with its traditions of freedom.

The Electors must have felt this; for they tried to protect themselves against it—but only in the naïve fashion native to the simple citizen who strays into high politics: by a legal document. They tried to tie the new Emperor's hands by an imperial capitulation in which he promised to respect all rights and privileges, to conduct his government and in particular his foreign policy in accordance with the advice of the Electors, to take up residence in Germany, to hold no diet outside Germany, to bring no one to justice save in his own country, to make official use only of the German and Latin tongues, to bring no foreign troops into the Reich, to involve the Reich in no foreign wars, and finally to set up a "Reichs-regiment," a national governmental body composed of the Estates. This virtually meant nothing else than that the new Emperor should abdicate the functions of government in advance. The naïveté of this document is incredible. It was an open confession of the terror in which the foreign Emperor was held, and an effort to seek protection from him behind—a sheet of parchment. As if an Emperor would ever have bound himself by such clauses when it was to his interest and within his power to have nothing to do with them!

That is what happened. There were few of the promises embodied in the imperial capitulation which Charles would not have broken, and in the end the German nobles found themselves obliged openly to rebel against the Emperor in order to free themselves from foreign domination. In this they were successful; but they were not successful in averting the lasting consequences of the election of 1519. This election drew Germany, that unpolitical, disunited, policy-less nation, into the maelstrom of the European struggles for predominance, in which from generation to generation it sank more and more into the condition of a subordinate factor, a simple bone of contention fought over by other states. That is the significance of 1519 : it was the reaping of what 1477 had sown.

This could never have been so fatal if at the same moment there had not broken out the gravest of internal crises over spiritual matters. The whole frightfulness of the calamity which the elevation of the Spanish-Burgundian Charles to the imperial throne involved becomes clear when we recall what had happened in the spiritual life of the German people (and was further to happen) just when, by the placing of a foreign ruler on the German imperial throne, foreign powers, with their own interests and ambitions and resources, obtained control of the destiny of Germany.

CHAPTER VII

THE REFORMATION

IT is usual to speak of the greater part of Germany's past in terms of decay. From this judgment the beginning of the sixteenth century has not been excluded ; and not only on account of the incontestable defects in the secular organization of the country : the great revolution in religious matters which began in 1521 was long regarded very generally and is still regarded by many as a result and an index of decay, spreading from elements of rottenness. This judgment is untenable. At the beginning of the sixteenth century Germany was very far from being in decay. The unbiassed student will be unable to reject the impression of a constantly intensified growth, beginning at the turn of the fifteenth and sixteenth centuries and crowned in the two centuries that followed with a splendid flowering in many directions.

The enormous increase of wealth is unmistakable. There had already been so great an enrichment that many phenomena are met with which have in more recent times been accepted as signs of economic repletion : big accumulations of capital, the formation of rings, and speculation are phenomena which around 1500 were familiar and have many times been described. Germany was still behind Italy, the Netherlands, and France in prosperity, although there are indications that the difference cannot everywhere have been very great. In the international money market, for instance, the Medici had lost pride of place about 1500 as the foremost banking house to the Fuggers of Augsburg. It is not, of course, to be inferred that every Strassburg or Nuremberg merchant was a millionaire ; property was certainly very unevenly distributed, and there were whole countries and states which were in poverty ; evidence enough that not everyone had his belly full is provided by the ease with which mercenary soldiers could be hired in the German Empire. There was never any shortage of this article, as there was in France, where in spite of the greater density of population there was no adequate surplus for military needs. On the whole, however, Germany was a land of comfort and especially of increasing prosperity.

Along with increasing wealth went increasing culture. Culture was a relatively recent acquisition. Down to the middle of the fourteenth century there had been not a single seat of learning except those which the mendicant orders had maintained here and there for their members, institutions necessarily of limited capacity and correspondingly limited influence. For learning and culture the German had had in those times to go to France or Italy; especially to France. In the past Germany's spiritual culture had lain under French guidance.

So also with poetry. As is well known, the epics of court poets and the songs of the Minnesingers were alike entirely imitative, largely actual translations from French sources. French material, often actual French works, were presented in French guise, and it is hardly possible to dispute the judgment of an authority like Gervinus, that the imitation—especially in lyric poetry—was very greatly inferior to the original. The Nibelungenlied is a great exception which merely confirms the rule.

The spell was not broken until towards the end of the fourteenth century. With the opening of the universities of Prague (1348) and Vienna (1365), France lost her monopoly of the imparting of learning. The great schism of 1378 in the Church, resulting in the loyalty of Germans and French to different popes, completed the emancipation. The German priest could no longer study or teach in Paris as he was now regarded as a schismatic, and German universities sprang from the soil like mushrooms after rain. Heidelberg, Cologne, Erfurt, Leipzig, Rostock, Freiburg, later Basle, Greifswald, Ingolstadt and Tübingen, and finally Wittenberg, competed with one another and with the elder sisters beyond the frontier. They did not attain the standard of the French seats of learning, much less exceed it, but they fulfilled their function entirely, and their existence had a result which was certainly not aimed at when they were founded : the higher learning, in spite of its cosmopolitan curriculum and its international loyalties, received a special, one might fairly say a national character.

The same thing happened in literature. The French

influence disappeared entirely. The Hundred Years' War had largely brought France herself back to barbarism; it had silenced her poets. The German nobility had become steadily narrower in outlook since the end of the world policy of the Staufen; and the intellectual lead had been taken over by the German burgesses in poetry, in the art of the Meistersinger. The two developments worked together to liberate Germany from the influence of French literature. Even amid the active literary life of the court of Charles IV, who had been brought up in the French tradition and had studied in Paris, there was no longer any trace of French influence. The vernacular literature and poetry of Germany between the middle of the fourteenth and the beginning of the sixteenth century is not of a high order, but in comparison with the very much more significant creative work of the twelfth and thirteenth centuries (always, of course, excepting the Nibelungenlied) it has the merit of being of the soil, purely German, in a word, national.

The same is true of the plastic arts. In the thirteenth century the French Gothic had taken Germany by storm with its style and technique. The art of the last decades of the middle ages was still Gothic, but no longer French Gothic. It had freed itself from foreign influence and had found its own German way of expressing German feeling. To this day the churches and town halls of that period bear eloquent testimony to the extent to which the German people had learnt to stand on its own feet in matters artistic. The young Goethe called the beginning of the sixteenth century the only period in which "Germany could take pride in having a native art of her own." Taking all in all, it may probably be said with justice that there was no period in which Germany's intellectual life belonged so entirely to itself, and gave expression to the specific character of the people with such freedom from foreign conceptions and influences, as in the decades which are described as those of the expiration of the middle ages.

There comes into the picture at the same time a special feature which distinguishes Germany from other countries. This is the astonishing spread of intellectual culture among the people. With the universities there flourished the middle schools and elementary schools, and when the invention of printing for the first time made the name of Germans famous all over the world in connexion with a great step forward in the arts of civilization, it gave Germany also the means for the participation of all her people in the achievements and battles of the intellectual life. This " German art " of theirs gave the German people a sudden advantage over all others, not in the greatness or value of the creative work of their thinkers, but in its diffusion through all classes.

What had happened was an awakening of the soul of the German people, to achieve greater and greater things from generation to generation in its search for its highest expression : this is evident from the names written at the beginning of the new century in the annals of German literature and art : Sebastian Brant and Hans Sachs, Albrecht Dürer, Matthias Grünewald, Hans Holbein. Not in every region were the same heights attained, but the powerful new impulse, the new life in every field, are unmistakable. Ulrich von Hutten was right when he cried : " The sciences are blossoming, the minds of men are awakening, it is a pleasure to live ! "

In everything one may discern the strongly-marked trait of a new national self-consciousness. It shows itself alike in the works of the learned and the ephemeral pamphleteering of the time. There was research into Germany's past, to show that the Germans had always been a people of great deeds and achievements, equal to any other people, even superior to the Romans. Had not Arminius, chief of the Cherusci, defeated the legions of Rome ! The times and the policy of Maximilian contributed substantially to the awakening and nurturing of such ideas. For the first time for generations the opportunity had come of once more taking a share in European affairs ; German soldiers fought under a German king in Flanders, Italy, Hungary, often victoriously, always commanding respect, and even if the result was disproportionate to the efforts expended the nation had at all events tested its powers and discovered what it would be able to achieve in more fortunate circumstances. In this soil Martin Luther's intensely German feeling struck root, and from it sprang Ulrich von Hutten's resolve thenceforward to write only in German.

This self-realization often grew into a quaint self-deification. The first book of German history is also the most chauvinistic that ever was written : Jacob Wimpfeling's *Epitome Rerum Germanicarum*. And understandably so : the less the reality corresponded with this high self-appraisement and these grandiose recollections, the more easily a justified pride gave place to vain extravagance.

This antinomy between ideal and reality could but arouse deep discomfort in thinking people. The more the claim was made to a proud past and to present reasons for self-satisfaction, the more bitter, necessarily, was it to realize how little the German counted for among the nations. It was impossible to fail to see the reason for this. The nations around Germany had consolidated themselves into single states ; the German had no national state. The imperial constitution was not sufficient to make one : it made the Empire powerless abroad, and dissipated its internal energies in feud and disorder.

This had been clearly realized for two generations past ; the more far-seeing had recognized that the existing conditions involved the ultimate danger of subjection to foreign rule. As early as 1433 Nicolas von Cues had written in his *Concordantia Catholica* : " A mortal disease has befallen the German realm ; if it is not speedily treated with a healing antidote, death will inexorably ensue. Men will seek for the realm in Germany and will not find it ; and in the time to come strangers will seize our habitations and divide them among themselves ; so shall we be subjected to another nation." Since the thirties of that century the need for a remedy had produced discussions of constitutional reform, discussions which were renewed from decade to decade but led to nothing. They could but lead to nothing, since the negotiators had irreconcilable aims. For the princes the reform was to be the means of assuring and enlarging their own share in the government of the realm. For that very reason the Emperor could but fight against it, and the towns also were naturally hostile to any growth in the power of the princes, which could but interfere with their own privileges. On the other hand, princes and towns alike fought against any strengthening of the centralized power of the Emperor. Consequently the discussions long remained fruitless.

A change came only when Maximilian found reason to meet the desires of the princes in order to secure the support of the realm for his European policy. But the results were very disappointing. All that happened was first the institution of a Supreme Court, to be formed from among the States—the Reichskammergericht; a Court which, for lack of funds, never functioned—and then the decree in the same year (1495) of a perpetual commission of the peace, which remained a paper measure as no executive organs were provided for the institution.

Inevitably the repeated and sometimes excited negotiations concerning constitutional reform awakened expectations and growing demands, and when the result brought disappointment the irritation was so much the greater. No one was content with the existing Constitution— neither the Emperor, since it afforded him no source of power, nor the princes, since it did not give them dominant influence, nor the nation, since the Constitution of the Reich was unable to stand comparison with those of neighbouring countries and left the future perilous.

Maximilian's Government had left the constitutional problem unsolved. State and nation existed in a state of political crisis, and the question was whether the tendencies making for further diminution of the central power through permanent institutions were to carry the day, or the Emperor would succeed in restoring something of his predecessors' power. Charles V yielded further at his election than his grandfather had done. The functioning of the Reichskammergericht and the administration of the commission of the peace were assured. With the actual institution of the Reichsregiment which Charles had promised, the princes would have triumphed completely over the Emperor. But only political children, such as the German princes then were, could have supposed that the Spanish-Burgundian world-emperor would feel bound by the assent which he had given. Those were times in which in the high politics of Europe promises were made and oaths taken only to be broken, alliances concluded only to be scrapped. Three years before Charles's election Machiavelli's *Principe* had been issued, reducing to dogmatic formulæ the statesmanship of the period as it was deliberately practised everywhere except in Germany. Charles V had no need to study the book to follow its precepts. Machiavelli had nothing new to tell any ruler or statesman of the period. The Germans alone had no notion of it all. The question of the German Constitution was thus bound sooner or later to become the subject of a trial of strength between Emperor and princes.

A second crisis which had broken out at the moment

of Charles's accession went much deeper—the religious, confessional one. It was by no means confined to Germany, the whole of the west passed through it. But it broke out first in Germany and its effects were deepest and most lasting there. For a century and more the church had been steadily losing its former position of command over the whole of men's lives, in secular and spiritual affairs alike. Growing education among the laity, the awakening of scientific criticism based on the study of ancient Rome and Greece, and the increasing dependence of the Pope on the secular powers had undermined the old respect for church and clergy. The church herself admitted and even emphasized her need of reform; she had held three reforming councils, but without getting anything effectual done; and all this brought grist to the mills of criticism. At the turn of the century men's religious needs were growing and their demands on the clergy increasing, and there increased concurrently the general dissatisfaction with existing conditions. They no longer suited the time; they were wanting in every aspect. The forms of service, with their strong admixture of superstition, were intolerable to any enlightened thinker, and the way of life of the clergy shocked the stricter lay sense of propriety. There was a widespread rejection of the claim of the clergy and the church to dominate public and private life.

This movement of opinion was to be found in all countries. In addition there was an element which was peculiar to Germany. Hitherto the Catholic Church had been a centralized monarchy, with the Pope as its absolute ruler. The churches of all countries had been ruled from Rome and made to serve her purpose. The fifteenth century had seen all this greatly modified by the reforming movements in every country except Germany. In England, as in France and Spain and even Italy, the state had been able to stand up in some measure for its own interests. Everywhere the nation had become its own master in matters spiritual. The nation had set its own limit to the extent in which it would bow to the authority of the external power wielded by the Pope. In Germany there had been efforts to achieve these reforms, but without success, for want of a strong centralized state able to put up the needed resistance to the Pope. Moreover, in 1448 a Concordat had been concluded which set limits to the exercise of papal rights of government, but these rights went considerably further than in other countries; and, in any case, the Pope regarded all this as a free concession of his own, and paid no great attention to it.

The emancipation of the churches in the western countries had diminished the revenues which the Curia drew from them. It was only natural that compensation should be sought elsewhere. It was found in Germany. The less France and England paid, the more was drawn from Germany. A favourite means for this was the Indulgences. In other countries they were scarcely tolerated; in Germany permission to issue them could be secured from the petty rulers by allowing them a share in the proceeds, and the expedient was a popular one and freely applied.

The situation was felt keenly. The difference was observed between the treatment meted out to Germany and the attention paid to other countries; it was, very naturally, even exaggerated, and there was a feeling of being bested, oppressed, exploited. The growing national consciousness turned emphatically against Rome, and the general criticism of the priesthood and condemnation of its privileges and power was joined to a hatred of the papal court, which took on the aspect of a foreign power that disinherited, oppressed and exploited the German people. In the meetings of the Diet complaints were directed constantly against the court of Rome. The *gravamina nationis germanicae* became almost a permanent item of the agenda, and were emphatically supported by the general population. Rome was the enemy of the German nation; if not its only enemy, at all events the chief one. This attitude found its classic expression in the writings of Ulrich von Hutten.

The latent crisis came to the surface on October 31, 1517, when Professor Martin Luther, of Wittenberg, an Augustinian monk, published his reasoned protest against the Indulgences. The gesture revealed the true situation at once. From being a purely personal and academic matter the case rapidly grew to a nation-wide issue, and when the Curia proceeded against the man for heretical teaching and he resolutely refused submission Doctor Martin quickly became the nation's hero. The controversy pushed him on further than he had intended to go. He was compelled to carry his views to their logical conclusion and to confess that the Roman church no longer possessed any authority which he could admit, that its whole claim to domination, its hierarchical system, even the distinction drawn between clergy and laity, were devoid of justification.

In saying all this he had spoken the inmost thoughts of countless fellow-men. His declaration was the signal for secession from Rome. The occasion of the issue of this epoch-making declaration to the world, Luther's disputation in Leipzig with Johann Eck in July, 1519, was separated only by a few days from the Emperor's election in Frankfurt. When Charles V appeared on German soil towards the end of the following year, he found Germany in the first stages of a religious revolution.

It is unfortunate for any people, at any time, to be associated in a single state with another people that is more numerous and stronger than itself. At the best its free development of its innate individuality is then hampered, generally suspended, perhaps entirely stopped. Such an association is particularly fatal in times of crisis, when the old is being sloughed off and the new pressing forward to the light. Never is it more important than at such moments that the people shall be able to develop according to its own nature, that it shall determine its own fate, in a word that it shall be free.

If the German people had been free in 1519–20, it is not difficult to imagine how things would probably have gone. There would first, as always, have been a split. Some would have cast themselves adrift from the Roman Church and found new forms of devotion; others, no doubt far less numerous, would have remained loyal to the old system. The two sections would have begun with violent mutual polemic but gradually learnt mutual toleration and recognition, and it would have been left to the future to decide whether or not the minority ultimately followed the example of the majority.

But Germany was not free. She had set a foreign ruler on the imperial throne, and this ruler was King of Spain. He was Spanish by nature, and even if he had not been he would have had everywhere to put first the interests of his principal realm, Spain. Even in Germany Charles V could only pursue Spanish policy.

This had at the moment a two-fold significance. On the question of the constitution, the new Emperor was forced to take up an even more decided attitude than his predecessors against the tendencies which found expression

THE REFORMATION

in the movement for the reform of the Empire. If the German crown was to be not merely a burden to him, if it was to further his political plans, he must strive to get Germany entirely into his hands. Thus the demand of the princes for a say in the government, and even in the determination of foreign policy, was bound to be extremely inconvenient to him. Even if he had not been autocratic by nature as he was, he would have been bound to set his face against all that had come to be regarded in Germany as definitely acquired rights and liberties of nobles and burghers, rights which every effort was being made to extend. It would have been impossible to expect Charles V to be willing to rule according to the constitutional ideas of his German subjects.

Still more acute was the difference of view on the question of the church. Personally committed to the ideas of Catholic reform which had dominated Europe in the fifteenth century, bound closely to the side of the Catholic Church by the whole disposition of the Spanish people and all the traditions of the Spanish State, Charles V could not but meet the religious movement which he found in Germany in a spirit of utter opposition. He was entirely unable to comprehend either the revolt of German nationalism against the domination of Rome or the claim to independence of personal judgment in face of the authority of the church. Even if he had had any personal sympathy with the German aspirations he could not have tolerated them without flouting Spanish opinion. The ruler of the empire which had been born and had grown to greatness in the fight for the Catholic faith against the Moors, and had built the faggots of the Inquisition into the foundations of its existence, the king of the nation in which the spirit of the Crusades still worked, could not expose himself to the reproach of anywhere protecting and favouring heretics against the church.

On the other hand, Germany was not altogether in a weak position in face of the Emperor. If only it were clearly recognized what was at issue, determined and united action might yet save the country's independence. Germany was much too necessary to the Emperor. Even the withholding of German forces, to say nothing of open revolt or the setting-up of an opposition Emperor, might be fatal to Charles. He found himself driven to show forbearance towards the German aims.

Such was the situation when, in January, 1521, Charles V opened his first Diet at Worms. The conflict of views at once became apparent. On the question of the Constitution the Princes demanded the imperial régime which had been promised. The Emperor, incautiously lifting the mask, replied that he was not to be treated as of less account than his predecessors, but of more, seeing that he was more powerful than they had been. "It is, therefore, our view that the Empire from of old has not had many masters, but one, and it is our intention to be that one." Finally a compromise was arrived at : the promised régime was instituted, but only for the period of the Emperor's absence and only for internal affairs. In return the Diet granted the Emperor the armed forces which he demanded, a splendid army of 24,000 men, ostensibly "for the Roman expedition," but really for the conquest of Milan and war against France.

In this very first step the princes exposed their political incapacity. If they saw through their opponent—and he made it easy enough for them—not a man nor a groschen should have been granted to add still more to his power, unless he renounced all interference in Germany's internal affairs, by some such device as the appointment of a King of Rome, to rule for him with plenipotentiary powers. But they had not the political insight for this, and the old-time disunion between the Estates of the Empire, the old dissension between towns and princes, did the rest; within three years Charles was in a position, acting from Spain, to end the new régime and to take the government entirely into his own hands. If the pressure of his ascendancy took time to make itself felt, that was due only to the international complications which kept the Emperor's hands constantly tied.

His very limited power was best shown by the manner in which he was compelled to handle the church question. Rome had excommunicated Martin Luther, and Luther had openly and solemnly burned the bull. Under the old law of the Empire—it dated from the time of Frederick II— the ban of the Empire ought to have been pronounced against the heretic. But it was out of the question to venture to proceed strictly in accordance with the law. For this monk had recently become the acclaimed leader of the majority of the nation in the fight against Rome. In August, 1520, he had published a manifesto : "To the

Christian nobility of the German nation, on the improvement of the Christian condition." In this he sketched a programme of religious reform for Germany, and called upon the princes of the Empire—" the Christian nobility of the nation "—to carry it out. In so doing he had expressed the deepest feelings of the whole people. Even those who disapproved of his theological dogmas and were alarmed at his revolt against the church, were very ready to adopt most of his proposed reforms, and here at least to go a long way with him. Consequently his friends had not much trouble in securing, contrary to all prevailing law and usage, a resolution of the Diet once more to interrogate this heretic condemned of the church before abandoning him. That was in itself a revolutionary step. The Empire itself was virtually on the way to becoming Lutheran.

Everyone knows what happened at the interrogation. Luther, with steadfast fidelity to his convictions, refused the recantation demanded. Not only that, but he refused to submit to the judgment of any ecclesiastical council: he declared his conviction that that was not the final authority. He thus threw away a very promising opportunity. If he could have brought himself to appeal to the decision of a council, he would have emerged from its interrogation as undisputed victor. The Emperor himself, brought up in the tradition of ecclesiastical councils, would have agreed, and the Estates of the Empire would have rallied to his standard. With the decision of the Council all would have gone well. On no question were the European Powers so at variance as on this ; already it had remained unsolved for seventy years, and the Pope above all would have done everything in his power to avoid summoning a Council. Luther's doctrines would thus have had time to spread, and when at last the Council met they would certainly have been too deeply rooted to extirpate.

One might be tempted to blame Luther for not realizing this and acting accordingly. But he was no politician ; he was concerned only to do what his own convictions bade, and no man can be expected to belie his own character in his actions. Nevertheless it was plain enough how matters stood. As early as April 19, immediately after the hearing, the Emperor had pronounced his personal judgment in a solemn declaration that he would protect the purity of the faith as his fathers had done before him. But he found himself powerless to take immediate measures against the stiff-necked heretic. Not until May 26, when most of the representatives of the States had gone away, did he venture to issue the ban against Luther and his adherents, prohibiting his teachings and writings, which had been drawn up in his chancellery on May 8. He had been afraid of opposition from the Diet or at all events from a strong minority, even of disturbances and appeals to force. So was the Edict of Worms issued—not straightforwardly, openly and in proper form, but secretly and surreptitiously.

Its execution, too, had its own special difficulties. Luther himself had been brought into safety, and the rest depended upon the local authorities. The great majority of them, however, championed the new ways of thought. Instead of stifling the movement, the Edict of Worms rather helped it to success. In 1521–22 the practical reform which Luther had demanded in his appeal to the Christian nobility began everywhere in Germany: the overthrow of the church authorities, the sequestration of church property, the abolition of celibacy and of the elevation of the host.

The Emperor could only look on helplessly. His hands were tied by the war with France, which assumed greater proportions every year. Germany's support was now indispensable, and any strong action, any offence to the feelings of the people, was out of the question. In the end Charles actually found himself driven to make war against the Pope as the ally of France. How valuable to him then (1526) was the German ill-will against Rome! Never had the recruitment of mercenaries been more successful than when the slogan became "Down with the Pope!" It was the storming of Rome by German foot-soldiers at Easter in 1527 which brought victory to Charles V. The Peace of Cambrai (1529) made him master of Italy; his opponents were driven off the field, and the Emperor was triumphant.

Now he could deal with Germany. In the stress of the fight she had had to be left alone. No notice had even been taken when in 1526, at the moment of greatest tension, the Diet of Spires expressly charged every Estate of the Empire to conduct itself in the ecclesiastical issue in accordance with the dictates of its own conscience: "as

THE REFORMATION

they would answer therefor before God and the Imperial Majesty." That amounted to formally turning over the religious issue to the decision of each province.

Charles had no intention of tolerating that for ever. Apart from all religious motives, he would no longer have been master in Germany if the decision in ecclesiastical policy no longer lay with him and each State could consider itself sovereign in this matter. Here constitution and church became a single issue. With a firm resolve to put an end to the new situation, Charles returned to Germany in 1530.

The preceding year had already shown signs of a change. Under pressure from the Emperor in 1529 the Diet at Spires had approved the execution of the Edict of Worms, but with the result that a number of its most influential members protested against a decision by majority vote reversing the unanimous decision of three years previously. The "Protesters"—from whom the name "Protestant" is derived—were already prepared to go to all lengths, and began to join together for the defence of their views in what soon became known as the Schmalkald Confederacy. The Diet at Augsburg, in 1530, failed to restore unity. The Emperor seemed determined to resort to force, and the Protestants to meet force with force. Thus the parties stood face to face with their hands on the hilts of their swords.

Yet sixteen years passed before the decisive appeal to arms.

We need not here give the explanation of this delay It was mainly due to the Emperor being involved abroad, as before. He found himself continuously engaged in a war on two fronts. The war with France flared up again, and in addition there had been war with the Turks since 1526. In the battle of Mohacs, on August 29, 1526, the kingdom of Hungary had collapsed, and King Louis met his death. He died childless, and so the settlement of the succession made in 1515 came into force, and the Emperor's brother Ferdinand became King of Bohemia and Hungary. It was certainly an increase of power for the house of Habsburg, but heavily burdened with the mortgage of the Turkish neighbourhood. The Turkish peril, which had previously been relatively distant, was now at the gates. The year 1529 saw the enemy before Vienna, and in the following years Hungary became the prey of Turkish conquest. The Habsburgs had to fight for this part of the inheritance if they were to remain in secure possession of Austria.

In such circumstances, the support of the Germans was quite indispensable. It was unthinkable to let loose civil war in Germany; the double external danger forced Charles to proceed very cautiously. He extended toleration, granted delay, permitted argument, sought to put off and to gain time. He put up with the expulsion of his house from Württemberg in 1534 by its opponents, the Protestants. All he could attempt was to prevent the Confederacy from growing further. First he must get rid of his external difficulties; then he would be able to attend to the German question.

There is no doubt—even contemporaries recognized it—that the Protestants did not in the least understand how to make the best use of their opportunity. Had they held firmly together and acted with decision they might have put the Emperor into a tight corner. They would not have needed to call in foreign aid, which would have its undesirable aspect; even without that they were strong enough. Their party was constantly growing by the accession of new supporters. It would only have been necessary to organize these firmly and to keep them always ready to fight. They never accomplished this, because they lacked the elements of political wisdom. They failed to realize their danger, and were unwilling to guard against the possibility of it. Their whole course revealed the political incapacity of the German princes, products of the petty state. Brought up against a statesman of European breadth like Charles V, these parish-pump politicians made a wretched display. No more, naturally, could be expected of their underlings, the clergy and the learned. None of them ever saw through the Emperor; they walked, indeed, straight into his trap. Of none of them was this truer than the one with the greatest repute of all for political intelligence, Philip of Hesse. It is well known how he became dependent on the Emperor owing to the immorality of his private life, his notorious bigamy. In his fear of the punishment which he had richly earned, he threw himself into the arms of the Emperor, and demeaned himself to an anxious subservience, thwarting the plans of his associates, when everything depended on unity and courage.

THE REFORMATION

One would gladly have dwelt longer on this picture. It has many features of resemblance to our own times. Never before were narrowness and pettiness, quarrelsome obstinacy and wrong-headed quibbling in the face of great and lasting duties and opportunities more repulsively in evidence. Anyone who wants to familiarize himself with the political character of the Germans of the sixteenth century—and unfortunately not only of the sixteenth—should study the history of the Schmalkald Confederacy. Inherited characteristics were reinforced by the new impulse of freedom of individual conviction in matters of faith. Since people had learned to listen to the Word of God and their own conscience in the ultimate, all-important questions, the inclination to subordinate themselves to others, to set aside their own special desires for the sake of common ends, if it had ever existed, had completely vanished. Each one thought only of his own safety, his own advantage; what became of the rest was a matter of indifference. It was not realized that only mutual defence accompanied by mutual sacrifices can save even the individual.

It was fortunate that for a long time their opponent did not see through their weakness. But it could not remain hidden from him for ever. The Schmalkalders were prevented by the apprehensions of the Landgrave of Hesse from admitting into their Confederacy the Duke of Cleves-Gueldres, who was in search of support in defending his country against the Emperor, and so lost even their connexion with England (1540–41). Then Charles recognized, as he himself writes in his memoirs, that it would not be difficult, that in fact it would be very easy, to deal with them.

From then onwards his attitude changed. Until then he had tried to keep the Germans quiet with half-concessions, in order to master the external situation first; he now reversed his policy. He adjourned his foreign disputes, concluded the Peace of Crépy with France in 1544, purchased an armistice from the Turks, and collected all his forces for the overthrow of the Protestants. In 1546 he launched the blow. The leaders of the Schmalkald Confederacy were put under the ban for disobedience and breach of the public peace.

We shall not follow the military operations. It is notorious how the political incapacity of the Protestants led to their complete defeat when victory was virtually assured to them. On Easter Sunday, 1547, the Elector of Saxony was taken prisoner by the Spaniards at the battle of Mühlberg, and shortly afterwards Philip of Hesse surrendered voluntarily. Charles was victor in Germany and over Germany.

He was now in a position to order Germany's affairs as he pleased. With all his great power, however, he did not succeed. The arbitrary fashion in which he handled the religious question, and at the same time made the princes feel his superiority, the ruthlessness with which his Government steadily moved towards Spanish dominion in Germany, and finally the unmistakable design of perpetuating the union with Spain revealed in his transfer of the Imperial Crown to his son Philip, led to the revolt of the German princes under the leadership of the Elector Maurice of Saxony. In April, 1552, the Emperor himself barely escaped capture in the mountains of Tirol. The restoration of the Imperial autocracy had come to grief.

But the price was high. It had no longer been possible for the Germans of their own strength to shake off what they now called "the bestial Spanish servitude." Foreign support had been necessary, and had had to be paid for. Under the treaty of Chambord (January 15, 1552) Maurice and his confederates had given their agreement to the annexation of Metz, Toul, and Verdun by the French king. At the moment of their rising, the French stroke took place. In a twinkling, Metz, the gate of the middle Rhine, was French. In vain Charles tried to recover these losses. In the late autumn of 1552, when his army melted away in the trenches before Metz, in the vain effort to re-take the fortress, he admitted defeat. Deeply disappointed and embittered, he retreated, and withdrew more and more from affairs, until finally bodily sufferings and the melancholy of his life's failure drove him into a monastery. He had long since left Germany to herself.

What might have been had from the beginning with wise, firm, and above all united action, had now been attained at the cost of long struggles and heavy losses. The development of German affairs continued to follow the customary paths, and the change to a unified state, which had seemed to be setting in with the accession of Charles, was given up. The Emperor was again pushed back into the part which he had played a century earlier, and the independence of the reigning princes and the free towns no longer had any bounds.

A corresponding solution was found for the religious question. The religious peace of Augsburg (1555) was hedged round with reservations and declarations, but the essence of it was its provision that in church matters the ruler of a province and not the Empire had the deciding voice. Each Estate of the Empire could choose its creed. In other words, the territorial sovereignty which for long had included the police, the law-courts, the army, and the finances, was now extended without restriction to the church as well.

This was undoubtedly in accordance with the steady direction of developments in Germany since the thirteenth century. It may be said to be a final step in the dissolution of the unity of the Empire. That may well be deplored. If the past could be changed to suit present needs, we might well say that the reverse process would from more than one standpoint have been better. A lasting victory of Charles V would have strengthened the internal unity of the Empire, would have restored its power abroad, and would thus have averted the serious dangers which more than ever threatened the nation from east and west. Many will consider that, if the restoration of the unity of the state was at issue, it would have been well secured even at the cost of the suppression of Protestantism.

The great question is only whether that was possible. No one in Germany would have agreed to it; all, without distinction of creed, would have rejected the idea. Only a foreign ruler could have harboured such designs. Even the princes and states which clung to the old church from conviction by no means demanded that the others should be forcibly compelled to recant. Bavaria, which from the beginning stood immovably on the Catholic side, was far from collaborating in the Emperor's policy of forcible conversion. She was repeatedly, from purely political motives, in opposition to him. The course of events thus confirms what had already been said: had the German people been left to themselves, they would very soon, perhaps as early as 1530, have arrived at a definite settlement along the lines of parity and tolerance, in consonance with their nature and their political conditions. That this was prevented for so long, and even in the end was only incompletely secured, is attributable to the foreign ruler, whose non-German interests made a different solution desirable. A complete victory for Charles would therefore have been possible only in the form of a complete subjection of Germany to Spain; and it will scarcely be disputed that at that price the unity of the state would have been too dearly purchased. For what would have been the value of the unity of the state if the German people could no longer remain true to themselves?

To that extent it must be admitted that the fall of Charles V was a piece of good fortune, and a necessity if the German character was to go on developing—that is to say, if the German nation was to remain in existence in a political sense.

On the other hand, there is no more preposterous statement than that which is often heard, that the emergence of Luther and the religious cleavage which he brought about caused or accelerated the dissolution of the Empire. The converse is true: it was because the Empire was already in a state of semi-dissolution that a permanent religious cleavage was possible. If the component states had not already become so powerful and independent, the religious question would have been settled in Germany, as in other countries, on centralised principles. But they had already attained an independence and power which made it impossible even for Charles V to compel unity of creed.

The only lasting result was that to the many elements of disunion which until then had racked the body of the German nation—differences of race, division into petty states, disunion between towns and nobles—the events of 1517 and after added the worst of all estrangements, that of creed. Nothing since has so powerfully influenced the course of German history as this difference of religious faith. It is still at work to-day; indeed it has increased in acerbity in recent times. Everyone knows what a pernicious effect it has had on our national destinies.

Is it not then justifiable, quite apart from personal attachment to one or the other party, and simply from the standpoint of the national interest, to deplore the beginnings of the cleavage, and to look upon the man who conjured it up as an enemy of his country? I do not feel that I can avoid putting this question, although the answer which I have to give can only represent a personal view, and one which makes no claim to objective validity.

It seems to me that here too we must resist the

temptation to correct the course of events even only in thought. It is of more importance to understand it. Such events as the German Reformation run their course from intrinsic necessity, and with Luther especially one gets the impression, as of few other men, that he could not have acted otherwise than he did. It was precisely in this that his moral greatness lay, and his title to our esteem and veneration. There might be more reason for blaming the German people for its failure to overcome in one way or another the cleavage which had arisen. But the same objection would be valid against this reproof : the German people, too, could act only as their own nature dictated. And nowhere more than in the history of the Reformation period does the character of our people reveal itself in its strength and weakness. It had to happen so, and realization of this must still the voice of regret.

Once, however, we realize this intrinsic necessity, we soon discover that there is after all nothing to regret. The religious cleavage, the need for living in harmony with those of another belief, has given the German national spirit a depth and an inward wealth which other peoples do not know.

If there is anyone who refuses to admit this consolation, because it amounts to envying an incurable invalid the spiritual benefit which he owes to his malady (the invalid will, on the contrary, always envy the healthy), I should like to give him something else to consider.

Religion is the ultimate and deepest expression of the life of the soul. Therefore every people has its own religion which corresponds to the character of its soul. This is true even of Catholicism, which seems so uniform. Catholicism is not the same thing in Germany as in Spain and Lower Italy, in France as in North America. Happy the nation which fate allows to choose its religion quite freely, in accordance with its inner nature ! It will then thrive best, and be able to develop its powers and capabilities in the fullest degree. Now it is a fact which no one can miss, that all the greater achievements in which the German people has had a share since the Reformation, creating anew and giving new impulses in its own fashion to world civilisation, have proceeded from the Protestant section of the nation. What the world knows as German progress is in essentials of Protestant origin, in spite of the large number of German Catholics. Nothing would be more preposterous than to conclude that Catholicism in itself is of little value. With the French and Italians it is the other way round ; there the great deeds all originate in the Catholic life of the people. It can therefore only be that, for the particular character of the German spirit, the Protestant form of religion is the more suitable, the more adapted to rouse and develop its powers and to fit it for its highest tasks. The exception which music appears to constitute, only confirms the rule. Music lives on feeling alone, and its language is therefore elevated above all conflicts of thought and will. German thought, however, and the German conscience are by nature Protestant.

If we look at things in this way, we recognize how necessary, in a still higher sense, it was that a large part of the German nation should break loose from Rome and seek its own path to the beyond. It was necessary, and it was a gain—in spite of all.

CHAPTER VIII

THE THIRTY YEARS' WAR

THE Peace of Augsburg had achieved two things: the victory of the princes over the Emperor both on the question of the constitution and on that of the church. Germany remained the country of political decentralization, one may even say of political dissolution, and she remained the country of religious discord. In the fight for the control of the Empire, which had lasted through the whole of Charles V's reign, the princes had not only maintained their position, defeating the Emperor's attempts to make himself a real ruler, but gained a very considerable increase of power. In all territories, both Protestant and Catholic, the prince became lord over the church. Where the Reformation had been adopted, that is easy to understand: the Protestant churches were everywhere national churches, their clergy state officials. Moreover, the confiscations of church property naturally brought a great increase in the power of the ruler. But in the Catholic regions as well the prince became the determining factor in ecclesiastical affairs, because without him the church would have been quite unable to maintain itself.

Accordingly, in the two next generations the Emperor was of less importance than ever; in spite of their wider dominions—the addition of Bohemia to Austria greatly increased the predominance of the latter over all the other states in area and population—the Emperors of the House of Habsburg after 1555 had lost their position of influence. They were in constant difficulties in consequence of the fight for Hungary, of which they possessed only a very small part, and where they were threatened by the Turks. They would hardly have been able to maintain themselves without the repeated assistance of the King of Spain. Thus it came about that the Emperors lost their leading position once more as completely as in the time of Frederick III. The princes, with their increased power, and impelled by concern for the maintenance of their particular creeds, pursued a considerably more active policy, especially abroad. This independent appearance on the part of Hesse, Saxony, Brandenburg, and above all of the Palatinate, at the foreign courts, in France, England, the Netherlands, Scandinavia, and Poland, working side by side with or in opposition to the imperial policy, was a new phenomenon.

It was a consequence of the ecclesiastical split, but not a necessary one. Germany would have been quite contented with the peace of 1555, if she had been left to herself. So far as Germany alone was concerned, 1555 might have been the conclusion of the epoch which began in 1519. That this did not happen, that the struggle was begun again after a time, was entirely due to the renewed and continuous interference of foreign powers.

The religious peace had prescribed that every state of the Empire might choose its religion, and thereby decide the religion of its subjects. An exception was made of the heads of the ecclesiastical states, the bishops, abbots, and abbesses. For these the change to the new faith was forbidden. This was the so-called " ecclesiastical reservation." The Protestants had not recognized it, and had not relinquished their opposition to the whole settlement, until the Emperor, in a personal declaration, the " Imperial declaration," gave an assurance that in the ecclesiastical territories the members of their Diets should have the right of going over to the Protestant creed. Accordingly, nobles, knights, and towns in a bishopric or in the territory of a monastery might become Protestant, while the Prince must remain Catholic. Thus, here too nothing stood in the way of the spread of Protestantism.

This was, however, only a concession by the Emperor for the time being, not a law of the Empire, and was therefore of doubtful validity and duration. The Protestants had contented themselves with it, in the feeling that even so they were already the stronger. This they were. We have the testimony, dating from 1557-59, of Venetian ambassadors, agreeing that actually nine-tenths of Germany was already Protestant, and that it was only a question of time before the whole country would belong to the new faith.

As a matter of fact, no attention was at first paid to the ecclesiastical reservation within the limits of the influence of the Protestant princes. This influence was uncontested in North Germany, there was no Catholic dynasty left there, and thus one North German bishopric after another chose a Protestant prince for its bishop. Although he was not consecrated, he ruled his principality as "Administrator." In this manner the bishoprics became younger sons' portions for neighbouring princely houses—a further increase of power for them. In the year 1577 this had gone so far that, in the whole of North Germany, Hildesheim was the only remaining exception to this rule.

But at that time Protestantism had already passed the zenith of its power, and the Catholic counter-movement had begun. In 1573, Prince-Abbot Balthazar of Dernbach in Fulda disregarded the imperial declaration and forced the Protestant knights of his domains to return to the Catholic Church. In 1574, Archbishop Daniel Brendel of Mainz followed his example in the Eichsfeld. In 1575, at the election of Rudolf II, the imperial declaration was not renewed. The " counter-reformation " had begun.

This did not proceed from Germany ; it was due to the missionary activity of foreigners, to the work of the Spanish Order of Jesus and the Roman Curia. The struggle of the Catholic Church to reconquer the lost territories had been actively taken up throughout the world. Its outcome was decided in the war between the Spanish crown and the rebellious Netherlands, in which neighbouring states took part and England finally turned the scale. In 1572 the revolt of the Provinces began ; in 1581 there followed their formal secession from Spain ; the year 1588 brought the decision with the annihilation of the Spanish Armada by the English. So the die was cast for the political, religious, and spiritual fate of Europe.

Germany took hardly any part in this, except through the soldiers who were recruited within her borders, to fight in either camp. In passive neutrality she looked on at the struggle, although her own fate was in the balance. Participation was made impossible by her constitution, and also by the character of German Protestantism. Its leaders had hitherto been Lutheran, but the west had become Calvinist, and, in true German fashion, the differences were once more assigned more importance than the common basis. This attitude was even accentuated when Calvinism, always bellicose, always aggressive, began itself to make conquests in Germany. When the Calvinistic Palatinate was energetically canvassing for support for its co-religionists in France and the Netherlands, that was an additional reason for Saxony to take the opposite side, fearing for her inherited leadership of the Protestants, if the Palatinate's creed were to win through.

There was, however, a case to be made out for the convenient neutrality policy of the Lutherans. If they were to join in the struggle of the Western Powers the war might spread to Germany and involve her in civil war. It seemed worth while to avoid this, so long as they themselves were not threatened. And they did not feel any threat, although, with a little more foresight, they might well have seen its imminence. The anxious avoidance of civil war, so long as they might have won it, ultimately brought its outbreak when their opponents were the stronger side.

It was these years that, under the protection of the religious peace and of neutrality, changed the face of Germany; and first in the sphere of the school and of education. In 1562, educated Germany was Protestant. The Duke of Bavaria had to renounce sending delegates to the Council of Trent, because he had no one in his country who could have represented him worthily among Italians and Spaniards. The few Catholic universities were deserted, and dragged out a dismal existence. Twenty years later all this had changed. The Jesuit colleges, themselves in the possession of the dominant Italian school, had quietly taken over the education of the upper classes, and a Jesuit training was now the more fashionable. Above all, they had trained a number of young princes to be tools which could be relied upon in case of need. The Catholic party was awake; it was advancing towards its goal in unity and with determination, under shrewd leadership. In the 'eighties a violent reaction had set in in full swing in many places. The first indications in the 'seventies have already been mentioned. The fight for Cologne, 1582–4, may be looked upon as a visible turning-point. When the Elector Gebhard Truchfess of Waldburg on his conversion to Protestantism found no effective support from his new co-religionists—just as had happened to the Duke of Cleves forty-two years earlier—and when Spanish troops from the Netherlands interfered and drove out the apostate, the whole future of the Lower Rhine and of Westphalia was decided. Cologne remained Catholic, and the Protestant Administrators disappeared from the

THE THIRTY YEARS' WAR

Westphalian bishoprics before the Spanish battalions. This should be borne in mind : Spanish soldiers built this cornerstone of Catholic Germany.

Meanwhile the flood of the reaction rose higher. What the loss of the Lower Rhine and Westphalia had not brought to pass was caused twenty-five years later by the case of a little Swabian free town. In the year 1608, Duke Maximilian of Bavaria, long the aggressive leader of the Catholics, forced the town of Donauwörth to accept the Catholic creed and annexed it. This at last produced concerted action by the Protestants for energetic defence. A section of them organized themselves in the same year, under the leadership of the Palatinate, in the Evangelical Union for the defence of the religious peace. Bavaria replied (1609) with the founding of the Catholic League. Civil war seemed imminent. It would have been a European war on German soil, for France and Spain were just about to come to blows.

But at that point the course of events slowed down. Henry IV was murdered (1610), and the entirely Spanish, and also mentally-diseased, Emperor Rudolf II, was dethroned by his brother Matthias (1611). This once more produced a respite. The new Emperor Matthias succeeded in preventing war by mediating between the parties. It looked as though the peace might still be saved if only Germany were left to herself. But that was not to be. If the Germans alone had been concerned, it is conceivable that, in spite of all, the peace would not have been disturbed. It was essentially the Spanish interference that brought war.

The Spanish Empire was then, under King Philip III, in its proudest flower. The ideas of Charles V were alive once more, the great fight against France was to be taken up again, and, in order to prosecute it the more vigorously, to be able again, as in the days of Charles V, to attack the enemy on his eastern frontier, the Spanish king was again to become German Emperor. This plan was finally abandoned, but only because a simpler way offered itself.

Emperor Matthias, with his weak policy of mediation, no longer satisfied the Catholic ambitions, and his rule in his hereditary domains threatened to lead to a fiasco. The archdukes accordingly plotted to set him aside. His successor was to be Ferdinand of Styria, the most docile of all the docile pupils of the Jesuits. His own country he had already driven back into the Catholic faith with fire and sword, proclaiming that he would rather lose land and people than tolerate the heretics there. Now he was to carry out the same work in Bohemia and Austria. For this it was necessary to have the help of the Spanish king, the head of the family, in dealing with whom the German line of the ruling house always played the part of poor relations. Spain alone could supply the very necessary money, and King Philip for his part was ready to give it, provided that a service was done for him in return. In 1617 an agreement was made : Spain pledged herself to support the elevation of Ferdinand if the Austrian possessions in Alsace were made over to her.

Matters were set going at once. Matthias was driven first out of Bohemia, then out of Austria and Hungary as well, and Ferdinand took over the Government. With him was introduced ruthless, forcible conversion. The reply of the population was universal open revolt. The famous incident at Prague, when Ferdinand's agents were thrown out of a window (May 23, 1618), was the dramatic episode which gave the signal. In a short time Ferdinand was driven out of Bohemia, and his life was hardly safe in Austria, when, in 1619, Matthias died, and the imperial title, the last thing remaining to him, thus became vacant.

In August, 1619, the Electors assembled at Frankfurt to choose his successor. Ferdinand was the only candidate. It was like an exaggerated repetition of the occurrences of a hundred years earlier. What had then threatened, and had with difficulty been prevented in 1555, would now come again, inevitably and for ever, if Ferdinand was elected. It was known what his designs were, known also that Spain stood behind him. The religious civil war and foreign intervention would no longer be avoidable. And yet it was done : on August 28, 1619, Ferdinand was elected almost unanimously. Only the Elector Palatine abstained from voting, after making a last attempt to avert the disaster by offering the crown to the Duke of Bavaria. Maximilian declined, as once Frederick the Wise had done. Destiny took its course. Very pertinently the Brandenburg delegates wrote to their lord : " As Jesu wept over Jerusalem, so must tears be shed over this election, in view of the disaster which will come to

THE THIRTY YEARS' WAR

Germany from it." And yet they had themselves voted for Ferdinand, in accordance with their instructions!

There is something incomprehensible in the spectacle of the Protestant princes thus drawing the noose round themselves and their cause with their own hand. The explanation lay probably in their character. Among all the princes of those days, there was only one single man of weight, Maximilian of Bavaria. All the rest, in both camps, were but mediocrities. And the poorest types of all were the very men who claimed, by position and tradition, to represent Protestantism. John Sigismund of Brandenburg and John George of Saxony were pitiful creatures; it would be difficult to decide which of the two was the more stupid. In this instance, at any rate, both acted equally foolishly and lamentably. To urgent dissuasions the Saxon even gave the classical reply: " I know no good will come of it, I know Ferdinand. But one man can do nothing; the matter must be left to God." Having said this, he ordered his delegate to vote with the ecclesiastical Electors! Fine morals, and still finer statecraft, which leaves it to God to make good the follies committed by his "all-highest" representatives on earth. In explanation of this stupidity, it was said that the Elector was completely drunk. Where the most important business is handled by such people in such a manner, one can of course be surprised at nothing.

Amongst the Protestant powers there was one which attempted to stand out against the rest. At the Palatine Court at Heidelberg, far-reaching plans were cherished and most energetic attempts made to carry them out. Here reigned the active, aggressive spirit of Calvinism, represented by the principal minister, Prince Christian of Anhalt, a resourceful man of the world. He had no lack of fiery enthusiasm and ingenious ideas, but was wanting in prudence and judgment. The Evangelical Union was his creation. It was, however, an organization which left much to be desired, even weaker and looser than the Schmalkald confederacy had been. It was an alliance of the powerless; the strongest of the Protestant princes kept outside it. This and other experiences ought to have made Anhalt cautious. Instead, he hit upon the fantastic idea of anticipating the threatened attack of the Imperial-Catholic movement by a counter-attack. He persuaded his master, the Elector Frederick, to accept the Crown of

Bohemia at the hands of the rebels. On August 26, two days before the election of the Emperor in Frankfurt, the Elector Palatine was chosen king in Prague.

That meant a life and death struggle with the Habsburgs, who would have to strain every nerve to regain Bohemia if they did not want to lose Austria and all its dependencies, and, of course, the Imperial Crown. The Elector Palatine ought not to have conjured up such a fight unless he at least knew that the bulk of German Protestantism was massed in its full strength behind him, and unless he could in addition count on foreign support from at least one of the Great Powers. Neither of the two was the case. The Protestant Estates left their co-religionist in the lurch from the beginning. Apart from the danger, which terrified them, there could be no attraction for them in making the Elector Palatine, of whom they were jealous already, King of Bohemia and perhaps Emperor. Saxony preferred to be neutral, and to accept from Ferdinand in payment the cession of Lausitz. There was not the slightest sign of help from abroad. Even the Elector's father-in-law, King James of England, had endeavoured to dissuade him. In such circumstances, with no better support than his own weak forces from the Palatinate and the Bohemian rebellion, the acceptance of the Bohemian Crown was a foolhardy and even criminal adventure.

For, how different was the picture on the other side ! The Catholic Powers had ranged themselves behind Ferdinand as one man. Bavaria and the League placed themselves at his disposal, Spain helped as much as she could—not a moment's doubt was possible as to the superiority of this party, both in resources and confidence. Thus the tragedy was completed with sinister rapidity. As early as November 8, 1620, everything was decided with the annihilating defeat of the Palatinate-Bohemian army at the White Mountain, near Prague ; the " Winter King " fled helplessly from the country, and Ferdinand was uncontested master of Bohemia and Austria. In both countries the population, previously in the great majority Protestant, was now with frightful harshness forced back to Catholicism. The " conversion " was in great part nothing else than depopulation. But the backbone of the German Austrians was then broken. Even a nation of sterner stuff than this race would not pass through such an ordeal of violent conversion, in which all the more capable and independent individuals were exterminated, and emerge from it spiritually unscathed.

For all Germany, too, the battle of the White Mountain has the significance of a day which settled the whole future. Bismarck once said that the thought of how different everything must have been if the result of this battle had been otherwise had given him a sleepless night. And indeed it is beyond conception what the consequences of a victory of the Protestants would have been. Just imagine what it would mean if Austria had been Protestant and the Habsburgs driven out, with no footing in Germany—this family, which down to our own days brought nothing but ill, and always the greatest ill, to the German people; God grant that its melancholy and tragic part has now at least been played to a finish! The religious cleavage, if not removed, at least moderated and kept within limits; no conflict of creed between north and south, and therefore probably no insuperable differences left—it would have been too good to be true. And it is, indeed, only the dream of a sleepless night. For it to have been possible, the German Protestants would have had to be quite other than they were. Being what they were, it is more than doubtful whether even a victory for the Bohemian and Palatinate arms would have borne its full fruit. It was but natural that, as it was, they should fail of victory in the field. Victory would have required not only more soldiers and abler generals, but above all wiser states and princes. Thus it cannot be said that the chance of battle decided in a single day the course of affairs for centuries. It was no chance happening, it was by the merciless logic of facts that Frederick lost and Ferdinand won. All that happened on that day was a sort of trial of strength.

The war over Bohemia did not yet affect the rest of the Empire. But from it came the punishment of the Elector Palatine. He was outlawed, and the Duke of Bavaria was charged with the execution of the decree. This brought the war into the Empire. That could have been avoided, there were plenty of ways and means of making the Elector Palatine, who had at once fled abroad, permanently harmless without turning Germany into a theatre of war. But the Emperor's allies wanted their price. Bavaria demanded the Palatinate land and the Electorship, which had been promised her; the Spaniards wanted Alsace and the Rhenish Palatinate. The chief persons in the play, the Jesuits, demanded the Catholicisation of the most powerful country in South Germany.

Thus the war was continued, and the Bohemian war became the Palatinate war. After two years that too was concluded; the Palatinate was Bavarian and Spanish, and was to be Catholic. But even now the matter was not to be at an end. The fact that the Protestant troops which had recently fought in the Palatinate had retreated towards North Germany, served as an excuse for the League, the Bavarians, and the Jesuit wire-pullers, to carry the war and forcible Catholicisation into North Germany as well. This is the real beginning of Germany's tragedy. For now foreign countries also intervened on the other side. The appearance of the League troops in Lower Saxony, whose own forces could offer no further resistance to them, and the possibility of seeing even the north of Germany mainly Catholic again and at the beck and call of the Spanish world power, amounted to a summons to arms for the neighbouring Protestant countries, the Netherlands, the Scandinavian States, and England. Coalitions were formed, armies recruited with foreign, Dutch or English money, and Germany became for the second time, as four hundred years earlier, the chessboard on which the great game of European rivalries was played out.

The first attempt to check the victorious course of the Catholic arms was a complete failure. In the north, Denmark was to do the work, in the south, Transylvania and the Turks were to attack the Emperor in the rear. But the Turks were held by Persia, Transylvania alone was too weak, and Denmark broke down completely. The army of the League under Tilly gained the mastery of Lower Saxony, and the Emperor's General, Wallenstein, advanced irresistibly as far as Jutland. The peace of Lübeck in 1629 laid the whole of Germany at the Emperor's feet. Ferdinand II was Emperor as none before him, not even Frederick I or Henry VI, had ever been.

In Wallenstein's head there arose fantastic plans. The Emperor was to make himself the master of the princes, the sole ruler in Germany, to abolish the imperial election, introduce a hereditary right to the imperial throne, build a fleet in the Baltic and link this up with the Spanish naval armament. Yet remoter plans included the subjection of Italy and a crusade to put an end to the power of the Turks.

Even for so much of these dreams as was realizable—and they were not all chimeras—the limited, unimaginative Ferdinand had no taste. He was dominated by another ambition—the re-establishment of the Catholic Church everywhere in Germany. If he had been willing to follow Wallenstein's suggestions, he would have had to turn above all against his present allies, Bavaria and the ecclesiastical Electors, and to forget the religious issue. His choice lay between making full use of the political possibilities opened up by his military successes, renouncing religious reconquest; or concentrating on the latter at the cost of abandoning any attempt at the revision of the constitution of the Empire. But the former alternative did not exist for Ferdinand. He probably quite failed to understand the brilliant ideas of his great general. Accordingly he refused to see him, and limited himself to issuing the Restitution Edict (1629), which demanded nothing less than the return to the State of the possessions which the Protestants had held in 1555.

If that had been carried out in full, there is no doubt that Protestantism would have been eradicated from the greater part of Germany. It would have sunk to be a tolerated sect in some of the North-German secular principalities, in Saxony, Brandenburg, Brunswick, in the same way as the Hussites had, at an earlier date, been tolerated in Bohemia. How long and to what extent it would then have maintained itself is very questionable. In time it would perhaps have sunk to be a religious curiosity like the Waldenses or the Mennonites. It would have had hardly any influence on the intellectual progress of the west. Germany in general would have settled down intellectually and in every other respect to the Bavarian and Austrian type.

In 1629 this fate seemed almost inevitable. The country itself no longer had the strength to avert it. There seemed to be nothing left but a more or less heroic martyrdom. The escape from this was due simply to foreign intervention.

The Emperor's successes, even within the modest limits which Ferdinand assigned to them, still meant a huge threat to his neighbours. Three of these, the Netherlands, England, and Denmark, had already been put out of action. Those most threatened, France and Sweden, had not yet taken a hand.

To France, in view of the union of the two branches of the house of Habsburg, what had happened in Germany amounted to a victory for Spain. If the situation endured, if the Spaniards maintained the position which they had gained on the left bank of the Rhine, then France was permanently encircled. To Sweden, the appearance of Spain, the Catholic Power, on the Baltic was a direct threat. The very existence of the Swedish Crown rested upon Protestantism and the mastery of the Baltic. Both were now jeopardized.

The whole course of modern German history was determined when these two Powers, France and Sweden, joined together to reverse what had taken place in the preceding years. To the year 1629 belongs the great memorial in which France's great statesman, Cardinal Richelieu, demonstrated to his king that it would be needful to intervene in the German struggles if France's independence and greatness were to be assured for the future. It was not easy for him to seek alliance with the Protestant King of Sweden for this purpose. But he overcame his religious prejudice; the community of interest was too strong, scruples had to be suppressed Thus the alliance, which was documented at Bärwalde in January, 1631, came to pass. Gustavus Adolphus of Sweden had already been six months on German soil; as early as 1628 he had prevented the capture of Stralsund by the Imperialists. Now he could prosecute the war on a large scale. For the one thing he had hitherto lacked, money, he now got from France.

A few months later (September 17, 1631) his victory at Leipzig gave the decisive turn to events. Not only was the whole of North Germany freed at one stroke, but the South opened its gate to him. In the next year his campaign led him to Bavaria, and he was planning a thrust into the heart of the Austrian hereditary territories. Then Wallenstein, whom the Emperor in his need again called in, came against him, and upset his plans. In November, 1632, on the battlefield of Lützen, in the moment when victory was in sight, the heroic career of the king came to an abrupt end in a soldier's death. The meteor from the north had set as suddenly as it had risen. But even the short time during which it had shone had sufficed to divert the course of Germany's destiny.

It has been maintained that Gustavus Adolphus died

THE THIRTY YEARS' WAR

at the right time for Germany. I cannot agree in this. Whatever his plans were, whether he wanted to be German King and Emperor, or merely the leader of the united Protestant States of the Empire, certain it is that his death was a misfortune for Germany. True, he was a foreign king, and had he had lasting success he could not have neglected the interests of his native land. But the greater those successes, and the stronger his position in Germany, the less would he have needed to make her great at Germany's expense. Sweden and North Germany belong together geographically, and are complementary, just as the two nations are closely related to one another. And Gustavus Adolphus was in descent and mentality as much German as Swede. Under him both countries could have made good, and if in the long run one had taken the lead, there can be no doubt that this would have been Germany, the larger as well as the intellectually superior. The political centre of gravity of a German-Swedish dual monarchy would, by the laws of nature, have been situated in Germany, and the accession of strength proceeding from the union with Sweden would have been of advantage to Germany, just as Sweden's own development would have been furthered.

All that was now altered, with Gustavus Adolphus removed from the scene before the play was at an end. Now France found herself compelled, if all her efforts were not to be in vain, to commit herself yet more deeply in the struggle, and accordingly to aim at still greater gains for herself. By themselves, without the brilliant leadership of the king, the Swedes were too weak, in face of the opposition of the German Protestant princes. When in 1634 the Swedish army suffered a severe defeat at Nördlingen, the principal Protestant states fell away from the alliance. Saxony made her peace at Prague in 1635, others followed. The Emperor granted an amnesty to all Protestants, and guaranteed the religious position of 1627. To many that seemed enough, especially as the Catholic League was now dissolved. The war would have died out if the issue had lain with the Germans. But France could no longer allow that; she would have failed of her object, the destruction of the Spanish position on the Rhine. She accordingly took the field with her own forces. In 1635 came her declaration of war on Spain. Deeper and deeper she plunged into warlike adventures in the following years, until finally, as the strongest factor, she dominated military events and consequently the peace negotiations. The results were fateful for Germany. For now the Franco-Spanish war was fought on German soil and peace concluded at Germany's cost.

We will only take a cursory view of the welter of events. The Swedish forces were growing exhausted, and were no longer of service save for short sudden moves and raids; the French forces were growing in strength. France, previously unwarlike, became militarized, developed her army and trained up generals in her service. From 1643 onwards, Condé and Turenne were at the head, and now the war drew towards its close. The end had really come when in 1646 a Swedish army under Wrangel from the north and a French one under Turenne, advancing into Bavaria from the west, joined hands. Only indecision and incapacity prolonged it until 1648. Two decisive blows at last forced peace; in May the Swedes stormed Prague, in August Condé annihilated a Spanish-Austrian army at Lens. On October 24, 1648, peace was signed at Münster and Osnabrück. This peace closed the epoch which began with 1519, and booked its results, as a tradesman draws up the balance of an account in his ledger.

In the religious question the peace of Westphalia brought nothing new in principle: the creeds retained equal rights as before. The only point was the delimitation of possessions. This was based on the position in 1624, whereas the Emperor had previously conceded only 1627. The three years make a great difference. The reversion to 1624 saved the greater part of the north German bishoprics for the Protestants, as well as Württemberg and the Palatinate on both banks of the Rhine. From the religious point of view, therefore, the war had been carried on since 1624 on the imperial side to no purpose.

This was still more so as regards the constitution. Every absolutist move which the Emperor had made was repulsed. The freedom of the Estates of the Empire was expressly recognized, their independence even in foreign politics documented in all form by the concession of the *jus foederis*, the right of making alliances. It was the consummation of self-government; the Estates of the Empire were independent, even if not sovereign. Was the Empire still a state? Was it not merely a union of states?

The theoreticians could dispute about it. Samuel Pufendorf, the greatest authority of the time on international law, designated this constitution, a little later (1667), as a "*Monstrum.*" Peculiar it certainly was. Anyone who had still taken this Empire for a living state could now learn otherwise. The peace of Westphalia was the death certificate of the German Empire.

Thus as regards the constitutional question too the frightful sacrifices of the war might have been spared, and again we may remind ourselves that it really broke out in consequence of Spanish intervention, and that it was only through the long years of activity of other foreign powers—Rome and the Jesuits—that the premises were created from which it could arise at all. Thus the Thirty Years' War was, in the preparation and the making, the work of foreigners in Germany.

It was only logical that it should be foreigners who profited by the war. The victorious powers, Sweden and France, demanded their indemnity—it was not yet necessary to cover up the nakedness of the demands with such fictions as "reparations" and "self-determination of peoples." They could help themselves, the booty lay ready. Sweden took what she wanted above all, the south coast of the Baltic in northern Pomerania; and in addition the mouth of the Weser, with the bishoprics of Bremen and Verden. France demanded and received the Habsburg possessions in Alsace. She had established herself there during the war, and did not quit the position again.

We must be clear about what these cessions meant—and they were cessions to foreign powers in both cases, although the Crown of Sweden became a member of the Imperial Diet in respect of the German territories transferred to it. In northern Pomerania and at the mouth of the Weser the best harbours that Germany still possessed were lost, since Danzig had become Polish and Hamburg had come under the influence of the King of Denmark as its territorial lord; he had also been Duke of Holstein since 1460.

And now Alsace too! Right from the beginning, Richelieu had kept in view this very acquisition, and had openly acknowledged its object in the memorial of 1629: " Pour acquérir une entrée en Allemagne," " to acquire a means of access into Germany." As early as that he had indicated Strassburg and Lorraine as the goals of the French advance. From here South Germany could at all times be kept in check, the South German princes drawn into subservience to France, and Austria threatened. The acquisition of Alsace was designed as a basis for war against the German Empire, and since then it has often enough served that purpose.

At the same time France came forward as surety for the constitution of the German Empire. The only record which formally regulates the relations of the Estates of the Empire to one another and to the Emperor, and their rights and duties in the old German Empire, is the peace of Westphalia, which is therefore a document of international law. The war was represented therein as a fight for the rights and liberties of the Estates against attempts at their suppression by the Emperor, and " German liberty " was now guaranteed by foreigners—the French and Swedish kings Germany had become virtually a French protectorate, and the French king the permanent secret anti-Emperor.

Other losses the treaty of peace merely had to confirm. These included the loss of Switzerland. She had felt herself to be a European power since 1475, and since 1500 had in practice no longer regarded herself as a part of the Empire. Now she secured her formal release. There was also a French interest at stake, for without recruitment in Switzerland the French army could not be kept at full strength. For Germany, however, this separation meant the loss, not only of valuable population, but also of her natural geographical frontier in the south, and of places, such as the town of Basle, which belong to her by position and communications.

A further loss was tacitly accepted: the independence of the Netherlands. There had never been any doubt that they belonged to the Empire, in spite of all the splendour of Burgundy. It was only their fight for freedom against Spain, and the fact that the Empire took no notice of it, that brought about their development into an independent, and then into a Great Power. We have forgotten in Germany how closely related to us are the people of the Netherlands, Dutch and Flemish: they are in reality simply parts of the German nation. In this case political developments have dissolved natural associations. And at the same time Germany lost the mouth

THE THIRTY YEARS' WAR

of her principal river. This too was the work of the Habsburg dynasty. Charles V as Emperor should have strengthened and revived the connexion of the Netherlands with the Empire, which had been loosened by the Burgundian domination. Instead of this, he bound them up closely with his Spanish kingdom, and thereby separated them from Germany.

One more loss we must mention here, as it belongs to the epoch of which we are speaking, although not to the peace of Westphalia—Livonia. It had been left to itself since the middle of the sixteenth century, and had fallen a prey to its neighbours. The Russian invasion in 1558 began the game, which ended in 1625 with partition between Sweden and Poland, Sweden annexing the north, up to the river Dvina, and Poland the south, the Duchy of Courland. Nothing was remembered of the rights of the German Empire.

There had once been a German Hanseatic League, which, in war and peace, dominated the Baltic and the whole of the north with its ships. What had become of it? Its trade received its first severe blow when the free town of Novgorod in 1479 fell a prey to the Tsar of Moscow, who took away their privileges from the German merchants and dissolved their association. After that the Hansa dwindled away. Here too Charles V took sides against German interests, in the Netherlands as sovereign and in Denmark as the brother-in-law and ally of the king. The rise of the Swedish Crown under Gustavus Vasa deprived the Hansa of light and air, and Elizabeth of England finally gave it its death-blow (1579) by withdrawing all its privileges.

No power remained in existence which could have prevented this, since there was no longer a German Empire worthy of the name. The conditions that made possible the peace of Westphalia robbed the German seaports of their independence. Lubeck and Hamburg, too, fell now entirely under Danish influence; Hamburg actually sank to be a Danish provincial town.

So ended the epoch which had begun with the union of Germany and Spain in 1519 under a common ruler. All the alarm felt at the election of the Spanish king to be German Emperor, all the sinister possibilities which the election had foreshadowed, had been frightfully confirmed and outdistanced by the course of history. The Empire had been dissolved, its frontiers broken down, its independence destroyed. In such conditions, and not only so, but impoverished, laid waste, and reduced to a land of peasants, it entered a new stage in its history. Had it any future, any hope left ?

CHAPTER IX

THE LOUIS XIV ERA

THE Treaty of Westphalia brought one epoch to a close, and marked the beginning of another. It ended the struggle between Protestant and Catholic and the disputes over the constitution of the Empire, and thenceforward both the cause of religious uniformity and the claims of the Emperor to absolute power were dead, abandoned things of the past.

For the people of Germany, the rule of the Emperor was replaced once and for all by the tyranny of the territorial princes. Their serene highnesses had an immense task to perform—nothing less than the restoration to life of a land in ruins; but they had at their disposal a far greater power than before. Whereas their only rivals for authority, the Estates, had become enfeebled through financial exhaustion, the princes—at any rate in the larger states, by which the fate of the nation was mainly determined—were in possession of the armed forces employed in the war, which they took care to retain after peace had been restored. Thus the standing army, the *miles perpetuus*, made its first appearance in Germany, a basis and support for local absolutism. Not that the estates were entirely abolished; the Diets and Committees remained in being, but in most cases only in the sense in which an old unoccupied building is allowed to remain standing; that is to say, they became ruins, interesting historically and occasionally picturesque and venerable, but of no practical value, if not actually a hindrance. Even in states like Württemberg and Hanover, where they clung to their existing rights and privileges with dogged tenacity, they played hardly any active part in public life and had to submit to the will and pleasure of the ruling prince in every case, unless, as occasionally happened, some foreign power came to their assistance. In theory the authority of the state was vested still in prince and estates jointly, but in reality the prince was master and controller of all the resources of government. In the eyes both of the outside world and of his own subjects, he was invested with all the insignia of a superior being—a minor Jehovah on earth.

The effects of this change can hardly be overestimated. In many respects, especially in the early years, they were certainly propitious, for the devastated country needed for its reconstruction strong individualities of unquestioned authority, and most of the German potentates accomplished great things in this respect. Even at a later stage, when the hardest times were over; there were many rulers of outstanding ability to be found among the innumerable territorial princes, small, medium and great. Of course, exceptions are always more noticeable than the normal rule, but it would be a mistake to judge of the state of things in general by the relatively few exceptional cases. Considered as a whole, princely autocracy was a benefit to the country, and in the circumstances it gave better results than the supremacy of the Estates would have done. It brought Germany onwards and upwards, which the impotent, selfish wrangling of nobles, prelates and town councillors would never have done.

At the same time the evil influences exerted by this new type of autocracy must not be overlooked. Absolutism is undoubtedly degrading. It may be bearable when viewed at a distance, but at close quarters it inspires either contempt or terror or a mixture of the two. We can see the ridiculous side in the empty grandeur of Prince Irenaeus von Siegharts-Weiler in Hoffmann's tale of "Growler the Tom-cat," still more in Reuter's "Serene Highness," that classic caricature of the pocket Dionysius who has to be careful not to drive too fast for fear of crossing the frontiers of his dominions. He seems to us like a turnip-ghost. But though such figures are harmless enough in the pages of a book, in the flesh they could order the death of any one of their subjects, and the sentence would be carried out. No wonder that the loving subjects trembled lest their prince should take too close an interest in their welfare. Frederick William I of Prussia, who vented his displeasure on passers-by in the street by ordering them lashes, who could with difficulty be dissuaded from putting his own son to death, in defiance of a judgment of his own courts, is a vivid illustration of the type, and Charles Eugene of Württemberg a still more glaring one.

The German townsman's fear of his all-gracious sovereign lord was deep-seated, and remained as a fixed obsession long after all real danger had evaporated. It may well be that this innate fear of the governing authorities has been largely the cause of the diffidence and lack of stability which has always differentiated the Germans in public life from all other civilized nations—and also of that sullen obstinacy of obstructiveness which is nowhere so much in evidence as in Germany. From this point of view the influence of the situation created by the Treaty of Westphalia has lasted up to the present day, and still persists.

It may be possible to interpret most of these phenomena as the ultimate outgrowth of long-established tendencies, as the ripe harvest of an earlier seed-time of German provincialism, but there is one product of the year 1648 which was unquestionably new, and that is France's intrusiveness in German affairs—her constant arbitrary interference, which had previously been unknown. There had been occasional relations between German princes and the kings of France, sometimes of considerable importance, as for instance the Treaty of Chambord in 1552, but these were mere episodes, transitory connexions. From 1648 onwards France's tendency to rule the roost in Germany became permanent.

An additional reason was that the princes were still, in the early years after the conclusion of peace, obsessed by the dangers from which they had just emerged, still felt the menace of the imperial power, and were all inclined to turn to France as their neutral protector. Hence she came to be regarded as the leader of the German opposition against the Emperor, and when Leopold I was elected in 1658 the French Government was able to confront him from the outset with an organised opposition party. A number of German potentates, led by the Archbishop Elector of Mainz, formed the Rhenish League (Rheinbund) in conjunction with France for the protection of their privileges against possible encroachments by the House of Austria. The league was joined within a few years by several other states, including even Brandenburg. It did not accomplish anything positive, but it was important as a sign of the times, keeping the Emperor perpetually in check under the direction of France, by whom the German princes were used as pawns. Thus it was under French tutelage that even Germany's domestic affairs were reconstructed in the period following 1648. The Emperor became a mere symbol of authority against which the Empire was in revolt, and the only real federal power became centred in the Imperial Diet, which was in permanent session at Ratisbon from 1663 onwards—a standing Congress of accredited representatives which hardly ever managed to pass a single resolution and in which the French delegate did all the talking.

France's formal justification for her continuous intervention in German affairs lay in the provisions of the treaty, signed at Münster on October 24, 1648, which regulated the constitution of the Empire and established the sovereignty of the Estates. The fact that the King of France was a party to the Treaty made him a guarantor of the constitution, and his guardianship of the rights of the Estates led naturally to a general supervision of German domestic politics. In practice, the exercise of this new role was facilitated by the predominance in Europe given to France by the Treaty of Westphalia, especially in relation to Germany. So far as German territory was concerned, she had obtained a footing by the acquisition of part of Alsace—not a very large part so far, neither extensive nor concentrated; merely the Habsburg domains, but an outpost from which she was able to exert a constant pressure. It only required extending, consolidating, strengthening, to turn that pressure into imperious compulsion.

This aim conditioned the policy of the French Government during the period immediately following the Treaty: to gain possession of the whole of Alsace, if possible the whole of the left bank of the Rhine, or at least that part of the Palatinate which lay on the left bank, and thence to dominate first Southern Germany and ultimately the whole country. Not that the French were primarily concerned with Germany itself. That impoverished, impecunious land was only valuable as a recruiting ground, and would serve for that purpose whether annexed or not. In itself Germany inspired neither cupidity nor fear. The fundamental motive was the old-standing enmity between France and the Habsburgs of Austria and Spain.

By the Treaty of Westphalia the Emperor had been forced to allow Spain to continue the war with France alone, and eleven years later France reaped the fruits of victory against her southern rival in the Treaty of the

Pyrenees (1659). The great fear of the men in power in Paris was lest the two Habsburg branches should be re-united when the Spanish line became extinct as was to be expected at the death of Charles II. In that eventuality the Emperor Leopold would be the heir to the whole of the Spanish monarchy, that is to say, Spain, Naples, Milan, Belgium and the American colonies. This would have been tantamount to a revival of the world empire of Charles V, and France resolved to oppose this at all costs. French counter claims to the Spanish succession were adumbrated on the ground that Louis XIV had married a Spanish princess, and it is understandable that to be able to put the resources of Germany in the scale against the Emperor in the conflict which was visibly brewing would have been a valuable asset to France. Her surest method of approach was to establish herself in Alsace and on the Rhine, so as to be in a position to invade Southern Germany at any moment and to march on Vienna via Ingolstadt and Regensburg.

There were probably further and more recondite calculations in Louis XIV's mind. He was consumed with self-satisfaction at his position of hegemony in Europe and was anxious to see it recognized and consecrated by some external symbol. He regarded himself as the lawful heir and successor of Charlemagne and hence entitled to all the dominions that the great emperor had once possessed. To be Emperor himself was his dearest wish, as it had been that of his ancestors in the thirteenth and fourteenth centuries. And even if this personal ambition were set aside, the traditional aim of ousting the Habsburgs from the imperial seat remained. To further that aim it was necessary to gain a controlling influence with the Electors, no less than four of whom had their seat on the Rhine, while a fifth, Bavaria, lay not far from the Upper Rhine. Hence Louis' policy was clearly to lay hands on as much of the Rhine as possible, and his people fully shared their royal master's sentiments. They regarded themselves as the successors and lawful heirs of the Franks, and wanted France to recapture the old limits of the Frankish Empire. According to this theory Germany rightfully belonged to the French, and the irreducible minimum of their claim was for their frontier to be extended as far as the Rhine. An idea which had previously merely flashed through the minds of a few crystallized and became the common talk of the many in the phrase " France's natural boundary is the Rhine."

Such in outline was the political situation in which Germany found herself after 1648 *vis à vis* her all-powerful neighbour, and events soon began to dot the i's and cross the t's when Louis XIV set about realizing his schemes. These schemes bade fair to succeed, and would have done so, if Louis had only had the strength of mind to restrict himself to one main object at a time and direct his whole concentrated attack on one chosen mark. If he had limited his aim first to bringing to an end the Habsburg monopoly of the Imperial Crown, then to obtaining the indirect control of Germany, and then to getting all the states on the left bank of the Rhine one by one under his direct tutelage, it is difficult to see how he could have failed to achieve each and all of these ends. He could put into the field forces of his own more than ample to deal with any opposition, and at the same time could count on receiving valuable support, for the German princes were only too ready to ally themselves with France. Their fear of Austria, their utter indigence coupled with a keen desire, inspired by vanity, to maintain their *état* and pose as Great Powers in miniature, aping the *Roi Soleil* in their military organization, their architecture and their court life, all combined to make them disposed to curry favour with France. Much could be got out of them by a gracious gesture combined with a tangible subsidy. In the last resort they would be moved by sheer fright if His Most Christian Majesty were to order his battalions to march on the Rhine.

In addition, France could rely on the support of Sweden, who owed her rise to the status of a Great Power to French assistance and depended on it to maintain herself in that position, and was hence obliged to adopt any and every hint that Paris chose to convey to her. Finally, Poland was generally to be reckoned as a supporter of some consequence against the Emperor. Thus the latter was confronted to the west, north and east either by France herself or by French satellites, and, to make the circle complete, France had in mind to arrange for an attack to be launched on the Empire from the south-east by the Turks. Ever since Charles V had relinquished the greater part of Hungary in order to have his hands free to deal with the Protestants, the Turks had been settled on the Danube and had even occupied the bridgehead of Buda on the right bank of the river. The Emperor called himself King of Hungary, but the title was an empty one, and Vienna had practically become a frontier city. It is true that the Ottoman military power was no longer as formidable as it had been, but it was still a potential danger through sheer weight of numbers, especially if France had attacked in the west at the same time. Germany could not have held out long in a war on two fronts. But the *sine qua non* of success was that France should have no other opponent to meet, and this condition Louis XIV failed to ensure. His ambition did not stop short at the annexation of Alsace, the extension of his frontier to the Rhine and the virtual control of Germany, he coveted Belgium and Italy still more, and was determined at the same time to make France the premier country of the world in industry, commerce, sea transport and colonial possessions. This programme aroused the hostility alike of Spain, the Netherlands, and Great Britain, and in the resultant struggle against a world in arms Louis was defeated. Only in regard to Germany did he achieve at least a partial success.

His first attack (1667) was directed against the Spanish Netherlands, his second (1672) against Holland. Not until both these enterprises had in the main proved failures did he turn on Germany, except for the prelude of 1670, when the Duke of Lorraine was forcibly expelled and his territories annexed to France. The period immediately following the Treaty of Nymwegen (1679) was devoted to the capture of Alsace.

This was undertaken by way of a civil action at law, before French special tribunals (*chambres de réunion*) in which the appellants sought to prove, with all those arts of sophistry, prevarication and false witness for which the French have always been famous, that those parts of Alsace which were still independent had originally been appanages of the parts which were now French. The upshot was the occupation of Strassburg in October, 1681.

This did arouse a certain amount of opposition in Germany. Many of the princes began to realize—not a few being personally affected through the " rectifications " which were taking place in their Alsatian possessions—that the danger of which they had always stood in fear was threatening them not from the Emperor's side but from that of France, and a sense of the impending menace grew apace. In those days, for the first time for many years, a wave of nationalist sentiment passed over Germany. The French exactions had aroused in the people a consciousness of their precarious position. A burning desire to put an end to it arose and called for satisfaction. War was within an ace of being declared. But Louis had stronger cards to play The movement was crippled by the obstruction of some of the leading princes, especially the Elector of Brandenburg, who was at that time wholly pro-French. The trump card was a Turkish advance on Vienna (1683). This danger was averted by the most determined efforts, and the victory of the imperial troops at the Kahlenberg saved Vienna and temporarily lifted the menace from the eastern front. But by this time the German stocks both of war material and of courage were no longer sufficient to permit of any military effort in the west. The Vienna authorities decided to give up Strassburg and Alsace, and in 1684 a twenty years' truce was signed with France, under which the latter retained everything she had seized. The Emperor was thus enabled to devote his whole attention in the next few years to subduing the Turks. By 1686 he had reconquered the whole of Hungary, then the Danube was crossed, and in 1688 Belgrade fell and the road to the Balkans was open.

For Louis XIV this was an additional reason for reopening the attack on Germany. He could not allow his natural ally Turkey to be put out of action permanently. He felt bound at least to take steps to consolidate his gains, and accordingly declared war again in 1688 with the object of conquering the Palatinate.

But he made a grave miscalculation. He now had to deal with the whole of Germany, and not only with Germany. His allies in that country had deserted him, for his brutal and hypocritical annexation of Alsace and seizure of Strassburg were still remembered; many had been influenced against him by the fact of his entering into an alliance with the Turks, and there were other reasons, such as the expulsion of the Huguenots. In the War of the Palatinate (1688–97) Louis had the whole of Germany against him for the first time, while concurrently a European Grand Coalition, headed by Great Britain, took the field against him. This was more than France could cope with unaided. She could not hope to carry on hostilities in Belgium, on the Rhine, in Northern Italy and on the high seas at the same time. To retrieve Lorraine was a small thing if Alsace was to remain French. Alsace too could have been recaptured, but it was not, chiefly because Austria's policy had once more taken an eastern orientation.

The Turks had resumed the offensive and retaken Belgrade in 1690, and the Emperor, seeing that his resources were not equal to ensuring success on both points, decided to concentrate on the war in the east and abandon the west. Alsace was sacrificed to save Hungary. His object was achieved, for the victory gained by Prince Eugene of Savoy at Zenta on September 11, 1697, finally disposed of the Ottoman menace, and the treaty of Karlowitz (1699) ceded the whole of Hungary to the Austrian crown. The eastern front was clear and secure, but the western front had been abandoned.

The Emperor's council had made the choice with its eyes open. During the discussions which preceded the final decision the Margrave Louis William of Baden-Baden, Commander of the Imperial forces, expressed his opinion as to the importance of Strassburg in the following memorable words:

"For Germany the possession of this city means purely and simply a lasting pledge of peace. For France it is a door constantly open for war, a door through which she can invade German soil as often as she wishes. Her motive in finding excuses for not restoring Strassburg to the Empire is perfectly clear; she is reluctant to give up her chief means of attacking Germany and the Empire at will."

But Vienna had decided in favour of abandoning Strassburg, and the reason is not far to seek. The danger in the east was far more real and menacing to the Emperor's own territories, and until it was eliminated, no expansion was possible, even in the west; and in Hungary rich new territories were calling out for capture compared with which the recovery of the little Austrian domains in Alsace was a negligible matter. The Emperor pursued a dynastic policy, and the Hungarian shirt was nearer to his back than the Alsatian coat. The result was that Strassburg and Alsace were left in French hands.

Among the German people themselves there was little disposition to question the Emperor's choice. The wars with the Turks were commonly regarded as a matter affecting the national honour far more than the wars with France, and the victories gained by Louis William—Louis of Turkey, as he was called—and by Prince Eugene aroused the greatest popular enthusiasm as national exploits. It may be assumed, too, that they were taken in some sense as a compensation for the very unheroic part which the nation was condemned to play in the west.

Once again an opportunity was to arise of redeeming past omissions. In 1700 the long expected crisis in Spanish affairs occurred through the death of Charles II without direct heirs, and in 1701 the resultant European war broke out, the War of the Spanish Succession. We are not concerned with its details, any more than with those of its predecessors, for Germany was in no way directly concerned. No German interest was affected in the original dispute, nor was Germany threatened or attacked. Yet she became involved in the struggle owing to two circumstances, first that the Habsburg claimant to the Spanish throne, Prince Charles, was the son of the Emperor and later became Emperor himself as Charles VI at the death of his elder brother Joseph I in 1711; and secondly, that the Elector of Bavaria, in his lasting hostility to the House of Habsburg, became an ally of the French king. A third circumstance, namely that France was in possession of Strassburg, turned Southern Germany into a theatre of war during the first phase of the struggle. The French aimed at striking a decisive blow at Austria by combining two converging lines of attack, from the Upper Rhine via Bavaria and from Northern Italy via Tirol, but this scheme came to naught owing to the French defeat at Blenheim in 1704. This put an end to hostilities on German soil, and even opened up a real possibility of reconquering the territory previously lost. By 1709 things had progressed so far that Louis XIV himself, disheartened by the never-ending series of military reverses he was sustaining, offered to restore Strassburg to Germany. But the extravagance of the Emperor's demands—he actually asked for the co-operation of French troops in subduing Spain in the interest of Charles of Habsburg—prevented peace from maturing at the moment, and as the next few years brought with them a complete change in the European political situation and the break-up of the Grand Coalition, that golden opportunity was irretrievably lost.

By the Treaty of Rastatt (1714) the Emperor secured

THE LOUIS XIV ERA

vast gains: Belgium, Milan, and the Kingdom of Naples. This Treaty definitely marks the rise of Austria from a mere German dependency of Spain which happened to be connected dynastically with the imperial house, to a fully fledged European Great Power. The Treaty of Baden, signed six months later between France and the representatives of the princes—Emperor and Empire were now actually functioning independently—not only left Germany without any compensation for all the sacrifices she had made but inflicted a further penalty in the loss of the fortress of Landau, which was destined to remain in French hands for another century.

Reviewing the Louis XIV era as a whole from the German standpoint, we may say that the chief result was to increase the French preponderance over Germany by the transfer of Alsace. All efforts at its recovery failed; but, on the other hand, France's plans for the complete subjection of Germany, including the extension of her frontier as far as the Rhine, likewise failed. Germany managed to assert her independence technically, and at all events did not become France's vassal.

Public opinion in Germany accepted the situation, on the whole, with equanimity. The first almost unanimous impulse of indignant resistance had evaporated. The weakening of the power of France as the result of the War of the Spanish Succession seemed to diminish the urgency of the menace from the west, and there was now no compelling reason for carrying on the opposition to France to the bitter end. In later years memories of Louis' predatory wars and of the twice repeated devastation of the Palatinate were to act as a ferment and foster a lasting Francophobia in the minds of the German people, but in the years immediately following the death of the French King little of this emotion came to the surface, and it had no influence on the course of European politics, On the contrary, it was not long before France largely recovered the old ascendancy over the German states which had been forfeited by Louis XIV's brutal rapacity. The Habsburg monarchy's rise to the status of a European Great Power revived earlier apprehensions lest too great a power in the hands of the Emperor might jeopardise the autonomy of the territorial states. What was more natural in such circumstances than that the princes should seek protection in the same quarter as their ancestors had done in the

Thirty Years' War ? In this way France gradually reacquired a troop of clients in the Empire by means of which she could combat the influence of Austria and keep the Emperor in perpetual check. The quarrels of the World Powers were reflected in German affairs, one group of princes forming a French party and another an Austro-British one, so that any recrudescence of the general European war, any conflict of interests between extra-German Great Powers, might easily have precipitated civil war in Germany. The state of things first brought about by the Thirty Years' War, that Germany formed the chess-board on which the Great Powers fought out their games, threatened to be perpetuated.

The danger was enhanced by the fact that a number of the states of the Empire were held by foreign rulers. The King of Sweden was a Prince of the Empire ; the Elector of Saxony became King of Poland in 1697, and in 1714 a Guelph of the Hanoverian line asecnded the throne of Great Britain and Ireland. There was thus a dual tendency for foreign countries to become inquiline in Germany, and for German dynasties to spread beyond the confines of the Reich. This was especially noticeable in the case of the Imperial house itself, which with its possessions in Hungary, Belgium, and Italy had already become much more a European power than a German state.

In the east the Louis XIV era wrought profound changes. The Ottoman menace finally disappeared, thanks to the conquest of Hungary by Austria. The might of Poland-Lithuania had already crumbled before the Turks were repulsed, and from that quarter no danger threatened. Yet the double front problem for Germany had not been disposed of ; it had merely entered a new phase—a far more serious phase, with Russia in the place of Poland. The great Northern War of 1700 to 1721 completely metamorphosed the position in Eastern Europe. The palmy days of Sweden came to an end through her internal instability, and she did not recover from the disaster of Poltava (June, 1709). She disappeared from Germany almost entirely, and only Rügen, Stralsund and Greifswald continued as a reminder that the best part of Pomerania had once been Swedish. In consequence the mouths of the Oder and Weser were freed, but at what a price ! Esthonia and Livonia were swallowed up by Russia, St. Petersburg was founded, and the Baltic thenceforward

THE LOUIS XIV ERA

came under the control of Muscovy, a Power of such vast extent and such incalculable potentialities as had never before been seen in Europe.

This struggle was also carried on partly on German soil. The King of Sweden's lordship over western Pomerania, and the fact that the King of Poland was also Elector of Saxony, resulted in the Russian armies advancing through Pomerania and Mecklenburg and as far as Holstein, and it would not have been surprising if they had stayed there. Peter the Great seriously thought at one time of laying hands either on the Duchy of Prussia or on Pomerania and Mecklenburg, and for a while his ambitions were centred on gaining control of the southern coast of the Baltic. Nothing actually came of this plan, but lasting traces of it remained in the form of family influences which the Tsar had acquired in Mecklenburg and Holstein by means of political marriages. A third party now grew up within the Empire, a pro-Russian party, on the lines of the pro-French and the Austro-British parties, and Germany became a prey to diplomatic partition schemes. Fortunately there was an unbridgeable gulf between France and Russia in their divergent interests in regard to Turkey. The French maintained their former relations with the Porte for fear of losing their trade in the Levant, while Russia had designs on the Straits. But for this conflict of interests, and if Paris and St. Petersburg had found it possible to come to an understanding in the eighteenth century, the whole future of Germany would in all probability have taken quite a different course.

In the last analysis, the fate which constantly threatened her was always the same—the danger implicit in her geographical situation, that is, the danger of being divided up amongst neighbours of superior strength. If at any given moment Franco-Russian rivalry in the Balkans had disappeared wholly or in part, and the two powers had made common cause, there was little to prevent their joint advance from the west and the east into Germany. The states as they existed in the eighteenth century were not in a position unaided to resist partition with any success. France could have expanded as far as the Rhine, Russia as far as the Elbe, and all that would have been left of Germany would have been a small buffer state—a somewhat larger Switzerland, but without the Swiss unity and stability. It might have become a British protectorate, or perhaps the southern half would have been a French " sphere of influence," while the upper half was allotted similarly either to Russia or to Great Britain. The process might in time even have been carried further, and the buffer state partitioned in its turn. In any case the German nation would have been eliminated as an independent and respected voice in the councils of the civilized world.

What actually happened was very different. With a sudden *volte-face* Germany turned her back on the past, threw over all effete traditions, and, taking with full self-consciousness a diametrically opposite path to that hitherto followed, struck out a new trail towards political unity and world power.

To do this required indeed a thorough-going break in historical continuity. A policy of conservatism, striving to maintain and develop existing characteristics in the political and social life of the nation and clinging to the historical bases of constitutional law, could in such conditions only have led to disintegration and national disaster. A revolution was required, by which the existing social structure would be destroyed, the Empire dissolved, and on and from its ruins a new edifice created. This was achieved, and the achievement is due to Prussia.

CHAPTER X

PRUSSIA IN TRIUMPH AND IN ECLIPSE

AMONG all the German territorial states formed by the chance accretion of inheritance and conquests, Brandenburg-Prussia is perhaps the most freakish growth. It came into being in 1618, when the Elector of Brandenburg succeeded to the Dukedom of Prussia owing to the collateral Hohenzollern line, which had ruled since 1525 over the remnants of the East Prussian house of the Teutonic Order under the suzerainty of Poland, becoming extinct. The Elector had already, in 1614, come into possession by similar inheritance of the Rhenish territories of Cleves, Mark and Ravensberg, and in 1648 the eastern part of Pomerania was acquired by Brandenburg, though Sweden retained the more valuable western portion under the Treaty of Westphalia.

These *disjecta membra* were made to live and breathe by a ruler of outstanding capacity, the Elector Frederick William, in the critical period which followed the conclusion of the Thirty Years' War. Strict and painstaking administration, high aims and a courageous readiness to take risks were the characteristics of the new state. Expansion or downfall seemed to be its motto, and indeed its strange geographical constitution seemed to prescribe some such guiding principle. For all his tireless efforts, Frederick William achieved little in the way of external aggrandisement. He failed to secure Western Pomerania despite his many military successes, because the whole endeavour was based on a political miscalculation, Louis XIV being determined not to allow his Swedish ally to be weakened in any way. The only effective way to the Pomeranian ports lay through victory in Alsace or the Netherlands; it was of no use to fight for them in Pomerania itself, to say nothing of East Prussia or Courland, where Brandenburg's triumphant soldiery had actually penetrated in pursuit of the enemy. The ambitious Elector only scored one definite success in foreign politics:

the freeing of the Duchy of Prussia from Polish suzerainty, attained as the result of fortunate generalship and unscrupulous diplomacy in the course of the First Swedish War, 1655-1660. But there was one other acquisition which came to him unsought—fame. The "Great Elector," as even his contemporaries had begun to call him, was the first heroic figure in German history after long generations during which the rulers of the nation had only varied the tradition of mediocrity by an occasional example of oddity. From the time of Frederick William all eyes were involuntarily turned towards Brandenburg-Prussia, the most powerful state in Northern Germany, the best governed, the most enterprising and, *pace* the Elector of Saxony, the leader of German Protestantism.

Frederick III, who succeeded to these consolidated territories in 1688, added lustre to the state by acquiring the title of King of Prussia, but in other respects his rule marked a retrogression. The national rivalries on the Baltic went on without any participation by Prussia, who thus missed an opportunity of securing the hegemony of northern Germany, and when Frederick William I came to the throne in 1713 it was too late to pursue a forward policy there. He had to content himself with salvaging from the wreck of Greater Sweden the more important part of western Pomerania, including Stettin.

We need not dwell on the great value of Frederick William's particular service to Prussia. He is deservedly famous for his creation of an exceptionally large and exceptionally effective standing army, backed by an administration of exemplary probity, frugality and technical skill. He was in many respects a typical product of the age; his general capacity was mediocre, and he had many unprepossessing qualities. But though he cannot be called an attractive personality, Frederick William I had one virtue which distinguishes him from his contemporaries, places him on a higher level and compels our respect, even our admiration, and that was his inflexible sense of duty. He regarded himself as the servant of the state rather than its master, and he was filled, in all that he did, with a sense of responsibility to a higher power, as if he himself were a mere functionary. The phrase coined by Frederick the Great, that a prince is only the first servant of his people, had already been put into practice long before by his father.

But in all this there lay no presage of any reorientation of German history. The change, when it came, was not the fruit of a natural development extending over an indefinite period, but the work of one individual, the intensely personal achievement of a man of genius. From the moment when King Frederick II, soon after his accession, made the regiments and the millions of thalers which his father had bequeathed to him serve the purpose of territorial conquest, the course of Prussia and German history entered a new phase.

In October, 1720, the Emperor Charles VI died, leaving no male heir. He had taken endless trouble to secure for his daughter Maria Theresa, by means of agreements with all the European powers, undisputed succession rights in all parts of his hereditary dominions, first formally asserted in the Pragmatic Sanction of 1713. But Prussia, under a new king still in his twenties, tore up the agreement she had made with the late Emperor by invading Silesia and announcing that his recognition of the Pragmatic Sanction was dependent on the surrender to him of that Austrian province.

This was the signal for the outbreak of a general European war. France took the opportunity to lay her hands on Belgium, and for the first time the Imperial Crown was wrested from Austria. At the initiative of Prussia and with the consciousness of French support the Electors chose, not Francis of Lorraine-Tuscany, the husband of Maria Theresa, but Charles VII of Bavaria. Without the support of Great Britain this would have been the beginning of the end for Austria as a Great Power.

We must pass over the complicated military and diplomatic events of the next few years, interesting and instructive as they are. We are concerned here only with the new creation to which these events gave birth—the acknowledged power of the state of Brandenburg-Prussia, which rose to such a level of influence that it took up a position in the Empire equal if not superior to that of the Imperial house of Austria. When the war of the Austrian Succession was brought to an end in 1748 by the Treaty of Aix-la-Chapelle, Austria had regained the Imperial Crown, but forfeited her old prestige. She had but two alternatives, either to stomach the rise of Prussia to a position of equality with her, if not of successful rivalry for leadership, or else to endeavour to redress what had happened. Maria Theresa chose the latter, but the Seven Years' War which resulted only went to prove that Prussia was now capable of facing a coalition of three Great Powers and had thereby made good her claim to be regarded as a Great Power herself. The Treaty of Hubertusburg, signed on February 15th, 1763, showed clearly that the Empire contained no longer one Great Power only, but two.

This was the fruit of the invasion of Silesia. That fine province, rich and flourishing, was like a sliding poise, the shifting of which from Austria to Prussia changed the whole distribution of weight in the Empire. Henceforward Austria could still, it is true, boast of the sole possession of the Imperial Crown, but side by side with her there stood always a potential anti-Emperor in the person of the King of Prussia. The Empire now had two leaders, and suffered for ever afterwards from the effects of this rivalry, which also tended to incorporate older, traditional differences; North versus South, and Protestant versus Catholic. A new danger was super-added to the eversent one of partition, that of internal disintegration.

In the situation thus created in 1740, and formally recognized in 1763, lay the seeds of several alternative possibilities. The two Powers might come to an understanding and govern Germany in a sort of diarchy. This course was very unlikely because of its inherent difficulties, since in such a relationship one party is bound to lead and the other to follow, and no Great Power is willing permanently to accept a subordinate role. Secondly, they might compromise on the basis of the division of Germany into two separate spheres of influence. But even this choice would have required a certain degree of self-abnegation on the part of the Emperor, and it was not reasonable to expect that he would adopt it of his own free will. Finally, one of the two rivals might overcome the other and either reduce him to impotence or expel him from the Empire. This again would open up further alternatives; the victor might either entrench himself in such a portion of Germany as he could make sure of holding —which would amount to partition—or else display sufficient mastery to impose his sovereignty on the whole country, in which case the unity of Germany would be attained.

One after another, each of these alternatives was tried, as if the Fates were carrying out an experiment, until finally the last-named became a reality. The process lasted a long time, for the mills of history grind slowly, but in the end the inevitable consummation took place. Inevitable, for was it not written in the stars which of the two rivals was to prevail ? An unprejudiced comparison of the qualities of the two states, then and since, will suffice to prove it. Austria was a variegated mosaic, a conglomeration of nationalities, with no stability or coherence, including, side by side with such highly developed peoples as the Germans and North Italians, rude barbarians like the inhabitants of Hungary ; having international storm-centres on all its frontiers, at odds with France in Belgium and Italy, at grips with Russia and Turkey on the lower Danube, and hence forced to develop a policy of cosmopolitan breadth superseding all narrower national outlooks, whilst lacking the power to pursue such a policy effectively. It was an object lesson which was hardly needed when Joseph II struggled to raise his dominions to a level of efficiency in the shortest possible time, while engaged in dealing with important problems in foreign politics. The complete fiasco which resulted was only what was to be expected. Contrast this situation with that of Prussia—a vigorous, disciplined force, progressive in every field of activity, wholly German in population, the champion of German interests concurrently with her own on every frontier, facing France on the lower Rhine and Poland and Russia in the east. If she only played her cards properly Prussia was bound to win.

All these potentialities were the logical outcome of Frederick the Great's enterprise in Silesia—a venture which he himself described as merely a display of youthful energy and ambition. It was not a product of natural historical development, nor was it inspired by traditional national policy. There was nothing forced or pre-determined about Frederick's choice of Silesia as an object for attack. It is true that it was an eminently desirable territory and that the idea of annexing it was not entirely a new one for Brandenburg ; but from this point of view of rounding off her salients, which was a necessity in every direction—for the Kingdom of Prussia in 1740 consisted of a series of disconnected strips of land—other objects would have offered a more obvious choice : West Prussia for instance, which would have lent her a little geographical stability to the eastward, or Hanover, which would at least have facilitated her communicaitons with Cleves, or still better, the Electorate of Saxony, which would have fitted most conveniently of all into her existing design. By comparison, the new acquisition, Silesia, was situated rather excentrically. It was merely the favourable opportunity provided by the death of the Emperor and the consequent reopening of the question of the Austrian succession that induced Frederick to cast his eyes in the direction of Silesia. If the Emperor had died a year earlier, or if Frederick had come to the throne a year later, the whole course of German history down to the present day would have been different.

It was not as if Prussia had been a predatory state up to then. Of all her acquisitions, only a part of Pomerania had been won by the sword; the rest had all fallen to her by inheritance. And for her to turn against the Imperial house was quite unprecedented. The state of Brandenburg-Prussia had hitherto consistently supported the Emperor, with very occasional exceptions such as occurred for a time under the Great Elector. There had been frequent differences of opinion, and Berlin had sometimes raised loud complaints, but it had always ended in devout submission to His Imperial Majesty. Thus Frederick, in launching his attack on the dynastic house, was flying in the face of all tradition, and the Austrians were dumbfounded. His daring in flouting convention in this way and his superhuman skill in maintaining his hold on territory seized by a *coup de main* were achievements of sheer personal initiative, which refute far more effectively than any philosophical arguments the illusory doctrine of strict causality in human history. They were the work of a man of genius, and men of genius stand outside the laws of normal development, simply because they are made of a different stuff and possess both greater capacity and greater will-power than the average individual, and by their will-power set up fresh standards for human development. It was the act of a man of genius which laid down for the history of the German nation the lines along which it was to proceed and along which it will inevitably continue to proceed.

And not only did Prussia create a new situation in German history by reason of the complete redistribution of power which her aggrandisement brought with it, she introduced a new note by reason of her specific attribute of militarism. All the German states at that time maintained standing armies, and though Prussia's was larger and more efficient than the others that did not constitute an essential difference between them. The important special feature about Prussia was that her army was kept up from her own state resources, whereas the others looked to some foreign power—France, Spain, the Netherlands, or merely the Emperor—to defray all or part of their military expenditure. They could not have existed without subsidies. Even the Great Elector and his son, the first King of Prussia, had accepted subsidies—the more the merrier—but Frederick William I's self-respect had rebelled against the custom. He resented being on the pay-roll of another monarch and hence being subservient to him; but at the same time he resented still more having to give up any of his soldiers. How these sentiments of his reacted on the finances of the state and on the whole administration, is well known. The nation's resources were laid under contribution remorselessly, but also everything possible was done to expand them. The rigid fiscal methods of the state were counterbalanced by a degree of paternal solicitude for its social welfare such as was unknown in any other country.

In time this forced economy gave rise to a new method of raising troops for the army. In view of the high cost of recruiting abroad, Frederick William began to adopt the plan of obtaining a considerable proportion of his soldiers from his own population. At first the system of voluntary enlistment was still maintained, but the recruiting officers were given definite districts from which to get their quota of men, and in this way there gradually developed a kind of conscription among the rural population. Frederick the Great was thereby enabled to wage his protracted campaigns chiefly with soldiers who were his own countrymen, and found that in addition to their other advantages they were more reliable, for they did not run away like foreign mercenaries. At that time this was a unique feature, and the ground was prepared for the subsequent introduction of universal military service.

The result of all this was that the people of Prussia developed a much closer relationship with the state than any other nation. This fact was demonstrated in the

Seven Years' War, when the heroic, indomitable resistance put up by the King of Prussia aroused the wonder and admiration of the whole world. This was only made possible by the solid support of his people, a support so unreserved that in the county of Ravensberg soldiers who deserted were denied the benefits of Confession and Holy Communion and refused admittance to their homes. However great the extremity, not one sign of treachery or secession was ever seen. The subjects of Prussia were willing, even eager, to make any sacrifice for their king and Fatherland—the first occasion on which the word could properly be used in this connexion. At last a German state existed which was accounted by its citizens worthy of the name of Fatherland. Only in Prussia, under the Great King, could a poet assert, as Hippel did, that " to be a Prussian is to be a patriot."

Thus from the outset this state of Prussia received the stamp which differentiated it from the rest and gave it a firm basis and a definite orientation. Latterly the depreciatory term militarism has been much employed, and, " Prussian militarism " has been held up to execration as a crime against the nation, a crime against humanity; but those who are proof against noisy catchwords will recognize that to single out the preferential treatment and the controlling status accorded to the soldier in Prussia and to imagine that this feature explains everything is, to say the least, a superficial view of the real significance of that state. The core and substance of Prussian militarism lay in this, that every individual, lowly or exalted, rich or poor, gave his entire adherence, with body and soul, money and goods, to the state and served it in life and in death. Such devotion could have existed nowhere but in Prussia, where the example was set by the king himself, where two monarchs in succession literally wore themselves out in the endeavour to enhance the power of the state—Frederick William died prematurely through overwork, and Frederick the Great was an old man before his time—where the greatest of kings called himself the first servant of the state, and his father habitually rejected unsound proposals with the words: " What would the King of Prussia say to that ? " Such states were not unknown in ancient history, but in modern times, and on German soil, Prussia was the first embodiment of this classic, Spartan-Roman spirit—an exemplar

PRUSSIA IN TRIUMPH AND IN ECLIPSE 167

which, if it did not constrain to emulation, must arouse a fury of jealous violence.

On the whole it cannot be said that the rise of Prussia to the rank of a Great Power had the immediate and general effect of improving Germany's position in Europe; in fact, the very opposite was the case in some respects. The constant rivalry and more or less open hostility of the two leaders in the Empire at first tended to enhance the influence of foreign Powers in German affairs, and the Empire was made to feel, even more than it had previously done, the repercussion of the division of Europe into two camps, a division which made for disagreement and ultimately for war. The immediate cause of the outbreak of the Seven Years' War, as is well known, was Frederick the Great's decision, in January, 1756, to abandon the alliance with France, and to seek the friendship of the British, who were actually engaged in hostilities with France in North America. On the other hand, Austria was at that time quite prepared, in order to secure the support of France and Russia, to see Belgium annexed to France and to abandon East Prussia to Russia, and it was no fault of hers that this scheme was not carried out, a scheme that would very probably have led to the loss of the left bank of the Rhine.

But on the whole, the dangers to Germany from the west were relatively unalarming during this period, owing to France's lesser absorption in continental problems and increasing internal weakness. Whilst France slowly drifted towards revolution and the pressure on Germany's western frontier relaxed correspondingly, that exerted by Russia in the east grew year by year. The struggle for supremacy between the two Great Powers within the Empire inevitably made their eastern neighbour in a sense the arbiter of German internal affairs so long as she knew how to regulate her policy so as to profit by the circumstances. The decisive effect of Russian intervention was very clearly shown in the Seven Years' War. But for the participation of the Russian armies, this war, if indeed it had actually taken place at all, would certainly have ended within a couple of years in the complete triumph of Prussia, who could then in all probability have annexed the Electorate of Saxony, or at least Lower Lusatia. The fact that Russia withdrew from the war in 1762 without claiming any territorial compensations—she had been in occupation of

East Prussia since the beginning of 1758 and Frederick had already seriously considered the idea of abandoning that province to her—finally decided the issue of the conflict and perhaps saved the life of the Prussian state.

Catherine II was a monarch fully capable of taking advantage of the opportunities offered by the situation, and it would have been but a natural sequel if the German states had then stood together to oppose the intervention of Russia. The pressure she was exerting was felt not only on the lower Danube, in the Balkans and at Constantinople, where it would inevitably end in hampering Austria in her natural lines of expansion, but also in Poland, where it came perilously near to the Prussian frontier, and threatened to block the Vistula and to cut off and doubtless finally to absorb the province of East Prussia. If Russia had succeeded in annexing Poland at that stage—West Prussia being still a constituent part of Poland—there is little doubt that Danzig would have been lost to Germany for ever, and that Königsberg would have shared its fate. These are reflections which the events of our own day have made of great importance. The common menace from Russia might well have brought Prussia and Austria close together; but a *rapprochement* was not practical politics, since Vienna was unwilling or unable to stomach the continued rivalry of Prussia. Accordingly, each Power vied with the other in currying favour with Russia. At first Frederick was successful, but it required all his genius to obtain any appreciable advantage from the relationship. He met and deflected the Russian designs for the absorption of Poland by proposing its partition among the three neighbour states, and thus managed, in 1772, to secure West Prussia for himself. Thus, even if Danzig, the pearl of all Prussia, was still missing—for Frederick was face to face with British interests there, since the volume of English trade with Poland made Great Britain averse to allowing Danzig to fall into Prussia's hands—a great deal had been done towards wiping out a heavy loss incurred in earlier troublous times and satisfying one of the most natural aims of the nation. For West Prussia was still essentially German territory—three centuries of Polish rule had not altered that—and by the efforts of the Prussian state administration it soon regained its former German aspect, and changed from a needy, neglected country into a rich and flourishing one. In this way Prussia was not only meeting her own requirements by attaining a geographical continuity the need for which had long been felt, but was also serving one of the paramount aims of the German nation by recovering lost territory, so that Prussian interests and the interests of Germany as a whole coincided. With all his genius, Frederick could not repeat that fortunate *coup*. Seven years later the handicap imposed on Prussian policy by the influence of Russia became evident despite the alliance which joined the two countries.

Austria, under the leadership of the young Emperor Joseph II, attempted to follow Prussia's example and expand at the expense of her neighbours, and took possession of a large part of Bavaria. Frederick opposed this attempt to disturb the existing equilibrium, and in 1778 the old warrior drew the sword again in the War of the Bavarian Succession—the " potato war " as it was called from its lack of any productive result. It cannot be denied that the campaign was conducted by Prussia with distinct lack of vigour and organization, but it was fated to be unproductive in any case since Russia would have prevented any substantial gains being derived from it. The Treaty of Teschen, which brought the listless war to a close in 1779 and left Austria with an insignificant acquisition of territory from the Bavarian succession and Prussia with none at all, was really the work of Catherine II. She had acted as "intermediary," in other words, as dictator, and the peace followed entirely the lines prescribed by Russian interests. These were to maintain the existing equilibrium between the two German Great Powers and to foster the existing divisions in the Empire, which left Russia the arbiter in German affairs and forced both Prussia and Austria to sue constantly for Russia's friendship and support, and to pay heavily for them.

It was solely due to Frederick the Great's personality that Prussia had become a Great Power, and undoubtedly that fact constituted an element of weakness, for structures erected by a man of genius are always a burden to his successors. The creations of mediocre minds can easily be kept going by men of average ability, but a monument of genius, for the very reason that it has not of necessity grown up in nature's normal course, requires for its early maintenance exceptional capacity and effort, until it has taken its place in the natural order of things. We have had a case in point in our own day. The work of Bismarck's creative genius has crumbled and decayed because the weaker generation which followed him lacked the ability required for its preservation and development.

Frederick the Great's successors were totally unequal to their task. It is rare for incapable rulers to find capable ministers, especially if they are convinced that they know best and must in any case act for themselves. Frederick William II, by no means uncultured, but unreliable, pleasure-loving and dissolute, was a despot with no sense of duty or responsibility, whose chief aim, in politics as in other fields, was to satisfy his royal vanity. His son, Frederick William III was quite the opposite, fully conscious of his duties, but also, and still more keenly, of his own deficiencies. Filled with a sense of his immense responsibilities and his inability to cope with them, he evaded definite decisions where they were most needed, neglected all his opportunities, and finished by getting himself into the very position he had most desired to avoid. So it came about that twenty years after the death of Frederick the Great the state of Prussia collapsed, not under the inescapable blows of fate or through intrinsic defects or faults—faults were certainly not lacking, but not by any means to an extent which made the *débacle* inevitable—but literally and actually through the defects and faults of its leaders, rulers and statesmen alike: through their incapacity, their weakness, and their negligence.

In Bismarck's " Reflections and Reminiscences," a book which does not set out to deal with German history in general, there is a passage (Part I, Chapter XII) in which Prussian foreign policy in 1790 and the Reichenbach Convention are discussed at some length. Some readers may have wondered why the great statesman considered it worth while to dwell in such detail on one isolated event of an age long past, and the digression may even have been put down as evidence of a certain diffuseness in the plan of the book. But both criticisms would be mistaken. The events which took place in 1790 were momentous in their range and lasting effect, and determined the course of history for many years ahead, and it was Bismarck who first drew attention to their importance, more than two generations afterwards. Their significance lies not in what was accomplished, but in what was neglected. A great opportunity was missed which was never to repeat

PRUSSIA IN TRIUMPH AND IN ECLIPSE 171

itself in the same favourable conditions, an opportunity of carrying on and completing the work begun by Frederick the Great. It was left unutilized, and the year 1790 is a milestone in German history for that reason; because the policy of Frederick the Great, the natural and only healthy policy for the Prussian state, was then abandoned.

It was only by a great effort that the aged Frederick had contrived during his last years to maintain the position which he had secured for himself and for Prussia. His alliance with Russia had lost its value more and more. Joseph II had virtually displaced him in 1781, and thenceforward, secure in his powerful backing, devoted his attention to increasing Austrian power and prestige in Germany. He conceived the plan of extending the Habsburg territories at the expense of Bavaria and compensating the Elector by transferring his rule to Belgium. He also secured the appointment of his brothers as Archbishop Electors, thus increasing his own influence in the Empire, and now ventured to adopt the full demeanour of an Emperor *vis-à-vis* the smaller "Estates." Frederick countered these moves by organizing the rulers of the medium and smaller states in a League of Princes (1785) for the defence of the Imperial Constitution under the leadership of Prussia; and this achieved its purpose for the time being, for Joseph abandoned his designs on Bavaria. In the following year, however, Frederick passed away.

Released from the inhibition caused by the influence of Frederick's personality, Joseph embarked without delay on fresh schemes of the widest range. In alliance with Russia, he opened hostilities against Turkey (1788), aiming at her utter destruction, and the partition of the booty between the victors. But the necessary military successes were not forthcoming, the war grew more and more burdensome, the Austrian forces were immobilized in a campaign to which no end could be seen, and the country's resources were threatened with exhaustion. At the same time, as a result of the Emperor's ill-conceived reforms in Belgium, an insurrection broke out in that country (1789), while Hungary showed signs of following in Belgium's footsteps. When Joseph II died on February 20th, 1790, brokenhearted at the realization that "all his plans had come to naught," Austria was in a position of hopeless embarrassment. Her accomplice Russia, similarly involved in the war with Turkey, was at the same time hard pressed in the north as the result of a successful attack by Sweden. In Poland, too, the spirit of independent nationalism was active, though for the last time. Reforms in administration and education had given birth to a new impulse for the regeneration of that nation in decay. There was a movement to throw off the Russian suzerainty, abolish the elective character of the kingship, and institute a hereditary monarchy. No more perfect opportunity for Prussia could have been imagined. She could have driven Austria out of Germany and Russia out of Poland, and assumed the hegemony in both countries. The rulers of the north German states were at that time by no means averse to entering into permanent alliance with the King of Prussia and acknowledging him as their leader. Charles Augustus of Weimar, for instance, advocated with all the enthusiasm of youth the transformation of the League of Princes into a North German Confederation with Prussia at its head, and this alone would have checkmated the Emperor in Germany for good. In Poland the idea of seeking Prussia's protection against Russia was eagerly canvassed. Might it not still have been possible to restore that nation to political health so that it would have served as a buffer against the Russian colossus instead of being used by the latter as its battering-ram? Might not a combination of Prussia, Poland, and Sweden have been strong enough to drive Russia back from the Baltic and so remove the constant pressure on Germany's eastern frontier? Be that as it may, even if remoter aims like this were left to Fate and only immediate problems of security taken into consideration, the time called for big decisions and prompt action. It was a question of setting the seal on Frederick the Great's achievement by destroying Austria as a Great Power and so eliminating her once and for all as a potential rival. The rising in Belgium and the insurrectionary movement in Hungary provided an excellent opportunity, and one well-timed blow with the concentrated military resources of Prussia would have sent the whole edifice toppling, so that the further developments would have followed almost automatically. It is hardly to be doubted what line Frederick the Great would have taken, while Bismarck has himself described how he would have dealt with the situation.

Even Frederick William II was not insensible of the

PRUSSIA IN TRIUMPH AND IN ECLIPSE

greatness of the opportunity, but he lacked the capacity to use it aright, and there was no one in his entourage who could supply the missing qualities. The result was a diplomatic tragi-comedy which is probably unequalled for its mixture of the lamentable and the ridiculous. At the head of his already mobilized army, which was about to invade Bohemia, the king found himself obliged at last to sign the Treaty of Reichenbach (July 27th, 1790) which gave him nothing but the empty triumph of having "dictated" the peace between Austria and Turkey and rescued the latter from partition.

The whole conception which had formed the basis of Prussia's political advance was thereby thrown over. The principle of resolute hostility to Austria was abandoned, and many years were to elapse before any fundamental change took place in the relations between the two Powers. For a time they worked hand in glove, but the intimacy was an unnatural one. Their rivalry had not disappeared, even though they had tacitly agreed to ignore it, and it poisoned their attempts at co-operation. In regard to Poland, Austria and Prussia eyed one another with profound mistrust, and when, in 1792 and 1795, the Second and Third Partitions were negotiated, each endeavoured to overreach the other, and grudged any gain which the other obtained, so that Russia was placed in a position of preponderating influence. All three Powers had a bite of the cake, but Russia's share was by far the largest and best. Here again Prussia's policy was as ill-conceived as it could be. Instead of supporting and strengthening Poland, she thought only of swallowing as much of her territory as possible. The acquisition of Danzig and Thorn in 1793 was justifiable as being a real gain, but to take over in 1795 all the territory up to the Vistula and the Pilitza, and to make Warsaw and Byelostok German towns, was to secure an accession of weakness, not strength. Only the superficial growth of the state in square miles was considered, not the difficulties of administration to which that growth gave rise—Prussia became very nearly a semi-Polish and a semi-Catholic state—and still less the fact that Russia had gained still more and had thereby become still more dangerous. Berlin had lost its political vision.

And to secure this more questionable gain, the most fatal blunders had been perpetuated, or at least permitted, in western Europe. While Prussia and Austria, having come to an agreement at Reichenbach, were carrying out in precarious collaboration their land-grabbing schemes in Poland, the problem of Germany's western frontier, an open question since the days of Louis XIV, was coming to a head again. France was putting forward her old claim for the Rhine.

The influence of the French Revolution on Germany's internal politics did not show itself until some time afterwards, and then only gradually. At first little was done in Germany beyond following, either with enthusiasm or with abhorrence, the progress of the drama which was being enacted on the Seine. Poems were written and orations delivered on Liberty and Tyrannicide; trees were planted here and there to commemorate the Liberation of the People; there was a certain outflow of emotion on behalf of Equality and Fraternity, and expectations ran high in some quarters that a new Heaven and a new Earth would result from the victory of French idealism. But very little was actually done—one may say nothing at all. Two whole generations were to elapse before any open imitation of the French example was seen in action on German soil. Hence one cannot say that 1789 opened up any new era for Germany. On the contrary, a careful examination of the position of Germany in regard to revolutionary France will show that the Revolution, far from introducing any fresh element into the relations between the two countries, actually revived a century-old process which had been in abeyance for a considerable time, set it in motion again and carried it to its designed conclusion.

Louis XIV had conceived, but failed to execute, the plans of overthrowing the Habsburg Empire, expelling Austria from Germany, subjecting the German states to French suzerainty, and obtaining possession of the left bank of the Rhine; with the ultimate aim, barely formulated even to himself, of appropriating the Crown of Charlemagne. It was precisely the same designs which the statesmen and military leaders of the Revolution set before themselves, and actually realized. The guiding principles of their foreign policy were identical with those of the old monarchy, the only difference being that they put them into practice with greater vigour and consistency, and consequently succeeded for a time where Louis had failed. Therein lies, in fact, the abiding greatness of the French Revolution, and the reason why it prevailed and left its mark on history; that it linked itself up, as regards all national and international problems, with the traditional policies of the greatest ages of the past—policies which the old regime had laid itself open to the reproach of neglecting and betraying. Napoleon, the heir and executor of the Revolution as he has been aptly called, once said to a Prussian negotiator: " I shall play the part which Richelieu assigned to France." Such was the loyalty, the fully conscious loyalty, of Revolutionary France to the old national traditions.

It is unnecessary to point out that one of the main features of these traditions was hostility to Germany. The war which began in 1792 is pretty generally recognized to-day as having been planned and instigated by the leaders of the Revolution and not, as it has commonly been represented, forced upon them. They needed an external enemy in order to retain both the nation's allegiance and their own position as its leaders, and from the very outset they formulated the aims by which they expected to arouse popular enthusiasm: the annexation of Belgium and the left bank of the Rhine. When the first campaign ended in October, 1792, in the provisional retreat of the Austrians and Prussians, speakers in the National Convention in Paris openly boasted of their intention of absorbing all the territory up to the Rhine. Danton, at that time the most powerful personality in France, declared, on January 31, 1793, amid thunders of applause: " I repeat, it is futile to arouse apprehensions lest the Republic should become too large in extent. Her frontiers have been fixed by nature, and we shall reach out to their fullest limits—on the Rhine. It is there that our boundaries are fated to be placed, and no power on earth shall keep us from our goal." And a few days later Carnot gave expression to similar views: " France's traditional and natural frontiers are the Rhine, the Alps, and the Pyrenees. The outlying parts were only torn from her by brute force. According to all generally accepted principles it could not be regarded as mere lust of power on our part if we welcome as our brothers those who were formerly members of our family and seek to reknit ties which were only broken by the lust of power of our enemies in the past."

This, then, from the very beginning, was the prize for

which the French Revolutionary War with Germany was fought, a hopeless struggle for Germany, for the newly developed idealism in the Empire was a more serious handicap for her energies than ever the constitution of the Empire had been in earlier days. The friction between the two Great Powers which went on below the surface, even when they were banded together in a joint enterprise, was the chief reason why France was able not only to realize her old aims but temporarily to go far beyond them, and also why when she was ultimately beaten back she was able to retire from the struggle without loss.

The *rapprochement* between Austria and Germany, for which the Treaty of Reichenbach had paved the way, developed into a regular alliance against revolutionary France, with the object of rescuing the king and queen and preserving the monarchy on a constitutional basis. So far as their actual interests were concerned, Austria was defending her Belgian possessions, but it was not clear what practical end Prussia was pursuing. She was said to be fighting for Germany, but it was a half-hearted fight. She was full of suspicion of her ally—a tribute which the latter repaid with interest—and kept one eye continually on the east, lest Austria should come to some secret understanding with Russia to rob her of her gains in Poland. The campaign followed the kind of course that might have been expected in such circumstances: retreat followed advance, defeat alternated with success, and no decisive victory was attained, simply because there was no proper co-operation between the allies or between the two armies. Frederick William II had given up any personal attendance at the seat of war by the autumn of 1793, and, disregarding his self-assumed championship of the German nation a year before, announced in a manifesto issued on September 21, 1793, that he intended thenceforward to devote himself exclusively to the interests of Prussia. He would have done better service to the German nation if he had realized those interests more clearly and pursued them more effectively at the proper time. After this he concentrated on protecting his acquisitions in Poland, and a year later the last of the Prussian troops were withdrawn from the west, leaving the Austrians alone to defend the Rhine, which was finally lost. In constant fear of being overreached in Poland unless all her available forces were available there, and in addition harassed by utter financial exhaustion, Prussia made peace with France by the Treaty of Basle, April 5, 1795. She then completely dissociated herself from the affairs of the Empire, and abandoned all opposition to the annexation by France of the left bank of the Rhine, merely stipulating that France should assist her to obtain appropriate compensation in Germany proper for the loss of territory incurred in the Lower Rhine.

Both at the time and since, many harsh things have been said about this " betrayal of the cause of German freedom," and it must be freely admitted that, from the standpoint of Germany as a whole, the Prussian king's action was entirely reprehensible. If the best interests of the Empire are taken as a criterion, then it is undoubtedly true, as a pamphlet of the day put it, that Frederick William II played the part of a Judas. But the question is whether he could reasonably have been expected to take the best interests of the Empire as a criterion for his own actions. If he had, he would have been very different from his contemporary brother-monarchs, not excluding the Emperor himself, who engaged in secret negotiations with France for a separate peace on the basis of Austria's giving of Belgium in exchange for Bavaria. This was practically the same as what Prussia did, the only difference being that the Austrian negotiations were abortive. The attitude was the same in both cases, but the degree of success attained was different.

As a matter of fact, it would have been quite unjustifiable to require Prussia at that time to subordinate her policy to the interests of the nation as a whole. So long as everyone else, including the Emperor, worked for his own ends, why should Prussia alone have been expected to be nationally-minded ? The idea was quite unwarranted from the point of view of practical politics. There was no obligation on Prussia to take up the role of champion of the German nation ; indeed, she would not have been able to, as she lacked the necessary power. This had just been demonstrated in the campaign against France, which was a failure because there were two protagonists, two leaders, instead of one. Of course, if Prussia had been Germany's sole leader, if Austria had withdrawn or had been ejected from the Empire, the situation would have been very different ; but there was no question of this, the opportunity which presented itself in 1790 having been let slip. This shows the lasting effect of the fatal blunders committed in that year; for all subsequent events had proceeded with merciless logic from those blunders, from the Treaty of Reichenbach and its sequelae. Hence one can hardly condemn the Peace of Basle root and branch. It was, in the last analysis, unavoidable, and, consequently, in all the circumstances it was justified —which only goes to prove how chary one should be of condemning one particular action or one isolated decision in high politics, however blameworthy it may seem. In most cases it will be found that the position is like that of a game of chess when one piece is captured : the loss is merely the result of mistakes committed earlier in the game, and one cannot blame the player for it, seeing that he is unable to remedy the previous wrong moves. Such, at all events, was the position of Prussia in 1795. Her policy at that juncture was certainly mistaken and deplorable, but this was not a sudden failing, but the outcome of a deterioration which had been in progress for five or six years. The price paid for the earlier mistakes, however, increased with each successive year.

It is true that the consequences of Prussia's withdrawal from the war against France were as bad as they could possibly have been. Austria went on fighting alone, side by side with Great Britain, for two years longer, but her losses were correspondingly heavier, and when she found herself confronted with Napoleon's superior generalship her defeat became a rout. By the Peace of Campo Formio in 1797, she was forced to follow Prussia in consenting to the abandonment of the left bank of the Rhine, and when she ventured to reopen hostilities the victories of Napoleon and Moreau at Marengo and Hohenlinden (1800) decided the issue. The Peace of Lunéville (1801) sealed the fate of Germany, for all that followed merely developed the same themes, and led ultimately to the dissolution of the Empire.

One of the provisions of the Treaties of Basle and Lunéville was that the rulers who incurred losses of territory owing to the surrender of the left bank of the Rhine should receive compensation elsewhere. After protracted negotiations, the bargaining ended in the *conclusum imperii* of February 25, 1803, issued by a Committee of the Diet, which involved a complete revision of the map of Germany. All the ecclesiastical principalities disappeared, with the single exception of the state of the Arch-chancellor, and were added to the territories of Prussia, Bavaria, Württemberg, Baden, Hesse Darmstadt and Nassau, while shortly afterwards the small secular fiefs and Imperial towns were similarly mediatized. This redistribution of territory connoted the suppression of the old Imperial Constitution and hence the *de facto* deposition of the Emperor. With the secularization of the ecclesiastical domains the Imperial party in the Empire—the group whose loyalty could still be chiefly counted upon—disappeared. The Empire became a federation of states of medium size, and the Imperial house had lost its mainstay.

Formally, these decisions were Imperial decrees; in reality they were based on instructions from the French Government. The fate of the individual principality—whether it should survive or be absorbed, and how much of it should be transferred to which other states—all depended on the humour of Napoleon, whose line of action had been broadly agreed upon with the Tsar of Russia. The traditional French policy of crippling the Emperor by supporting the princes had reached its triumphant fulfilment. Austria made one final attempt to resist it, but was beaten to her knees again at Austerlitz in 1805. The end came in 1806, when the enlarged states of southern Germany proclaimed their autonomy, in other words, their secession from the Empire, and formed the Confederation of the Rhine under the ægis of France (July 10, 1806). Francis II retorted by relinquishing the title of Holy Roman Emperor—and the Empire was no more.

Prussia remained, and seemed to gain in stature by contrast. She had gained more than any other state except Baden from the division of the secularized domains in 1803, and the absorption of the church lands in Westphalia had brought her a considerable extension of territory. So far she had succeeded in keeping northern Germany free from warlike operations. In effect, therefore, Germany was now divided into two halves, one Prussian and the other French. This was a painful experience for Germany, but not necessarily a bad thing from Prussia's point of view. Shrewd and determined leadership might have enabled her to extend her gains still further, consolidate the whole of northern Germany, and then gradually seize favourable opportunities for liberating the south. Some such policy was clearly indicated—so clearly, in fact, that even the Prussian Government could at last hardly help making a half-hearted attempt to adopt it.

The position was not without its difficulties, however. The menace from France in the west had its counterpart in that of Russia in the east. Each demanded Prussia's adherence and support against the other. It was a situation calling for wisdom and, above all, for courage and prompt, adroit action. Unfortunately these qualities were all conspicuous by their absence in governing circles in Berlin. Frederick William III, surrounded by men of weak character, and himself averse to any bold decision for fear of antagonizing one or the other of his neighbours and being forced to declare himself openly, neglected every opportunity, fell out with Napoleon, found himself left in the lurch by Alexander I, and had to bear the full brunt of a war which he had shrunk from undertaking even in alliance with other Powers. His fate was that of every ruler who makes the maintenance of peace an end in itself—namely, to be forced into war and to be defeated. Any country which forgets that international politics are a fight for power will inevitably tend to relax its fighting efficiency and, if it is none the less forced to fight, will assuredly be defeated. Such was the outcome of Prussia's pacifist policy. She had the misfortune to lose the Commander-in-Chief, the Duke of Brunswick, who fell mortally wounded at Auerstadt, and the military incapacity of the king and his generals led to the destruction of the Prussian army at Jena (October 14, 1806), and consequently to the destruction of the Prussian state, for the belated intervention of Russia could not now avail to save her ally. By the Treaty of Tilsit (1807) Prussia lost all her territories west of the Elbe, had to disgorge all her Polish acquisitions, was burdened with an army of occupation in her fortresses and an enormous indemnity, and was deprived of her own military equipment. Western Germany on the right bank of the Rhine became French, partly by simple annexation and partly through the creation of vassal states such as the Kingdom of Westphalia and the Grand Duchy of Berg.

Even this did not exhaust Napoleon's intended vengeance. He had set his mind on the total elimination of Prussia, but abandoned this project in face of the opposition of the Tsar, who wanted a buffer state, however weak, left between his own dominions and those of France as a kind of fireproof curtain. But for this, the partition of Germany would have been carried out in its entirety, from west to east. Even as it was, Germany as a figure of any importance in European politics had been simply wiped off the map.

There was still an Austrian state, but this had been almost completely separated from Germany. Its population consisted chiefly of Slavs, Magyars and Italians, and its interests lay anywhere but in Germany. There were also some smaller German states, but they were vassals of France, bound by treaty to provide troops and money whenever needed. The territory actually held by France herself extended as far as the Elbe. The visions of the contemporaries of Louis XIV had become realities, the Empire of Charlemagne was restored to life, and Napoleon, whose work it was, could wear with every justification the Imperial Crown which he had assumed in 1804. The Crown of Germany had passed into French hands, and, as if to silence all doubters, French had been introduced as the official language from Westphalia to Hamburg.

A careful study of the history of the preceding centuries will show that this result was not an arbitrary one, due to the capricious fortune of war, but the logical consummation of a long and unhappy development. France had long reached the stage of consolidation as a national state, while Germany as a whole had been drifting for centuries towards dissolution. A clash between two such antagonists was bound to be fatal to Germany unless prompt help had come from outside. Doubtless weakness and unintelligence in Germany's rulers had been a contributing factor, but after all are not such disabilities inseparable from human affairs? Certainly they have never been lacking in German history. How rare are the exceptional circumstances in which the right man is found in the right place and political capacity functions unhampered!

In this case it would have been safe to prophesy that if ever the tried vigour of France should come into conflict with the disintegrating marcescence of Germany, the latter's last remaining resources would assuredly be wasted, since the inherited inefficiency of her ruling class would be found to employ them at the wrong time and in the wrong place. But even the inadequacy of Frederick William II and his son was not surprising. Anyone familiar with German history might have expected it, for it was quite in the direct line of tradition and development.

History had run its predestined course, and there was now far greater reason even than in 1648 to ask: Had the German race any future, any hope left?

CHAPTER XI

THE GROWTH OF NATIONAL SELF-CONSCIOUSNESS

On July 7, 1807, the Treaty of Tilsit was signed between France and Russia. Prussia was forced to submit to the situation thus created, and the subjection of Germany was complete.

This was the outcome of the considered policy of the princes and their governments. It was not the result of a momentary lapse or of a sudden overwhelming blow of hostile Fate. They had laboured towards this end for centuries, one generation of statesmen taking up the work from another, continuing the same policy in logical development, marching steadily towards their goal despite occasional setbacks. It is hardly an exaggeration to say that July 1807 marked the provisional climax of a process commenced six hundred years before. The dispersal had reached its maximum. It was not entirely complete, but the only remnants that retained an illusory autonomy and still kept alive the memory of an independent Germany were in somewhat the same position as Poland between the Second and Third Partitions.

In the following winter a course of lectures was delivered in Berlin and published very soon afterwards under the title of " Addresses to the German Nation," by Johann Gottlieb Fichte. The philosopher's message was intended, as he explicitly stated, for " the German people in general, setting aside and disregarding all those divisions and distinctions made between different sections of the one nation by the unhappy political events of the past centuries." He expressed the hope that his words might " awaken in the minds and hearts of Germans throughout the country a spirit of determined activity." In face of the disasters brought upon Germany by the action of her rulers he called upon the nation to seek its own salvation.

Was Fichte justified in thinking that there was a German nation whom he could address in this way? Not long before, Lessing's friend Nicolai had given a negative reply, calling the spirit of nationalism in Germany " a political monstrosity," and from the point of view of legalism and political realities he was right. But these considerations were no longer supreme. Nicolai had failed to take account of the changing spirit of the age. His mind was overshadowed by tradition and closed to new influences, and events were soon to prove him wrong. There was a German nation and a national spirit, and it was due to these new forces that the disaster was repaired, that liberty was restored to Germany in fuller measure than ever before, and that the path to unity was opened up.

Before 1806 one can hardly speak of a German nation. On one occasion only had the people of Germany ever shown a sufficiently united front to be regarded as a nation, and that was in the period from 1520 to 1525, when a deep-seated popular movement, embracing all classes of the population, overthrew and broke for ever the domination of the Church. In that great event the nation itself had assumed the leading part, had taken charge and swept the rulers along with it. But after that it resumed the position of a chorus, accompanying with more or less apt comment the action of the play, but exercising no influence on the course of events, and the desolation which the Thirty Years' War left behind it completely incapacitated the nation for any sort of corporate activity. When it is recalled that the population of Germany at that time had fallen to a mere fraction of what it had been, and that the area of land under cultivation was reduced to an appalling extent, there is no room for surprise at the lethargy and pettiness which characterized the life of the people for the next hundred years—rather is it a matter for astonishment that they should have recovered from this terrible disablement so comparatively quickly.

In the age immediately following the Thirty Years' War nationalist sentiment occupied a smaller place than ever in German history. For all practical purposes it was non-existent. The national self-consciousness was, as it were, hibernating. In political life no sign of it was apparent. Occasional catchwords, like the saying, " Remember you are a German," falsely attributed to the Great Elector, Frederick William of Brandenburg, had no practical significance, but were merely pretty phrases with no influence on men's conduct, certainly none on that of the Great Elector. The wave of indignation at the predatory schemes of Louis XIV spent itself and was forgotten, proving that nationalist sentiment was still undeveloped, a transitory emotion, not a constantly effective and inspiring force.

In literature, in art, in private life, the position was the same. How could national self-consciousness flourish amid the general abasement, the ever clearer realization of Germany's insignificance compared with other countries ?

A change began to be noticeable about the middle of the eighteenth century. The nation began to revive. It was still poor, much poorer than its neighbours, but there was enough to live upon and it was possible to think along creative lines again. The spirit of Germany raised its head once more, and tried its wings. There was a feeling analogous to the reawakening of nature after her winter sleep when spring comes into the fields. And perhaps the same influences were at work. Perhaps it was the very fact that the shackles of penury were beginning to drop from the nation's limbs, giving greater freedom of movement and wider vistas, that led to the rapid, exuberant development of creative power dating from the middle of the eighteenth century, which seems, and always will seem, like a divine miracle.

We cannot dwell here upon that glorious spectacle, but merely pause to express regret that it has never yet received the critical valuation it deserves. Even Hettner's monumental " History of Eighteenth Century Literature " is inadequate in its treatment, for the author's exaggerated predilection for the cosmopolitan, pan-human ideals of intellectual and political freedom prevents him from dealing with sufficient care with the other element of resurgent national sentiment and self-consciousness. Yet there can be no doubt that in the classic period of German literature beginning at about 1750, which in the main, to be sure, was inspired by the great wave of neo-rationalism which at that time was influencing the whole of Europe, there was a secondary *motif*, not so pronounced perhaps but none the less perceptible—that of Nationalism. Besides the ideals of " Humanity " and " Freethought," there was the striving to be German, and in the course of time, with the growing self-confidence and self-respect, a certain pride in being German.

Take the very first poet whose fame spread throughout the whole of Germany—Klopstock, with whose name the school books commonly begin the list of the German "classics." How full, how downright, replete—perhaps even swollen at times—Klopstock was with patriotic feeling! Before making up his mind to take as the subject of his long poem the Divine Incarnation, he had had thoughts, while still a student, of composing an epic based on the story of Arminius. Fifteen years later (1759) he wrote that "a young poet with a sense of his mission must choose his subjects either from contemporary history or from his country's past." He took a naïve pride in regarding himself as a pure-blooded descendant of the Cherusci—a claim rather calculated to arouse a smile nowadays—saying that "we owe it entirely to the Cherusci that the Germans do not now speak a Latin dialect like the French." In his Odes we hear again— or, rather, perhaps for the first time in German history— resounding praises of self-sacrificing devotion to the Fatherland. It behoves us more than ever to-day to recall the words with which Germany's first great poet greeted his country in the year 1786:

> "Laurels of endless age thy brow adorn!
> Thou marchest with a step immortal, leading
> The van of nations . . .
> Spare me! I love thee, O my Fatherland!
> One silent longing thrills my faltering heart;
> Oh, to be worthy of my Fatherland!"

And this truly national poet did not omit to castigate as it deserved his countrymen's worst failing, their xenomania, in an ode written in 1781:

> "Un-German Germans! slight your country's worth
> And stand agape in thoughtless admiration
> Of all outlandish things! Remember this:
> The foreigner whom you delight to honour
> Gives honour not again to foreigners
> But cold contempt for your subservience."

This national self-assertion of Klopstock's was a claim that was barely justified. What had Germans before his time contributed to the common stock of Western civilization? Only once had they put their shoulders to the wheel of progress, when Luther gave the first impulse to that great movement which inaugurated a new age for all the nations of the West. Since then Leibnitz had plunged all educated Europe into amazement at his marvellous intellectual gifts, but otherwise the Germans had made very little stir in the world. But now, how quickly the scene changes! In 1744-5 Klopstock conceived the idea of his "Messiah," and the first three cantos were published in 1748. In 1755 Winckelmann's essay on the "Imitation of Greek Works" appeared, announcing the arrival of the greatest of all connoisseurs and critics of classical art and inaugurating a new period in European culture.

In the same year Kant began his career as a lecturer. In 1771 Goethe started "Faust," in 1772 "Gotz." In 1779 Lessing's "Nathan the Wise" appeared—the purest, noblest and most perfect expression of all the great thoughts that had inspired the age of enlightenment throughout Europe. In 1781 Kant's "Critique of Pure Reason" was published, while 1774 saw the birth of the first German book ever printed which found its way immediately into every civilized country, aroused world wide enthusiasm, was translated into every language, and took its place at once in the classic literature of the world—Goethe's "Werther," which even Napoleon took with him on his Egyptian campaign. Already an unprejudiced observer would have admitted that, although the French might insist with redoubled vigour that their language was supreme and their literature familiar in every country in the world, they had been outstripped and an age of German intellectual supremacy had dawned in Europe.

It is common knowledge that this quickening of the German spirit was accompanied, perhaps conditioned, by a conscious, almost passionate rebellion against the tyranny of French taste, which had up to then kept Germany, as it were, in swaddling clothes.

Everyone knows, too, the name of the boldest and most successful fighter of this War of Liberation of the Spirit—Gotthold Ephraim Lessing. The herald of intellectual enlightenment was at the same time the herald of national freedom. One thread runs through the fabric of his whole life's work—war on the French artistic canvas, war on the French artistic dictatorship, war on the French artistic taste! Both in the field of theory and in practical achievement he fought and overcame French influences—in his "Letters on Modern Literature," in which he deprived Gottsched, the apostle of the Parisian art-gospel, of his self-affixed halo ; in his "Hamburg Dramaturgy," in which he pulverized the strange idols with the hammer of the iconoclast, and finally in his immortal " Minna von Barnhelm," in which he banished from the German scene with a noble gesture of proud dismissal the Frenchery that had threatened to take root there. What inimitable self-confidence re-echoes in his exclamation : " There isn't a play of Corneille's that I wouldn't undertake to improve on ! " He was conscious of the superiority of the Germans' mentality over that of their western neighbours.

The first beginnings of classical German poetry are nationalistic, German in conception, substance, and form, German in their conscious aims. The youthful Goethe is in this too the aptest spokesman of his age. He went on, it is true, to seek his ideal for art and life in the Greek world, but his earliest enthusiasm was for a German old master, Erwin von Steinbach, and the material for his first drama was taken from the history of Germany at the time of the Reformation. What is more, he took the theme for his chief life-work, in which he was to depict with such consummate art the unsatisfied longing of the human soul —a thoroughly German *motif*—straight from an old German chap-book. And the culmination of a stage of development which had lasted nearly two generations was reached when Schiller, in his " William Tell," sang pæans in praise of the love of free nationhood. It was he who gave classic expression to the emotions which had been seething in the heart of German poetry since Klopstock's day, in the famous lines :

> " Cleave staunch and true to thy beloved country
> And wear her ever in thy heart of hearts ;
> For in her soil is rooted all thy strength."

This rich florescence in the realm of thought, in poetry, and in philosophy had its equally striking counterpart in that branch of art which more than any other reflects the inner life of a nation, in music. The undisputed sway of Italian music had been acknowledged in Germany perhaps even more readily than elsewhere. In the second half of the eighteenth century a movement began, soon to be crowned with complete success, to liberate the country from this foreign influence, to create a vernacular of song as well as of speech, to discover a specifically German tone-language for specifically German emotions. The seed was first sown at Mannheim where the Elector Charles Theodore and his intendant Dalberg, already patrons of nationalism in the theatre, lent their influence to forward the establishment of the German opera. With astonishing rapidity the new " German Music " attained a high pitch of excellence and a reputation which spread throughout Europe. An English peer, Lord Fordyce, who was traveling in Germany at this time, has left on record his opinion that the tactics of Prussia and the music of Mannheim placed Germany in a position of superiority over all other nations. The Emperor Joseph II of Austria also encouraged the new movement as an integral part of his grand programme for developing the renovated and modernized Austrian Empire so as to secure for it the undisputed leadership of the German nation. In 1776 he founded a " German National Theatre " in Vienna, and discontinued the performances of the ballet and Italian operas, in place of which the " National musical play " (*Singspiel*)—in other words, the German opera—was inaugurated in 1778. Berlin had had opera in German since 1771, despite the Great Frederick's predilections, which were all for Italian taste in music, as for French in literature.

But Vienna had the pre-eminent good fortune to shelter the supreme genius—Wolfgang Mozart—who was able to satisfy by his compositions the deepest needs of the nation. Mozart, though a pupil of the Italians, was intensely conscious of his German nationality at an early age, as is seen from certain very emphatic passages in his letters. " Germany, my beloved country, of which I am proud " he wrote on one occasion. He was incensed at the thought of the Italian language being used in the German theatres. " Is not German every bit as suitable for singing as French or English ? " he asked. " If there were one solitary patriotic German in the profession things would take a different turn. But then," he added with caustic irony, " perhaps our National Theatre which is sprouting so merrily might flourish and come to flower, and that would be an everlasting blot on Germany's fair name if the Germans were seriously to set about thinking in German, acting in German, talking in German, and actually singing in German ! " As it happened he himself led the way, and the whole nation joined in the chorus. His " *Entführung aus dem Serail*," produced for the first time in Vienna on July 16, 1782, is the first of German operas, and at the same time a masterpiece of enduring merit, while in the " Magic Flute," as Jahn says in his biography, the dying composer " uttered, as it were, the ' Open Sesame ' to all the profoundest riches of national art. The nation recognized this, for the opera became instantly and everywhere popular as no work of serious import in music had ever done before."

And as in the realm of poetry, so here, in super-abundant measure, the products of the national genius became, so far as their best and even second-best specimens were concerned, the common possession of the whole of the civilized world. Gluck, Haydn, Mozart, Beethoven, and their many successors, are universal in their appeal. It soon became a matter of general agreement that Germany was supreme in musical composition. Music came to be regarded as pre-eminently a German art, and Italy's supremacy was a thing of the past, a memory only. The day of the German had arrived.

There is one special feature about this Golden Age of the German intellect that cannot fail to evoke our regretful longing to-day, perhaps more than at any other period. It is the striking unity of the nation in philosophy, poetry and music. These were neither North Germans nor South Germans, neither Saxons nor men of Swabia, but only Germans. What is more, and almost unbelievable nowadays, the new renaissance even overcame the clash of creed. Sectarianism dropped into the background to such an extent that only a determined search reveals its faint vestiges. It is a profoundly significant fact that the first History of the German People worthy of the name of history was compiled by a Roman Catholic priest, Michael Ignatz Schmidt.

This energetic, creative, self-confident people, essentially one in spirit, yet lacked an external material form. The realization of inward unity coincided with the loss of all hope of political unification. Not that Germans had previously been cut off from all sources of political self-esteem. Frederick the Great of Prussia had provided some compensation for the lack of a nation-wide state organism with a compelling voice in world affairs. He himself was alien in outlook to the German culture of his day, but by his achievements and his whole personality he was responsible perhaps more than any other individual for awakening and fostering the spirit of nationalism throughout Germany. His indirect influence on the native literature, too, as no less an authority than Goethe himself testified, was immensely stimulating, since every nation needs an heroic figure to crystallize its exuberant creative impulses, and Frederick was the hero of the whole German nation. Schopenhauer has said that the only real happiness lies in being conscious of one's own powers. That is the explanation of the delight taken by a nation in its great men ; it sees in them the embodiment of its own strength.

For the first time for centuries Germany was able to taste this pleasure when a Prince of German blood, a man who in spite of all idiosyncrasies ranked as one of their sons, extorted an unwilling admiration from the whole world, including even his enemies. No matter how their governments opposed and thwarted him, the common people everywhere rejoiced in his victories in war, and revered him in peace as the sage ruler who led the way and set the standards for other states in the working out of the most enlightened ideas of this age on the art of government and social well-being. Prussia under Frederick the Great marched in the van of progress with her liberal, modern spirit of tolerant humanitarianism, well expressed in her Common Law, and through her Germany took the lead in politics as well as in the arts.

Not everyone was satisfied, however, with this surrogate for national unity, and some betrayed their disappointment in singular fashion by making a virtue of necessity. It was such an advantage, such a blessing, not to be cabin'd, cribb'd, confined within a national state. The German's fatherland was the world, the German nation the true Cosmopolis, the German the purest speciman of *genus homo* and the great protagonist of all human idealism. Lessing had these notions in his mind when he called patriotism heroic weakness ; Schiller, when he counted himself fortunate in having lost his country and gained the world in exchange.

It was France's pretension at that time to be every educated man's spiritual home, to provide a world language and a world culture, but the Germans asserted still higher claims as priests of true liberty, apostles of free thought, custodians of the sacred flame of humanity. Achim von Arnim, in his essay on Folk Songs, published in 1805, referred to Germany as the greatest nation of modern times as though this were quite a self-evident fact.

Even in Fichte's addresses there is that same underlying assumption, when he assigns to the German nation this role of champion of the world's freedom, as though if Germany were to fail humanity would be brought to ruin.

There followed the collapse of the Empire, the overthrow of Prussia, the period of foreign domination. Short-lived were the glories of the nation of Cosmopolitans, who had imagined that they could do without a national state with its inevitable element of coercion and wholesome discipline. The disenchantment was terrible, but on the more balanced minds of the nation the effect was bracing in the extreme. Even in the most unexpected quarters the new doctrine of hard facts found remarkably rapid acceptance. The high-falutin' *Schwärmerei* for Mankind and Pure Humanity blew away like fog before the east wind, and its place was taken by the healthy natural emotions of patriotism and pride of race, attachment to the past and longing for political independence. "The spongy heart of a lover of all nations is beloved of none," said Herder, who more than most men had made himself at home among all the peoples of the earth. And Friedrich Schlegel expressed similar sentiments when he deplored the over-emphasis on æstheticism, the fantastic theories and sheer formalism which seemed to have taken possession of all cultured minds during the previous half-century, shutting out entirely all serious thoughts of God and Country, all memory of past glory, and consequently destroying the spirit of vigour and loyalty in the nation.

No one felt this more intensely or expressed his feelings more strongly than Heinrich Luden, of Bremen, who at Goethe's invitation became Professor of History at Jena University in 1810. In his "Observations on the Confederation of the Rhine" (1808) he had written in bitter grief: "The most vital elements in my mind and heart lie buried beneath the ruins of the German nation." In his lectures he directed his compatriots' attention to the past history of the race as an antidote to cosmopolitanism and xenomania. "We were the first in Christendom; we have become the last. We have ceased to be Germans." Let us therefore "bend all our efforts towards the one thing needful: the Fatherland." Achim von Arnim sounded the same note. "The study of our past history should enable us to broaden our self-knowledge and deepen our confidence in the destiny of our nation. It may have been right for Germany to spend a long period in quiet un-self-assertive development, but now the assaults from without render it essential that she should awaken to the consciousness of her mission in the world and resolve to fulfil it."

Such was the mental and spiritual soil in which the work of the poets Kleist, Rückert, and Körner took shape. They were a direct reflection of the emotional reaction of the best minds in the nation when they saw Germany relegated from a leading place among the peoples of the world to which they regarded her as entitled, to the very lowest. Yet the best minds were in a small minority, and the despot who held Germany in the hollow of his hand laughed at such notions. "What have the feelings of Westphalian peasants to do with politics?" asked Napoleon when he was informed that popular feeling was running high.

He was not far wrong. Feelings by themselves are impotent and hence of no account for the statesman. Schill's Volunteer Corps, Rückert's "Sonnets in Armour," and Körner's "The Lyre and the Sword" had no real influence on events. Feelings, even the deepest, sincerest emotions, are like steam which, if it issues without restraint, evaporates and leaves no trace behind. But just as steam can lift obstacles and drive machinery if it is compressed and controlled, so feelings and opinions can become a vital force in the life of a people—a force capable of bursting the stoutest bonds—if only they are run into the boilers of a state machine and controlled through the tubes and valves of a wisely planned organization. The national movement in Germany needed a state to adopt it and take over its aims, and in that event there was no limit to its potentialities. If it were left to itself it would inevitably run to waste.

Let us imagine for a moment that the subjection of Germany at the hands of France had taken place a century earlier, that is to say under Louis XIV, instead of under Napoleon. Would there have been any revolt, any liberation? It is doubtful. There are good grounds for the assumption that French would have become the language of all educated people in Germany, and that German would have sunk to the level of a patois as it did in Alsace. Even as it was, Fichte had reason to feel it a duty, as he did, to fight with all his powers of eloquence for the maintenance of the vernacular as the vehicle of the national character. Many of his contemporaries among the men in power, as for example Frederick William III of Prussia, could only express themselves haltingly in German, and even Stein used French in conversing with his family. It was still a comparatively short time since it had first been thought worth while to study the German language and to take any pains to speak and write it correctly. It would not have been altogether astonishing in those circumstances if German had died out as a literary medium before Lessing, Goethe, Schiller, or Kant had shown what could be expressed in the language and what the nation who spoke it had it in them to express. Barely two generations had passed since the Germans had first acquired a proper sense of self-respect and of their potentialities as a nation, and even now this sense was anything but universal. Not only was the French rule at first not generally recognized for what it was, a brutal, overbearing tyranny—even Görres, who was afterwards such a powerful advocate in the cause of liberation and rehabilitation, as a young man welcomed the French troops on their entry into the Rhine Provinces as " Neo-Frankish brothers," and spoke in favour of the union of the Rhineland with France—but even in later years the servitude was not felt as such at all by many Germans. Even Goethe, looking back on this period between 1806 and 1813, could call it " one of his best times."

There never was any general revolt against the French, never any mass rising inspired by bitter popular resentment. The masses knew nothing of Francophobia or national resentment, such as aroused the Spaniards to fury at about the same time. Germany as a whole bore the servitude with equanimity, and Napoleon and the French knew that they had nothing to fear from the German common people. Subsequent experience showed that they were not mistaken. The defeated Emperor came back through Germany with no military guard ; and the remnants of the Grande Armée, half starving, frozen, and in rags, who escaped to Germany, were let through unscathed, whereas according to all justice and equity not one should have been permitted to leave German soil alive and free. No, Germany was not Spain. It would have been quite impossible to get up a popular war, or even a general rising. When the revolt came it was practically confined to the educated classes, and was led by the university students. It was mainly (not entirely, it is true) from the middle classes that the bands of volunteers were recruited who fought and won the battles of the War of Liberation.

Yet the battles would not have been won, and the volunteers would in all probability never have had an opportunity of displaying their prowess, unless there had been an organized state to which they could offer their services and which could make use of them for the benefit of the cause they had at heart. This state was of recent origin, having a history of but two generations, but that had sufficed to fit it for its predestined purpose. Prussia, the only purely German Great Power, the heroic state of the Great Frederick, had a record, for all its brevity, that could never be wiped out, memories that were an ever-present stimulus to action. It had been sadly mutilated until nothing but a torso remained, but life was not extinct; the old spirit still lived on, more fervent and more tenacious than ever in times of prosperity

If in 1807 Prussia had disappeared from the map of Europe and her administrative machinery had been destroyed, who knows whether there would ever have been a German revival? It is probable that the blood of the finest of Germany's sons would have flowed to no purpose in a few easily suppressed revolts, as is indicated by the fate of Schill and his adherents, of Baron von Dörnberg, and of the Black Band of the young Duke of Brunswick. But Prussia still lived and had not forgotten her past. She was bound to devote all her energies to planning the overthrow of the French domination and her own recuperation. No other German state of any weight had the same inducement as she. Austria too was mutilated and humiliated, but Austria could still exist and look forward to a future within her new restricted frontiers. Bavaria, Saxony, Württemberg, Baden, Hesse-Darmstadt, had been gainers, had flourished in the warmth of Napoleon's favour, lived by it, and now clung to his coat-tails. Prussia alone could not exist if she remained as she was; she was Prussia no longer and could look forward to no prospects of self-development. She had only two alternatives—to seek to regain the lost ground, or else to go under. Thus the force of circumstances singled her out for leadership in the War of Liberation, and every German who still had faith in his country's future turned his eyes towards Prussia.

It is no mere chance that the ranks of Prussian statesmen and generals at that time include so many eminent figures of non-Prussian origin. Stein and Hardenberg, Niebuhr and Eichhorn, Blücher, Scharnhorst and Gneisenau were all foreigners who had entered the service of Prussia because of their belief, even before 1806, that Germany's future lay chiefly in the hands of that state. They remained with her subsequently because it became clear that only Prussia could create any sort of a future for Germany.

They were not to be disappointed. Prussia did finally recognize her mission and espouse the cause of Germany; but what a prolonged struggle was needed to persuade her! We cannot here describe in detail the stages of this development, but one point must be emphasized because it is not only characteristic of the situation in Germany at that time but also a novel phenomenon: throughout that period of 1807 to 1813 it was the educated, thoughtful stratum of the population which was the active, driving force, while the king and his government stood for caution and obstruction. The impulse came from below and only carried the ruling classes with it after a great effort. The men in power were fully conscious of the unprecedented and alarming nature of this procedure. It was like a foretaste of revolution for subjects to think of urging upon their prince the adoption of a policy which they had originated. The king saw every reason for caution and procrastination, and he hesitated to the very last.

The decisive step, the deed of power that led to the nation's emergence from servitude to France after the *débacle* of Napoleon's army, was the achievement of a general who interpreted the orders he had received somewhat arbitrarily. By the Convention of Tauroggen, concluded on December 30, 1812, by General Yorck on his own responsibility, the bare possibility of a national recovery was snatched from defeat at the eleventh hour—a possibility which the king had consistently and ultimately neglected and would have continued to neglect if matters had been left to him. The Proclamation " To My People " and the alliance with Russia were similarly forced upon Ferderick William III against his will.

But with or without his co-operation the desired development took place, and Prussia took her place at the head of the national movement. She was not a brilliant leader, for the king was too weak to triumph over all the adverse conditions with which he was faced. It was his subordinates, the spokesmen of the nation, to whom he allowed very little freedom of action, whom we have to thank for saving the situation. So it came about that in this heroic drama the chief part was played by a ruler who was anything but a hero. " He was a hero *malgré lui* " might be the epitaph of King Frederick William III of Prussia. Körner was right when he wrote :

" This is no war of kings and potentates ;
We are Crusaders, 'tis a holy war."

But the fact remains that Prussia, thanks to a popular rising on a scale seldom seen in modern history, and, so far as Germany was concerned, only paralleled in the Tirolese revolt of 1809, struck the mighty blow which loosed the French fetters from Germany's limbs. It was Prussia, too, who supplied the military leaders whose energy and resolution secured the victory. The battle of Leipzig, which finally shattered the power of Napoleon over Germany and over Europe, was the work of Blücher and Gneisenau, as was the battle of Waterloo, which drew down the curtain on the Epilogue. And to purchase these successes Prussia made greater sacrifices than any other country. That mutilated, exhausted land contributed to the joint struggle an army of 280,000 men, the largest of all in proportion to population, and this Prussian contingent was, as Clausewitz put it, the steel point on the iron wedge, which cleft the giant. For all these reasons, the War of Liberation stands out as the greatest service which the Kingdom of Prussia rendered in and for Germany, and 1813 as the *annus mirabilis* of Prussian history.

It has been my endeavour to illuminate the fundamental causes of the great change which dates from 1813. I am not concerned to narrate the events themselves, for I hope I may assume that my readers are already familiar with them, or if not that they require no special exhortation from me to devote themselves to a serious and intensive study of that period, for it has lessons of supreme importance for us all to-day. God forbid that history should one day have to report of the present generation that they forgot and neglected the message and the high example of the years 1807—1813 It is shame enough that we have had to experience the same misery over again, to learn the same lesson a second time !

The War of Liberation did not secure for Germany everything that her patriots had hoped. If their dreams had come true a new Empire would have emerged from the war, inheriting all the old Empire's power and splendour and influence, but none of its defects, outwardly safeguarded by strong and well-defined frontiers, and unified inwardly under resolute autocratic leadership. But the reality bore a very different aspect, and it must be admitted that this was unavoidable. Even if the men who at that time held the fate of the nation in their hands had been other than they were, they could not have fulfilled the demands which the more enlightened citizens were making. For them to be able to, the Liberation movement would have had to arise under quite different conditions, and to take quite a different course. It would have had to be a duel between the oppressor and his victim, a struggle in which the other Powers would have been content to be spectators ; and the nation which set itself free would have had to be united in structure, in outlook and in aspirations, resolutely pursuing one common aim.

The very opposite was the case. If Germany had been left to herself and obliged to rely on her own unaided strength, she could never even have begun the war of Liberation, to say nothing of winning it. It is true that her forces were the deciding factor and clinched the issue, but only through being thrown into the scale against France in a war the main burden of which had been borne by Great Britain and latterly by Russia also. British and Russian interests could not therefore be without influence on the Peace which was to settle, among other things, Germany's future Constitution.

The fact that these foreign interests actually played an authoritative and decisive part in the settlement was due to Germany's own inner lack of cohesion. For what was Germany in effect ? Geographically a fluctuating conception, politically a mere memory. Who was included in it, who was not ? Even Prussia could not give a clear answer, for the Kingdom of Prussia proper had from the outset been a sovereign state standing outside the German Empire. Was Austria still part of Germany ? She had in fact seceded in 1806 and was even then planning to get rid of the outlying territories which still recalled her former close association with Germany proper, the last of the so-called Austrian Netherlands. Thenceforward her centre of gravity lay in Hungary, on the Adriatic, and in Northern Italy, and she was chary of entering into any possibly compromising and onerous relationship with Germany or German affairs, remembering the complications with France which had previously resulted from such connexions. If Austria could thus be now regarded as separate from Germany, Great Britain could not, the King of England being also the Elector of Hanover.

Hence it is easily understandable that foreign countries should have had such a decisive voice in this settlement of Germany, and that the interests of other nations should have been paramount, while the demands of the Germans themselves remained unsatisfied. Take the foremost and most vital of their requirements—security of frontiers. There was a clear enough awareness in many men's minds in 1814 that the opportunity had come of settling old scores with the hereditary enemy who had held the key to the south-west gate of Germany for 150 years. "Strassburg and Alsace must be restored to Germany!" was the insistent cry of all patriots who held no official positions of responsibility; while professional soldiers like Gneisenau and prominent members of the ruling class like the Crown Prince of Württemberg recognized and emphasized the necessity of such a step for Germany's peace and quiet. But nothing came of it, simply because Austria did not support the demands, while Russia and Britain, basing their attitude on mistaken calculations regarding the so-called Balance of Power in Europe, preferred that this thorn in Germany's flesh should not be removed.

The upshot in the east was just as unsatisfactory. The frontier resulting from Russia's absorption of nearly the whole of Poland was so unnatural, and so unfavourable to Prussia, that Wilhelm von Humboldt, Prussia's delegate at the Congress of Vienna, made the not unjustifiable comments that it constituted a direct invitation to Russia to take possession of the mouths of the Memel and Vistula, and that the original province of (East) Prussia would almost be better off if Russia were to annex that too.

This was the result of the circumstances in which the war had been waged and the peace concluded: the precarious position in which Germany had been situated for so many generations was not only not improved, but rendered even more critical than before.

As for the internal situation of the German polity, it was still more hopeless. Formally it was the outcome of an agreement between various states. By a treaty signed on June 10, 1815, by representatives of all the governments, the German Confederation was brought into being—a body which was thenceforward to take the place of the defunct Holy Roman Empire. As a matter of fact, this solution had been laid down already by the Treaty of Paris of April 30, 1814, in which the belligerent Powers had decided that a federation of sovereign states should be formed in Germany. All that remained for the Germans themselves to do was to work out the details in much the same way as a department elaborates regulations under an Act passed by the legislative authority. It was quite in line with this procedure that the Treaty concluded by the German states was subsequently embodied in the final Act of the Vienna Congress. It thereby became, as it were, part of the public law of Europe, but from Germany's point of view this was merely a confirmation of the unpalatable fact that she was under the tutelage of Europe, that is to say, of Great Britain, Russia, Austria—and France.

Looking at the position in this light, it would appear that the heroic struggles of the Liberation years, with their immense sacrifices and super-human efforts, really ended in a negative result. The main object, deliverance from the foreign yoke, had, of course, been attained, and a disturbing and incongruous episode was thereby brought to an end, but nothing more than that. Nothing had been done to secure and promote the further development of the German nation. It is a strange reflection—that the War of Liberation, one of the greatest and most glorious memories of the German race, cannot be regarded as epoch-making, for it added no fresh or permanent contribution to the whole. It was an incident which rounded off an epoch—the epoch of the dissolution of the Empire. Whether a new epoch of consolidation was now about to open was the great question with which the German nation now advanced into the future.

CHAPTER XII

PRUSSIA'S SHARE IN THE STRUGGLE FOR UNITY

IN the decisions arrived at in 1815 regarding the future constitution of Germany there was nothing that savoured of novelty. They simply embodied a logical, frank recognition of conditions which, foreshadowed for generations past, had actually taken shape by the close of the previous century and had undergone a provisional settlement in 1806. The final dissolution of the Empire received historical acknowledgment and in its place arose the Confederation (Bund), a mere federal union of autonomous states. But this was only the first and somewhat belated, formal recognition of a state of things that had existed for scores of years—a mere juristic consecration of the *fait accompli*.

The bitter sense of disappointment which this consecration aroused in the hearts of the most fervent of German patriots is very understandable, and yet it must be admitted that they had only themselves to blame for their disillusionment. They had looked for more than it was reasonable to expect in the existing stage of political development. To demand of statesmanship the integral fulfilment of political ideals within a specified period argues a complete misunderstanding of the very nature of statecraft. The statesman is not a wizard; he can only create within the limitations of the material provided and of the natural laws governing the growth of human societies.

After all, what better solution could have been devised in 1815 ? The idea of Germany as one complete comprehensive, unified state was not practical politics at that time; was, indeed, unthinkable. The average South German scouted it as fantastic—did not the King of Württemberg express his indignation at this " ridiculous notion " of trying to make a " so-called national unit " out of the multifarious German peoples ? Even in the north a patriot of such distinction as Heinrich von Schön, one of the leading spirits in the struggle for the liberation of Prussia and of Germany, dismissed it as superfluous and unnatural. Indeed, how was it possible to imagine a united Germany ? Apart from a shoal of other difficulties, it would have had to include not only Prussia and Austria but also Great Britain, by virtue of her Hanoverian possessions, while the larger of the southern states— Bavaria, Württemberg, Baden—with their recent accessions of territory, were intensely jealous of their new sovereign status, and were assuming the proud airs of European Powers.

If it be granted that unity was unthinkable, what other shape could that better solution have taken which the patriots dreamed of in place of the Confederation ? It is hard to say. Their demands were distinguished more by lofty emotional appeal than by practical perspicuity. Many of them were not entirely clear what they really wanted, and, in so far as they did know their own minds, it is very doubtful whether the realization of their aims would have represented any improvement on what actually happened. Even a man of the calibre of Baron Stein persisted obstinately in advocating the restoration of the Imperial throne and of the sittings of the Imperial Diet (Reichstag) in Ratisbon, which could only have tended to strengthen the influence of Austria—not only an unhelpful but positively a harmful result, as the experience of the past three centuries had sufficiently demonstrated. It is therefore pardonable that a poet such as Arndt, in his well-known song, " Where is the German's Fatherland ? " should have been unable to reply precisely where that Fatherland was situated. For if his words " where'er the German tongue is heard " were taken literally, their message either amounted to this, that the German's Fatherland should be co-extensive with the whole earth and hence know no boundaries, or else that, at the very least, Transylvania, Livonia, the peasant settlements in southern Russia and certainly German Switzerland should be included. Indeed, Arndt was not the only one at that time who seriously advocated the reabsorption of Switzerland into Germany.

It is really fortunate that all these vague aspirations of well-meaning dreamers had, as it happened, no influence at all on the decisions arrived at ; for these, practical statesmen with clear heads and sober judgment, if without genius, were actually responsible. No doubt there were certain minor aspects in which these decisions might have been improved upon; Hardenberg's slipshod methods and Frederick William III's clumsy obtuseness must have placed obstacles in the way of complete success in many instances. But taking it for all in all, the Confederation, in the form it finally assumed, was the best that could have been attained in the circumstances—or, what comes to much the same thing in politics, the least bad.

Its one chief virtue was that it put an end to all illusions regarding the true state of Germany. So long as the venerable façade of Emperor and Empire remained in being, the man in the street, with his unreasoning attachment to tradition, could still indulge in make-believe as to the untold glories the edifice contained; now it had collapsed, and its complete and utter emptiness was revealed inexorably for all to see. Germany as a state, in the sense in which the French, British, Prussians, Spaniards formed a state, was non-existent. The Germans were only a second-rate nation, comparable to the Italians. And subsequent events only brought it home to them more clearly that, despite their utmost endeavours, they would never succeed in building any better, more hopeful future on the basis of their existing status. The German people were confronted with the choice between meekly continuing in this state of political nonage and resolutely creating for themselves a national organization such as other racial groups already possessed.

Hitherto a realization of their own smallness had made them content to accept the position, merely draping themselves in the obsolete finery of a bygone national grandeur. Their political status reflected accurately enough the dull level of insignificance to which the nation as a whole had declined since the Thirty Years' War. It is true that memories of the remoter past challenged this conception of the German character. Not only that, but the past half century had shown them that they had no reason to fear comparisons with any other people, might indeed even claim precedence over all others. There was, in fact, a glaring contrast between the two aspects, inner and outer, of the life of the German people : in the region of the spirit free, adult, unsurpassed ; in the earthly struggle for existence despised, disregarded, pushed aside—here a Crœsus, there a pauper.

To make a virtue of necessity brought cold comfort. Bitter experience had taught them that to be "citizens of the world," cultured cosmopolitans, a nation of pure humanitarians, meant being liable at any moment to be enslaved and destroyed by an unscrupulous neighbour for the simple reason that "might is right." There was no guarantee against a repetition of the treatment the German people had received between 1792 and 1813 if the settlement of 1815 were to be regarded as final. Injustice is the inevitable lot of the defenceless, and the sense of their impotence had entered into their souls.

The Confederation did succeed on paper in evolving a military establishment of a kind for itself. This happened in 1821, the sixth year of its existence. The Confederate Army was to consist of ten Army Corps, numbering in all 300,000 men, but no provision was made for unity of command, or even for uniform training or the development of an *esprit de corps*. It is fortunate that the German Confederation was never called upon to conduct a war! The goddess of Victory was not likely to have smiled on this patchwork army, as variegated as the map of Germany itself.

The essence of the matter was that since the criterion of effective influence in international relationships is always military power, the German nation as a whole could take no part in the direction of European affairs. In fact, an English statesman expressed this fact with brutal frankness, when he told a Prussian diplomat that the Germans were an "emasculated nation."

It might have been thought that if the Confederation itself was lacking in influence, that of the two Great Powers among its membership—Austria and Prussia—would be some compensation. But that too was an illusion. The latent rivalry of these two Great Powers within the Empire had been a fatal handicap ever since Frederick the Great's time, and this calamitous schismaticism had been inherited by the Confederation. True, a whole generation elapsed before it developed into a definitely hostile clash, for Prussia continued after 1815 to adhere, even more strictly and unswervingly than before, to the line of policy she had adopted 25 years before in the Reichenbach Convention. Her watchword was still agreement and co-operation with Austria, and all memories of Frederick the Great seemed to have faded away. It was as though the traditions of ages long past had resumed their sway, when fidelity to the Imperial house had been one of the guiding principles of Prussian statesmanship. With Frederick William III, indeed, the impulse towards unity went so far as to make him say on one occasion to his representative in Vienna: "Tell Prince Metternich I regard him as my Minister also!" It is not surprising, therefore, that in the hands of a statesman of such intellectual pre-eminence as Metternich the "collaboration" of the two Powers steadily developed into a position in which Austria led and Prussia followed with more or less docility, notwithstanding occasional signs of reluctance. This was taken as a matter of course in Vienna. One of the motives of Francis I in abdicating from the Imperial throne had almost certainly been to blunt the edge of the rivalry between Austria and Prussia. He announced that he had no desire to lord it over other nations; but he added that he did not intend anyone else to lord it over Austria. That meant, in practice, that Austria expected to be *prima inter pares* in the Confederation, and not only formally or academically. Vienna had not forgotten who had last worn the crown of the Holy Roman Empire, and was disposed quietly to assume that it still rightfully belonged to the same wearer. Austria had renounced Imperial splendours, and now looked to all the German states, the largest not excluded, to pay her the compensatory meed of willing subordination.

But the question began to arise how long such an attitude could be maintained by Prussia, even granting the utmost goodwill on her part and the most loyal sentiments in her rulers. For in the life of a nation individual human predilections and sentiments are of little account, as history shows over and over again, compared with its instinctive needs, its political interests. And in this case, the interests of Austria and Prussia in regard to Germany and the Confederation were not identical; they were, indeed, incompatible.

The Emperor Francis and Metternich had succeeded in moulding the Confederation into a shape which subserved Austria's ends. It offered some sort of protection at least against an attack from France; it was a buffer which would meet the first shock. In the event of war with France (which still remained the hereditary enemy in the eyes of Vienna) a certain interval would be bound to elapse before Austria felt the blow, even if the military resources of the Confederation proved of no avail. Moreover, Prussia could be relied upon, if only in her own interest, to take over the task of meeting the first onslaught and to carry it out with the fullest determination. From Austria's point of view this was all that was needed. No further degree of cohesion or greater striking power was called for from the Confederation or even desired, seeing that any such improvement would have been difficult to attain without stirring up the old rivalry with Prussia. The Confederation as it stood, in all its debility and ineffectiveness, was just exactly what best suited Austria's convenience. Her policy was therefore to oppose any attempt at giving it greater power and stability, and she accordingly seized every opportunity to do this.

On the other hand, if France happened to revive and seriously pursue her old designs on the Rhine, Austria's interests would not be directly at stake and, not having anything to lose, she could make concessions to the French there if necessary. And similarly if Russia thought fit one fine day to espouse the traditional cause of the Poles she had taken under her wing, and to agitate for the reunion of all Polish territories, with further outlets to the Baltic at the mouth of the Vistula and Niemen as Russo-Polish rivers—again Austria's withers would be unwrung. She could contemplate with equanimity an advance by her eastern neighbours into German soil, so long as compensation were offered her elsewhere. Austria's main interests lay outside Germany, in Italy, in Galicia, in the Balkans, on the Adriatic. Even if she had wished to champion Germany's vital aims, she could only have done this by neglecting her own.

Prussia's case was quite different. She had no interests outside Germany, and everything that closely concerned Germany also closely concerned her. Among the innovations introduced by the Congress of Vienna had been a fresh geographical conformation for the Prussian state. Of the Polish territory it had lost, only the province of Posen had been restored, enough, however, to reinforce Prussia's traditional sense that it was her mission to keep watch and ward against the east—the function which had been the making of the Hohenzollern state. Her compensation for the Polish lands surrendered was found on the left bank of the Rhine. This made her a more direct

THE STRUGGLE FOR UNITY

neighbour of France and hence a guardian of the western frontier as well as of the eastern. The old problem of the double front, which runs like a thread through all the centuries of German history, had now become a vital question of Prussian statesmanship.

Thus while Austria had adroitly extricated herself from direct participation in Germany's life and death problems, Prussia's very existence was henceforth intimately bound up with them. In defending her own borders to the eastward and the westward she was at the same time protecting the limits of the possessions of the German nation as a whole. At both ends of Europe she stood guard over the most threatened outposts, constituted by the sheer necessity of the struggle for existence the champion of the whole German race.

But Prussia's resources were not adequate to equip her to perform this task in any and every eventuality. For this reason, if for no other, she could not possibly rest content with the Confederation in its original form. In the event of war with one of her neighbours, to say nothing of the possibility of a combined attack, Prussia would have had to bear the whole brunt of the fighting on Germany's behalf, with constant uncertainty whether Austria would come to her aid or not. No assistance could be counted on from the Confederation. It was consequently inevitable that Prussia should set her mind from the very outset on securing such a modification of the Confederation's powers and constitution as would enable it, or possibly force it, to take its fair share of the defence of Germany. The only effective measure of protection for Germany, and hence for Prussia, lay in a drastic reform of the military resources and organization of the Confederation.

A similar position confronted Germany in her commercial life and her means of communication. Economic unity is dictated to Germany by the very facts of nature. Nowhere within her borders is there any insurmountable barrier to communication, such as the Alps or the Pyrenees constitute, while many large waterways and innumerable minor rivers provide natural arteries in every direction. To divide north from south it would be necessary to block the Rhine halfway along its course. To separate east from west would mean a similar violation of the Main and the Danube. The only part that could be cut off without damage to nature's close-knit design would be the region east of the Elbe, including the littoral and hinterland of the Baltic, with the lower courses of the Oder and Vistula. But there are no extraneous grounds or reasons for suggesting the separation of this territory from the rest of Germany. The broad plain which spreads out eastwards from the Weser makes the union of eastern and western Germany seem like an axiom of nature.

Nevertheless, this country, designed by nature to be one unit, had to wait centuries before it attained unity in its means of communication. Even in the early days of its history this lack of co-ordination had been keenly felt. In the forefront of the petitions for the reform of the Empire put forward in the fifteenth century stood the demand for a common coinage, and the abolition of artificial barriers to communication set up by individual rulers for their private advantage and to the detriment of the common weal. This desire had remained unfulfilled, and the Empire lived and died, economically as well as politically, under the banner of Particularism—the doctrine of the sovereign independence of the individual state. When the day of reconstruction dawned, patriotic citizens again put forward the old demands: one coinage, one customs organization, one commercial policy, throughout Germany! But the Congress Act which set up the Confederation took no notice of these requirements. The states were now sovereign powers, and any limitation of their prerogatives in this sphere would be out of harmony with the principles on which the Confederation was founded. In this way economic particularism too received a kind of statutory recognition.

It was impossible that things should remain in that condition. This view was held in every quarter, particularly among the common people, who felt the pinch most directly. The political insecurity which arose from the Confederation's military weakness was a contingent danger, an object of solicitude for the thoughtful; but the senselessness of breaking up the country's naturally unified system of communication was a daily, an hourly experience for all, felt in a spot which even for a German is a sensitive one—his pocket. It is, therefore, not surprising that a movement to redress the evil came into being within four years of the inception of the Confederation, when, in 1819, Friedrich List founded the " Society for the Promotion of Commerce." The Society did not at first command any great support, but it revealed the existence of a pressing need, to which even the states themselves could not fail to do justice ultimately. Economic particularism, egoism in commercial policy, was found to be to their disadvantage, because it brought poverty in its train. If the separate German states were to continue to set up customs barriers against one another, to carry on internecine commercial warfare, it meant surrendering at discretion to the economic supremacy of the great trading nations, particularly Great Britain. One result of particularism was to make Germany a prey to British capital. Thus economic unity was imperatively demanded by the national instinct of self-preservation, no less than military unity.

Austria had no concern for this vital interest of the German nation any more than for those previously referred to. She formed one large homogeneous, rich, and on the whole, self-sufficing economic unit, with adequate means of disposing of her products, and with harbours of her own. She did not stand in need of any closer relationship with Germany, and was bound to regard the development of the Confederation into a unified trading community as merely a threat to her own markets. For Prussia, on the other hand, the existing situation was intolerable even more than for the other German states. She had not even reached the stage of territorial consolidation, being split up geographically by Hanover, Brunswick and Hesse-Cassel into one eastern half and one western, while in the midst of the eastern half lay the enclaves of Anhalt and Schwarzburg, sovereign principalities each with its own separate foreign policy regarding customs and commercial relations. The term "world politics" had not been invented then, or these potentates would in all probability have laid claim to a world policy as well as a European one. Thus for Prussia the economic union of Germany, like the unified command of the German armies, was an object of self-interest, one might even say a condition of her very existence.

To sum up, the interests of Prussia in every field were coincident with those of Germany as a whole, and consequently at variance with those of Austria. The old-standing antagonism between the two Powers had its source in the very nature of things. It might remain latent for a time, but it was bound to come into play sooner or later. It called for a solution which might be postponed, but could not be deferred indefinitely.

These presentiments found isolated expression even during the Congress of Vienna. The most perspicacious minds of the time realized even then that the problem could only be solved by brute force. An anonymous writer in 1815 ventured to give public utterance to his conviction that civil war was the only remaining hope, "since this settlement must inevitably lead to a struggle for supremacy in Germany." Clausewitz was even more forcible and more definite. "There is only one way," he said, "for Germany to attain political unity, and that is by the sword. One of the states must bring all the others into subjection." And that this one state could be none other than Prussia was also clearly recognized at the time by many thinkers, long before Paul Pfizer, in his "Correspondence between two Germans" (1831), had the courage to bring forward the question for open discussion. In 1817 Gersdorff, a colleague of Goethe's in the Weimar Ministry, indicated with remarkable acumen the course events were destined to take. Prussia should unite the more influential and enlightened of the German states in a league with a thoroughly efficient military constitution, paying due regard to their rights and privileges, and should then compel the rest of the states to join. Only thus, he said, would the real needs of Prussia, of her allies, and of the German nation as a whole find lasting satisfaction. The words seem like the utterance of a seer, but they were only the fruit of a shrewd perception of reality, combined with a reminiscence of Frederick the Great's League of Princes. Greater Prussia was, indeed, fated to take the lead and assume command, at first in part, then in the whole of Germany, or else reconcile herself to oblivion. The great work begun by Frederick the Great, which had been destroyed by Napoleon but revived by the War of Liberation, had to be completed or it would fall into ruins a second time and doubtless for ever, carrying Germany with it.

The task was rendered appreciably more difficult by reason of the changes brought about in southern Germany by the Napoleonic régime. Here, in place of the old colourful patchwork of diminutive "Estates of the Empire," there were now only four largish states, just big enough to justify the illusion of their separate sovereign existence. The reorganization had been effected by the fiat of France,

THE STRUGGLE FOR UNITY

and the Congress of Vienna did not disturb it. This had been the price paid for the adhesion of the southern states in the war against Napoleon.

It is important to remember this fact : that the grouping of the states of southern Germany, which has persisted right down to the present day, was the work of France, and was designed to subserve French interests. The main idea was to set up a military screen between France and Austria, or rather a series of shock-absorbers, each of which could, if necessary, be played off against the others. This is the secret of the descending order of magnitude displayed from east to west ; Bavaria, the largest of the states, was to act as a buffer against Austria, Württemberg against Bavaria, while Baden and Hesse, being near the French frontier, were the weakest. In this way southern Germany lay permanently open to French invasion from the direction of Strassburg and Weissenburg, and the rulers of the four states would have to think very carefully before allying themselves with Austria in the event of a clash with France.

In matters of internal German politics this arrangement had another effect. The monarchs who held sway in Munich, Stuttgart, Karlsruhe and Darmstadt were primarily concerned for the preservation of their realms and their sovereign rights, and stood in constant fear of being mediatized. This made them the instinctive opponents of any attempt to tighten up the bonds between the German states in the direction of effective unity, and the more it became clear that such a consummation must be Prussia's natural aim, while no danger of the sort was to be apprehended from Austria, the more they developed an instinctive aversion to Prussia, the " bully " who might one day swallow them up. Metternich was soon adroit enough to convince them all that their privileges would be safe for ever with Austria, and southern Germany thus grew to be the most formidable obstacle to the cause of German unity.

In the north, too, there were states who felt themselves to be in the same position, but only two, Saxony and Hanover. The rest were too small and weak to be able to offer any serious resistance to absorption by their biggest neighbours ; for Reuss or Gotha to do battle for their full sovereign rights would have been absurd. Thus, while the north was ripe for unification, and particularism could only survive there as an exception, southern Germany was particularist to the core and was both determined and able to remain so. There all the traditional outlook of the German petty states survived in these larger communities, which were just large enough to have a separate organic life and to maintain it, and the rooted German tendency to " keep oneself to oneself " and go one's own way found not only a soil ready prepared for it, but a semblance of justification. The Governments of southern Germany instinctively adopted an attitude of hostile aloofness towards Prussia as the state predestined by nature to demolish this framework of self-complacency, the ideal of Philistinism the world over. It is true that there were occasions, such as in 1830 and again in 1839-40, when a French invasion seemed to threaten and appealing glances were sent from Stuttgart and Munich to Berlin, the only source of effective help and protection. But no sooner had the danger passed than the old somnolent habits of mind were resumed, and the southern states were filled up with loyalty to Austria, the " Imperial House," and hostility to Prussia, the " bully " and upstart.

In such circumstances it is well nigh miraculous that the primary need of the nation, that of economic unification, did none the less find fulfilment. The process was certainly a slow one. It was not completed until January 1, 1834, by which date practically the whole of the internal toll-barriers had been abolished, and all Germany (with the significant exceptions of Hanover, which was under British rule, and the three Hansa cities, Hamburg, Lübeck and Bremen, which were under British influence) combined to form one single commercial unit with unified control of external policy—the German Customs Union (Zollverein).

It is not to our purpose here to dwell on the laborious negotiations, with their red tape methods and repeated setbacks, which paved the way for this achievement. Anything and everything in the way of obstacles which could be erected by jealousy, envy, petty pusillanimity and ignoble selfishness, was resorted to in order to block the Prussian project. Attempts were even made from outside Germany to sabotage the scheme. France and Great Britain, the latter especially, took up the cause of the autonomy of the smaller states with an anxious benevolence that was really touching, while Metternich took the opportunity to spread the news in London that Prussia was seeking to " set up a miniature continental blockade" and to "turn everybody in Germany into Jacobins." Yet the firm determination and dogged patience of the Prussian officials in charge of the negotiations overcame all these difficulties, assisted by the pointed arguments for urgency that everyday experience supplied. At the same time it would be wrong to imagine that the Zollverein was a sort of natural growth which took shape from inner necessity without any human creative impulse. It was both in design and in execution largely the work of one man of outstanding capacity, the Prussian Minister of Finance, Motz, who with far-sighted independence of judgment realized fully from the outset the momentousness of the step it was proposed to take. His aim and expectation was that on the basis formed by this economic unification " a truly united Germany " should be built up, " free and self-reliant both in her internal and her external relations, *Borussia duce et auspice Borussia.*" He did not live to see this consummation of his hopes, but when he died in 1830 he could at least say with pardonable pride that the work he had set his hand to was sure of ultimate triumph, which could only be deferred for a few years longer.

It is a pertinent question to ask ourselves what would have become of Germany if this decisive step had not been taken in time. For at that stage in history this earth was on the brink of such a drastic upheaval of her economic life as had never before been experienced, namely, that caused by the introduction of steam power and railways. In 1835, only one year after the Zollverein had been established, the first small railway was opened in Germany. From 1837-9 onwards more and more and longer and longer lines were built, and soon the whole of the German soil was linked up by this new means of transport. The age of coal and iron began, giving Germany the opportunity of turning to account one of her greatest hidden treasures, her rich coal-fields. German large-scale industry came to birth, and a new source of prosperity was opened up. None could guess at that time with what lavish profusion this source would one day flow or what metamorphoses it would bring about in the way of living and the very characteristics of the people. But for the Germany of the 1830's, but lately emerged from the sufferings of the Napoleonic wars and now painfully endeavouring to extricate herself from impoverishment by sheer hard labour, it was of immense moment that she was no longer almost entirely dependent on the products of her agriculture and their export, but could also pay her way by skilled industrial labour.

As a result of this, the process of recovery from the period of the Great Wars showed for the first time a marked acceleration at the end of the 'thirties. The worst destitution was abolished, the spirit of enterprise awakened, and the latent capacity of the nation found fruitful application thanks to the wide vistas opened up by the new force of steam power.

How could that have been possible in a country divided against itself economically and commercially? The Zollverein had created the conditions in which alone the new technique of transport and trade could be exploited, and the first result was not slow in showing itself: the former exclusive control by British capital steadily gave place to native enterprise. The foreign yoke was lifted from German national economic life so soon as the nation ventured to appear in the markets of the world as a unified Power under the leadership of Prussia.

These considerations alone are amply sufficient to dispose of the popular fallacy that the years following 1815 were empty and uneventful. This is another instance of that tendency to underrate certain epochs of history which we saw operating on a larger scale earlier in this survey. We drew attention then to the fact that the so-called "dull" centuries after 1250 were in reality of greater importance in the history of the nation and more full of meaning for the present day than the most flourishing period of the old Empire. Similarly, and still more emphatically, it must be stated that the decades immediately following on 1815 were one of the most pregnant ages in German history. The events and incipient developments of those years live on in the present, and their effects will be felt for a long time ahead. The foundations of the Germany of to-day and of the generations immediately to follow us were laid in those years.

Amongst these foundations, the expansion of the organic structure of the German states occupies a foremost place.

It is not always realized what constitutes the actual backbone of a true state. The view is still widely held that the exercise of a constitution, politics in the ordinary acceptance of the term, the activities displayed in Parliaments, National Assemblies and the like—that these are the mainspring of the nation's political life. This explains the exaggerated importance which is so often attributed to so-called constitutional questions, franchise demands and matters of that sort. Yet one simple reflection is sufficient to show that this view is erroneous, namely, that there have been many states totally lacking in what is generally known as political life which have been by no means negligible. For in reality what to-day is called politics is only one particular form of the struggle for power in a state. This struggle is always going on, in all ages and in all countries, and will continue to go on, but it takes many different shapes. The actual life of a state may be quite independent of this struggle, for the vital element is the administration, which consists essentially of the body of officials by whom the administration is carried on. Where the Civil Service or its equivalent remains uninjured, a state can, as history has often demonstrated, survive profound and drastic changes in its Constitution, but it is doomed to extinction if its administrative machinery is destroyed, whether by internal dissolution or as the result of external attack.

In Germany's case this backbone of national life—administration, officialdom, call it what you will—was created in the opening decade of the nineteenth century and has lasted up to the present day, sustained the tremendous shock of 1918 and in a large measure lived it down. It is significant to reflect that the elements of disruption, whose *bête noire* is Law and Order, have always directed their main attacks at this stronghold.

When the settlement of 1815 had been given effect to, it was not necessary to begin at the beginning as regards administration. In most of the states the groundwork had already been laid in the decades immediately preceding. In Baden, for instance, excellent work had been accomplished over a period of nearly fifty years during the long and beneficent reign of the Grand Duke Charles Frederick; in Württemberg under King Frederick I, and in Hesse-Darmstadt under the Grand Duke Louis, preparatory reforms on somewhat similar lines had been in progress since 1806, and in Bavaria Count Montgelas had been equally active. But much remained to be done before Germany could be said to have put her house in order. It was a question of adapting the whole administrative organization not only to the territorial reshufflings brought about by Napoleon's strokes of policy and by the Congress of Vienna, but also to the demands of a new generation with fresh needs and fresh aims. This was no light task, but not even the harshest critic could assert that it was badly performed. When it is remembered that up to quite recently the German administrative system was regarded throughout the world as unrivalled and frequently referred to as a model, a substantial part of the credit should be assigned to the rulers and statesmen of the 1815 period who reformed and developed the machinery of government in their respective states. Incidentally, this fact might justifiably count in diminution, if not refutation, of the traditional charge of political inefficiency so often levelled against the German people.

The hardest task of all, and the most successfully accomplished, was that of Prussia. She too had passed through a period of reform prior to 1815. Impulses dating from the time of the rationalist revival (*Aufklärung*), and inspired by the humanitarian idealists of that age, had acquired an immensely increased momentum from the effects of the political collapse. The Prussia that stood its ground on the battlefields of Grossbeeren, Leipzig and Waterloo was in many respects already a reorganized state. But the new order was still so embryonic, so unfamiliar, and the effects of the territorial readjustments arranged at the Congress of Vienna—the shifting of Prussia's centre of gravity to the westward—so profound, that it may justly be asserted that a tremendous effort of real statesmanship was needed to give life and stability to the new organism.

The first and most important task was to weld the reconstituted state into unity, to combine the old and new provinces into one unified whole, to turn Saxons, men of Posen, Westphalians and Rhinelanders into Prussians. That was accomplished—a brilliant achievement on the part of the Prussian Civil Service—and a generation later the unity was so solid that even a revolution could not shake it.

Perhaps the most impressive feature in this *magnum opus* of Prussian statecraft is its successful blending of the old and the new. The Prussia of the eighteenth century, the Prussia which received its deathblow at Jena,

THE STRUGGLE FOR UNITY

had been a military autocracy. But the dark days of Napoleon's rule had proved that the state had a soul which had not perished with its body, the army. A state has this in common with living organisms, that its most valuable asset is the capacity for constant and progressive adaptation in structure and external functions, to changing conditions of existence. Prussia had shown herself to be possessed of this capacity by achieving a process of self-regeneration in the most unfavourable circumstances conceivable, namely under the yoke of foreign domination. The far-reaching reforms planned and executed from 1807 onwards under the leadership of Baron Stein, especially the liberation of the peasants and the organization of municipal government, which might well be called the liberation of the townsmen, raised Prussia at one bound to the most advanced position she had occupied since the palmy days of Frederick the Great. When she entered upon the War of Liberation in 1814, she was the most modern of all the German States. Even after 1815 she retained that rank so far as administration was concerned. The Prussian administrative system was the best in Germany, and led the way also in allowing the class of the future, the bourgeoisie, the widest possible scope within its well-defined sphere of activity. It was this freedom from government interference which made possible the economic revival of the 1830's.

Yet, with all these concessions to the modern spirit, Prussia had succeeded in preserving what was most valuable in the age that was gone. She remained a military state, and even intensified that classic sentiment of loyalty to which we have previously referred: the feeling that the citizen owes everything to the state and should be ready at any moment to pay his debt, whether with his property, his fighting power, or his very life. In taking over from the French Revolution the idea of compulsory military service, Prussia was in reality merely giving a practical exemplification of something which had been part of her own very nature since the time of Frederick the Great, and even earlier. Yet this was at the same time the most modern of innovations. To carry out Scharnhorst's plans in their entirety meant that every male citizen, so long as and as far as he remained fit, would be ready at any time to take part as a trained soldier in the defence of his country. All class distinctions would be automatically abolished, equality would become a reality and, to use a modern catchword, a nation in arms would form the basis of a really national polity.

It was with the nucleus of such a citizen army that Prussia fought for and won her own and Europe's freedom. After victory had been achieved she did not pursue her conquests or increase her armaments—the general poverty made that impossible for the time being—but on the other hand she did not lay aside her weapons as all the others did in sudden exhaustion. The principle of universal military service was safeguarded and the efficiency of the army as a striking force was carefully maintained, so far as funds allowed. Prussia remained a military state, but in a fresh sense; she was no longer defended by mercenaries but by her own valiant people, and the Prussian army became henceforward a unique training ground for the spirit and character of the nation.

It has become the fashion to condemn this new form of militarism, of which at first Prussia was the sole exponent among the German states, on the ground that it made the nation un-self-reliant and robbed it of inward freedom. People point to the fact that so many Germans in everyday life are lacking in firmness both in their convictions and in their courage in acting up to them—lacking in character, in short, or in what Bismarck used to call "civil valour"—and argue that this comes from their having had their moral stamina undermined in the army, where obedience is the only law. I am convinced that those who put forward arguments of this sort are guilty of confusing cause and effect. How do they account for the undoubted fact that the strongest individualities and most decided characters that Germany has produced in recent times have very largely come from the army? No doubt they are outweighed by the large numbers who are lacking in self-reliance and decision, but such cases are surely rather due to inborn natural defects which even the discipline of the army could not remove and which only became more apparent under its influence. Under the hammer steel is hardened while lead is simply crushed. If it is thought that the foundry of the Prussian Army produced too many soft lead pellets, is that the army's fault? Would it not be fairer and more accurate to say, on the contrary, that the fact that an institution existed in which the soft lead of natures of the rank and file were given an opportunity of mixing with the steel of superior

THE STRUGGLE FOR UNITY

individuals, could not fail to have a beneficent influence on the national character as a whole ?

In a few years' time we shall, unfortunately, have an opportunity of seeing whether the proportion of stronger characters in the German nation has increased or not since the " dangers " of militarist training have been removed. I fear the result will not bring much satisfaction. For I am convinced that the Germans, with their innate tendency to indiscipline, mental and physical, their sluggish temperaments which put up with so much and are so apt to fall into mere phlegmatism, that the Germans above all nations stood, and still stand, in special need of a training establishment in which the primary lesson taught is the strictest, wholehearted performance of duty. It was just this lesson that formed the core of that much-abused thing Prussian militarism, and which made it the wholesome leaven for the whole German nation that it was. God grant that it may continue to exercise its beneficent influence in the future, if not in actual reality, at least through the power of tradition from father to son and son's son.

At the same time as this development of administrative technique was taking place, during the years following 1815, a force of a very different, not to say antagonistic, nature was growing up—that of party politics. Like the rest of the continental nations, Germany had known nothing of parties up to then, except in the realm of sectarians, theology. They could not have come into being within the old form of political structure, consisting of the monarch and the estates of the realm, for the only possible lines of division were either that of the estates as a whole versus the monarch or that of one group of the estates versus the rest. But when in France that form of government was brought to an end after the Restoration, political parties began to spring up there. They consisted of groups of individuals and social classes which, uniting in the name of so-called " principles " or " programmes," were animated by similar political views, desires, and demands, and aimed at getting the reins of government into their hands by means of joint action and a common tactic. The natural arena for such a struggle was the National Parliament set up on the English model under the Constitution granted in 1814 by the restored Monarchy.

These events in France had their influence on Germany

too, and a most pernicious influence it was. Germany had had no revolution. The transition from the old social and political structure based on the " Estates " to the modern basis of personal freedom and the legal equality of all citizens was carried out without any upheaval, owing partly to the wise measures adopted by the Governments and partly to the natural progress made in the education and economic sense of the people. In many cases the new forms of political life were linked up with traditional ones ; for instance, the new popular assemblies in Germany still bore right up to 1918 the old name of Diets (*Landtage*) or even the quite inappropriate one of Estates (*Stände*). In these circumstances, and as the actual conditions in Germany differed from those of the nations to the south and west, it would have been desirable for the new order to have found its own appropriate forms in harmony with the existing conditions, but that was not to be. The example of France proved to be too strong, and it was followed slavishly.

It cannot be too strongly emphasized that all that has been known in Germany for the past hundred years as home politics is not a natural unadulterated product of her own familiar conditions, but has from the very beginning been subject to the influences of foreign models, primarily French and secondarily, and by way of misunderstanding, English—influences which one cannot help calling mischievous and demoralizing.

One of the chief of these was the innovation of a party system. The groups of people with an axe to grind who now began to form parties in Germany, with the object of influencing and reconstructing the state in this way and that according to their various desires, needs, and views, revealed themselves from the very outset as imitations of French models. Their very labels were imported— Conservative, Reactionary, Liberal, Democrat, finally Socialist—nothing but French neologisms. (The fact that some were borrowed by the French from Spain is immaterial).

Let there be no mistake : this aping of the French has caused untold mischief and confusion, and is still doing so, for the simple reason that a foreign model cannot be arbitrarily imposed on the conditions of another country. For one thing, it suggests the completely erroneous idea that the party system in Germany is just as clear-cut and homogeneous as it is in France. In point of fact, Conservatism in southern Germany has never been the same thing as Conservatism in the north, while the Democratic Party in the south still has little more than the name in common with its homonym in north Germany. Again, as handed down from the past century *à la française*, Democrat and Conservative should be opposites. Yet in many a little town in Swabia it may be noted that membership of the Democratic Party is by no means inconsistent with an absolutely pigheaded conservatism. And finally, the most pronounced line of division of all, that between different sects, found no place at all in the French paradigm.

The problems, in fact, round which political strife proceeded in Germany in the period following 1815 differed entirely from those of her neighbouring country, but the incongruity passed unnoticed, and all with one accord set themselves to imitate the French. In France all the various factions contending for supremacy in the state came from one social stratum, that of the Upper Ten, more especially the moneyed bourgeoisie thrown up by the Revolution and the remains of the nobility and leading clergy. In Germany at that time there was, apart from a few exceptional cases, no higher bourgeoisie of this new type. The middle-class element, even including the University intelligentzia from which its leaders came, had not yet, generally speaking, risen above the level of a petty bourgeoisie. It duly assumed the label of Liberalism and took up an attitude of opposition to the tutelage of the monarchical, bureaucratic and police régime, but it really had no justification for challenging comparison with the Liberalism of France, with which it had nothing in common but the fact of being "agin the Government." The struggles of party politics in France at that time were disputes between different shades of the same primary colour, like the quarrels of a family over a legacy. In Germany, parties were aligned in opposing camps, since the chief issue was the survival or the abolition of the existing type of Government, that of monarchy based on officialdom.

In France parties strove to participate in the Government, in Germany to overthrow the Government. The French Opposition was quite capable of forming a Government, in Germany such a notion was, at all events for some time to come, distinctly remote. Yet the Opposition parties in Germany took the French as their model in all respects. They could only think in French concepts, could only visualize their political ideals in forms which they saw and admired in France. Louis XVIII's celebrated Charter of 1814 represented in the eyes of the majority of a whole generation of Germans the zenith of political achievement and the goal of their own endeavours. It was felt to be imperative that the German states should have a "Constitution" *à la française*.

In many cases the Governments themselves went half way to meet these demands. From 1818 onwards "Constitutions" giving the peoples, through their chosen representatives, a certain share in the responsibilities of government were granted to Weimar, Bavaria, Baden, Hesse-Darmstadt and Württemberg, while the influence of the 1830 revolution in France led to the introduction of similar measures in Hesse-Cassel, Brunswick, Hanover, Oldenburg and Saxony. Thus Germany began to enjoy the benefits of "constitutional government," and the various political groups began to have an opportunity of trying conclusions on the floor of Parliaments chosen by popular suffrage.

It is not surprising that at first confusion reigned supreme. Some time had to elapse before men's ideas took definite shape and the various political tendencies were clearly differentiated one from another. The Democrats were all for setting up republics in which the ideals of *Liberté, Egalité,* and *Fraternité* should be put into practice. The Liberals were different; they wanted limited monarchies with Houses of Parliament on the English model, such as had recently been introduced in France and Belgium. But all of them looked to foreign countries for their political instruction and inspiration. For one set, Great Britain was the paragon of states ; for the other Paris was "Freedom's Mecca." Whenever native politicians in Germany held forth on Freedom and the Rights of the People, one could be quite sure that they were largely repeating what they had been reading in the French newspapers. Others, again, conceived a grand passion for Poland, another fighter for "liberty." They did not grasp that hers was a case which presented an entirely different problem, namely, that of the self-determination of one nationality at grips with another—a problem to which there was no parallel in contemporary Germany. But no !

THE STRUGGLE FOR UNITY

Liberty was Liberty. This most ill-used of words could act like a charm on the mind of any shopkeeper in Baden or the Palatinate who nursed a grievance against his Prince over some detail in the local police regulations, until he would see in the Polish nobleman in rebellion against the domination of the Tsar of Russia a companion in distress, a brother and a comrade in arms, fighting under the same banner. This was the classic age of xenomania in Germany, an affliction which found characteristic expression at a Festival of Freedom held at Hambach in the Palatinate in 1832, when the Polish flag was displayed side by side with the German colours and one of the speakers called for cheers for the three sister nations, Germany, France and Poland—Germany, forsooth, hobnobbing with her two deadly enemies !

But we of the present generation have forfeited the right to pass judgment over strictly on such aberrations as these. The Germany of to-day has fallen into far graver error, without even the excuse of ignorance, which was a valid one a century ago. The people who displayed that absurd enthusiasm for foreigners and their methods of government had had no political experience. Their procedure in developing their constitutional theories was much the same as that of the typical German in Heine's story, who could draw a camel without having ever set eye upon such an animal : they turned their eyes inwards and painted an ideal picture of the state of the world as it appeared in the depths of their sentimental imaginations. Most of them had never visited the foreign countries whom they were proposing to adopt as mentors. They went on singing the praises of English, French or Belgian legislation without the remotest idea of the real situation in those countries ; few suspected that it was very different from the conception formed of it in Germany.

That was the curse of German political life from the outset, that while it moved within the limited spheres of petty states, and petty bourgeois mentality, it constantly aimed at imitating the ways of the larger, homogeneous nations. This was the reason for the sterility of those early decades of German parliamentary life, which might otherwise have been of so much value as a training for the nation's political capacity. None of the Parliaments at Munich, Stuttgart, Karlsruhe or elsewhere provided any real education in political method, even for the most zealous of students, for the simple reason that no real political life existed in any of the states.

This could only have been remedied by one at least of the two Great Powers within the Confederation deciding to adopt this new form of government. It was quite obvious that Austria could not venture to do this, since the transition to parliamentarism was bound to lead sooner or later to the disintegration of that composite of discordant nationalities. Prussia's case was different. Her progress towards unity might have been stimulated by bringing together representatives of the peoples of the eastern and western provinces in joint session, where they would have become better acquainted and learned to compose their differences and work together in harmony. Frederick William III is alone to blame for the failure to seize this opportunity. He had publicly promised in 1815 that a representative Diet should be convened covering the whole of Prussia, and in 1820 had even issued a decree laying down that no further increase in the national debt should be incurred without the prior consent of the Estates as a whole. But he could not make up his mind to convoke the national Assembly. Like so many of his contemporaries he lived in constant fear of Revolution, and his ministers soon became infected with a similar demophobia. Some of the measures to which this gave rise constitute a phase in German history which one would fain forget. By the king's special order a campaign was carried on for years against "demagogues" who were either quite innocent of any tendency to sedition, or if not innocent, were entirely without a following. Not content with allowing her own Jacks-in-office to wreak their mischievous will on the population within her borders, Prussia, backed by Austria, induced the rest of the German states also to adopt a régime of police oppression which can only be described as unworthy and disgraceful. It was this period that gave Prussia—the Prussia of Frederick the Great, the freethinker—the reputation of a ruthless suppressor of free thought and unorthodox opinion, and thereby cast a blot on her scutcheon which has never been expunged to this day, but has eaten into it with subtle corrosion.

Such being the prevailing atmosphere in Prussia during the first decade after 1815, there was naturally no thought of convening a session of the Diet, and once the royal promise had been allowed to lapse, it never again came into the realm of practical politics. All his subjects could obtain from Frederick William III was a renewal of the promise; "I shall decide," he said, "when My decision to grant a Constitution shall take effect. . . . It is My subjects' duty to await the moment which I shall deem to be a suitable one."

Thus a golden opportunity was wasted. How easy it would have been for a strong, self-reliant Government to fulfil, without the slightest risk to the state, all reasonable demands of the people, which were at that time modest enough to be sure! It was still within Prussia's power to determine, both in degree and in kind, the concessions to be granted and to create a form of constitutional government, independent of foreign models, suited to her traditions and her real needs, which might have been taken as an example by the rest of Germany. Moreover, Prussia's ambition to be and remain the leader of the German states should have opened her eyes to the necessity for this decision, and for it to be put into effect without delay. The more perspicacious of her citizens realized this, and even the aged Blücher, who was assuredly no demagogue, nor even a believer in democracy, wrote: "Why should we fall behind Bavaria and other governments? It is clear enough: a Constitution must be granted." But nothing was done; the king's promise remained a promise and no more, and a fresh gulf grew between Prussia and the southern states—a gulf which proved more difficult to bridge than any differences of temperament or of manners and customs, a gulf nearly as broad as the divergence in religious outlook. The biassed notion took firmer and firmer hold on men's minds that southern Germany was the home of Liberty and Progress, while Prussia was the last stronghold of an effete despotism and was hindering the nation's free development.

The persecution of so-called "demagogues," which was carried on at the instigation of Vienna and Berlin from 1819 onwards, included from the outset among the objects of its pursuit the movement for German unity, which in the eyes of the governing classes was highly revolutionary and seditious—as in fact it actually was, though by no means consciously or intentionally. For six hundred years past it had been the fixed policy of the various state Governments to combat German unity. Treaty after treaty, of unimpeachable validity from the point of view of international law, had marked the stages in the progress towards the disintegration of the Empire, and finally, in 1815, a European Congress had declared German national unity duly dead and buried. Any movement to resuscitate it was flying in the face of the settled order of things, which was founded on the realities of history and consecrated by these solemn agreements. Such aims were revolutionary, were downright sedition, and their suppression a matter of course.

But this policy of suppression did not achieve its object; on the contrary, it was a contributing factor in strengthening and spreading the influence of the new ideal of national unity—the longing to realize all the national potentialities —especially among the younger generation. For the student associations, whose chief aim was to raise Germany to a level corresponding to her real merits, to be persecuted by police and courts of justice, and punished with dissolution and proscription, did not hinder the growth of their membership; it probably gained them adherents. Martyrdom, in this as in other cases, was the best form of propaganda. All young men born in Germany after 1815 grew up with the ideal of national unity, in some form or other, implanted in their hearts, inspired by memories of 1813; and, as so often happens, the lapse of time gradually lent an added grandeur to the historical events and deepened the impression they made on men's minds. Then came the year 1840, with its urgent threat of a renewed French invasion in the midst of general European complications. The struggle for the left bank of the Rhine was within an ace of breaking out again as in 1792. At the first breath of danger the smouldering fires of national sentiment flared up, and the German nation awoke to the full consciousness of its real position. Suddenly the realization came back that France was the hereditary enemy, came back stronger than ever and found expression in speech and song. Becker's verses about the " free German Rhine " were on everyone's lips, while the " *Wacht am Rhein* " (by Schneckenburger, 1840) and " *Deutschland, Deutschland über Alles* " (by Hoffmann von Falersleben, 1841) were at once taken up by the people and became national anthems.

In fact, the whole marshalled forces of actuality were pressing in the direction of unity. Political unification was not a romantic dream of youthful idealists, but a necessity of everyday life. It had to come, in fact it seemed to be coming as it were of its own momentum, especially since the Zollverein had largely succeeded in unifying the system of communication throughout Germany. As early as 1840 a French observer travelling through Germany gained the clear impression that unity was being re-established. "What a magnificent spectacle," he wrote, "it is to see a great people drawing together the scattered fragments of its heritage, recreating a sentiment of nationality, and, as it were, entering into full life again!"

Yet this unity could not be achieved without effort. The idea might go on ripening, the force of public opinion in its favour might gather strength, but before it could be turned into reality, a creative act of will was required, and this must come from one definite source. It became more and more clear that this source could be none other than Prussia. In spite of all the criticism levelled against the Prussian Government from all parts of Germany, Prussia was recognized more and more widely as the destined deliverer of the nation from the morass of impotent pettiness into which it had fallen. There was simply no other possible way of salvation; the stern logic of facts pointed to that solution only. Edgar Quinet, who knew Germany well and sensed the vast secret longing of her heart, realized this as early as 1832, and was alive to the danger which threatened his own country. He warned his compatriots prophetically: "Prussia will bring forth a Man!"

When Frederick William IV came to the throne in 1840 many thought he was the Man the nation had been wanting so long; but they were soon disappointed. Seldom has a ruler been less suited to the task that awaited him. He seemed oblivious of it, almost wilfully blind to it. The whole spirit of the age called emphatically for a bold grasp of the future; but Frederick William lived wholly in the past. He dreamed of German greatness, it is true, but it was the glamour of ages gone past that held his fancy. He sought the light, but it was that of sundown, of faded glories, whereas his people's eyes were fastened on the dawn of a promised day. The inherited rights of others were for him sacrosanct, but that he himself had inalienable rights in an inevitable future was beyond his power to conceive. He was prepared to carry out his functions as *archicamerarius* of the Holy Roman Empire, and hold the ceremonial basin at the coronation of a new Emperor chosen from the venerable house of Habsburg; but it did not occur to his mind that he himself had a stronger claim to the Imperial crown by the unwritten law residing in current living realities. Not a spark of Frederick the Great's spirit had descended to him—how could such as he bring that great one's work to consummation? When he found the task nevertheless thrust upon him, he merely succeeded in putting further obstacles in the way. This King of Prussia, through his whole temperament, was a curse to Germany, an eloquent example of the important part one individual can play in history by reason not of his qualities but of his defects.

At this point I am bound to ask the reader's indulgence for a short digression, in order to refute an argument which despite its constant and widespread reiteration is nothing less than a malicious falsification of the facts of history. It is still universally asserted that Prussia was like a bandit in the blind onset of her crude expansionist greed, only championed the cause of German unity for purely selfish reasons, and was only able to achieve her aims by brute force. This is the exact contrary of the truth. If there is one general charge which can justly be brought against Prussian rulers and statesmen, it is that they were not resolute, ruthless, and rigid enough in their pursuit of aims which were a pressing need and an imperious necessity not only for Prussia herself but also for Germany as a whole. If that falsely alleged spirit of domination had really been the guiding principle of the Prussian state, then the history of Prussia and of Germany since the reign of Frederick the Great would have had a very different tale to tell! All the sins of omission between 1788 and 1806, and that crowning blunder which we are about to relate, would have been avoided.

When Frederick William IV came to the throne it was already a matter of common agreement that the time was ripe for Prussia to bring her form of government into harmony with the spirit of the age. The new king himself was apparently conscious of this; yet it took him years to make up his mind to act, and when, in 1847, he at last took the fateful step, it was with a half-measure which satisfied neither progressives nor conservatives:

THE STRUGGLE FOR UNITY

the summoning of the "United Diet," or combination of the Diets of the various provinces in Prussia. From the point of view of the upholders of tradition this was going too far and represented a dangerous concession, while the rest of the country regarded it as too little, and not even the beginnings of a proper acceptance of their just demands. The assembly dispersed without having accomplished anything. Its chief claim, to be recognized as a constitutional representative body, with regular sessions and control of the national finances, was rejected by the king, not because he considered it inherently inacceptable, but simply because it was couched in the form of a demand. Such concessions could only be granted as purely *ex gratia* gifts from the Father of His People. For this reason, too, he deferred his approval of regular sessions until March 6, 1848, more than eight months after the Diet had been dissolved. This was merely the patriarchal whim of a mind saturated in absolutist traditions, but it had the gravest results. By that time the bloodless revolution of 1848 was already astir in most of the German States. The deep impression caused by the overthrow of the monarchy in France (February 24) had encouraged every Opposition and disheartened every Government. The old régime tumbled everywhere like a house of cards, and Liberal ministries, formed of the leaders of the *ci-devant* opposition parties, took over the reins of government. "Liberty" celebrated her triumphant entry into Germany.

And with "Liberty," it was expected that unity would be attained. The whole movement of 1848 had this aim in view from the outset. It demanded the political forms of government that existed in Great Britain and France, but on the basis of a national state organization such as these models already possessed. The process termed "Liberation" was thought to be the quickest route to national unity. The old governments had not been able, even if they had been willing, to create what the people demanded. Then the people themselves must take the job in hand, and success would be certain. Through Liberty to Unity, through Revolution to the Reich!

The Federal Diet in Frankfurt bowed its head to the storm, and set about initiating reforms, starting (March 2) by adopting the banner and colours of the nationalist movement, the old Imperial eagle and the tricolour (black, red, and gold) of the student organizations. In Vienna things began to get too hot for Metternich, and he resigned on March 13.

Prussia's golden opportunity was at hand : the harvest was ripe and calling for her sickle. The king had only to remain firm, to protect his own state from the reverberations of the general upheaval, and to march forward with calm determination to his goal, and he would have been hailed as the nation's leader. Austria was temporarily out of the running and was soon convulsed by repeated insurrections, with her provinces and separate nationalities in rebellion against the Crown and her whole polity in danger of disintegration.

The capitals of the other German States were in a condition of panic lest the lava-stream should flow on until it engulfed the royal and grand ducal thrones. Prussia offered the best, indeed the only protection against this danger, and there was general readiness to accept her leadership as the price of safety. The one thing needful was that she herself should escape the effects of the revolution. Whether she did this by a policy of repression or of conciliation was immaterial, but escape she must. A decisive act of will was required. This, however, was precisely what Frederick William IV could not provide. He shrank from the idea of assuming rights which were not legally his, from the idea of possibly having to use force against his royal brethren. Revolution was in his eyes the abomination of abominations, and to think that he might be placed at the head of Germany by a successful revolution was an affront to his sense of honour and dignity. Hesitant and infirm of purpose as he was, he knew exactly what he did not want but was not at all clear what he did want, and, as so often happens with such temperaments, he was compelled by circumstances to do what he did not want.

It is unnecessary to recount in detail how he failed in the first and most urgent task, that of keeping Prussia clear of the revolution. It would have been a simple matter. There need have been no 1848 in Prussia if the men in the seat of power had only shown a little backbone, a little *sang-froid*. But what with the king's weakness and the lack of self-possession displayed by his advisers, matters drifted on until open revolt broke out in Berlin on March 18, and on the following day both the city and its ruler were in the grip of revolution. One painful quarter of an hour in the king's council-chamber, and the royal troops marched away: the crown had laid down its arms.

From this moment onwards, Prussia followed the rest of Germany further and further down the slippery slope. It sounded like an ironic mockery when on March 21 the king, immediately after his humiliation at the hands of the Berlin mob, announced in a pompous manifesto that he was assuming the leadership of the nation in the hour of danger and that Prussia would henceforth be merged in Germany. What was the use to the nation of a leader who did not see where he was going and allowed himself to be pushed in directions he did not wish to take? Moreover, it was not a question of his leadership but of that of Prussia and of Prussia's fitness for the task. A state which was in danger of submersion, which could even announce its readiness to abdicate its position—for what could talk of " identity of interests with those of Germany " mean but that?—such a state could be of no help to the German nation, which needed nothing so much as a firm will and a strong right arm.

Prussia had to endure revolutionary conditions for six months—a senseless state of things in which only the capital and a few of the provincial towns participated, while the overwhelming majority of the people were strongly antagonistic and the pillars of the state—civil service and army—stood firm as rocks. When the madness passed, normal order was restored without the slightest difficulty. By November, troops were pouring into Berlin without meeting with any opposition, and the victory of the Crown was assured. In December the issue of a royal patent granting a constitution formally brought the revolution to an end. Prussia was herself again, although in externals she had changed. She had at last overcome her reluctance and donned the mantle of constitutionalism, but the frame beneath it and the living organism were full of the same unimpaired vitality as before—a vigorous, self-reliant, military and bureaucratic state. Nothing had been lost in the revolution save one irretrievable thing —a golden opportunity.

During the months that followed from March to December 1848 the other German states also regained their equanimity and lost their fears. The willingness to accept

Prussia's leadership was no longer so pronounced and, what is more, Austria had recovered. Here, too, after a severe struggle, in the course of which the Monarchy seemed for a while to be in process of dissolution, the Crown came out essentially victorious. Bohemia, Lombardy, and German Austria in turn were subdued by force of arms : a new ruler, Francis Joseph, and a resolute, clear-sighted statesman, Prince Schwarzenberg, had taken control, and under their leadership the old self-confidence and the old claims had revived. There was no compelling reason now for deferring to Prussia. The time when Dualism in Germany might have died a natural death and unity might have been secured without a struggle, was over—the opportunity had been missed.

It was in these circumstances that the authorized representatives of the German people properly so-called came forward with the proposal to set up a German Empire with a constitution of its own, irrespective of the separate states and their governments.

Since May 18, 1848, the German National Assembly, chosen by universal suffrage at elections held by order of the Federal Diet, had been sitting in the Church of St. Paul at Frankfurt. Its primary task was to hammer out a constitution for the united German Reich which it was hoped to set up, but it at once exceeded its terms of reference by taking the formation of the Reich for granted and proceeding to form an Imperial Government with an Imperial ministry presided over by a Vice-regent of the Empire (*Reichsverweser*). The members of this Frankfurt Parliament were unquestionably the ablest men in the country, the most distinguished in intellect, culture and character that Germany possessed. Yet their efforts can only be described as pitiable. For one thing, this Assembly, that undertook to express and enforce the sovereign will of the nation in face of the existing individual monarchies, had not the faintest shadow of any force behind it. This brand new Imperial Government had not even a single policeman under its control. The " Government," like the Parliament itself, existed in Frankfurt, as the Democratic revolt of September 1848 plainly showed, only on sufferance, under such protection as the Prussian and Austrian troops in Mainz were disposed to afford. On July 22 they had announced to the world at large, in stirring tones of eloquence, that " in foreign affairs their policy would be to see that Germany's honour and Germany's rightful claims took precedence over every other consideration." But as soon as Germany's honour and Germany's rightful claims in the Schleswig-Holstein question called for defence against Danish aggression, the National Assembly had to rely on the Prussian army, and when Prussia was forced by the intervention of Great Britain and Russia to abandon the war against Denmark the National Assembly had to acquiesce in the consequent sacrifice of Germany's honour and rightful claims. And such a Parliament had the presumption to attempt to impose a constitution on all the German governments, including those of Prussia and Austria, without their having been consulted as to its provisions!

It seems to have become the pastime of late to defend the ideologists of St. Paul's, Frankfurt, against the charge of doctrinaire unpracticality. It has been argued that both in their parliamentary discussions and in their constitution making they displayed the quality of true realists, shrewdly confining themselves to the limits of what was feasible. Such a defence has one justification, and one only, namely that their achievement was made up in every essential of compromises laboriously extracted from a number of violently hostile tendencies. The Assembly had no sooner commenced its task of consolidating the nation than every imaginable division, old and new, manifested itself with unrestrained intensity: Northerners and Southerners, Monarchists and Republicans, Prussophiles and Austrophiles, Protestants and Catholics took up attitudes of unconcealed mutual hostility. Infinite pains were needed to create something from all these opposing elements which should at any rate look like a whole on paper. In point of fact it was a mere conglomeration of mutually inconsistent propositions. For instance, the leadership of Prussia was to be safeguarded, but the German Austrians were not to be excluded. The Empire was to be essentially a liberal Monarchy, but to ensure the choice of a Prussian as Emperor Republican votes were required to outbalance those of the Catholics and the Austrians, and this led to such far reaching concessions in a democratic direction that the Monarchy looked like becoming a mere gaud.

One may judge from the foregoing what kind of a Constitution it was that came to birth at last on March 28

1849. It provided for the King of Prussia becoming hereditary (but elective) German Emperor, at the same time requiring that he should submit himself and his country to the directions of an Imperial Diet (*Reichstag*) elected on a purely democratic franchise, leave his own dominions and take up his residence in Frankfurt— in other words, abdicate the throne of Prussia ! Still more was expected of Austria, for only her German speaking provinces were embodied in the new Empire, while the rest of her dominions remained outside. The Emperor of Austria, therefore, was to accept a position of inferiority in Austria proper to the King of Prussia and the elected *Reichstag*, and only remain undisputed sovereign in Hungary and Italy. Is this patchwork of contradictions to be regarded as the work of realists ? In parish pump politics it may be accounted a great trimuph to arrange a temporary compromise between irreconcilable opposites. True statesmanship bears constantly in mind that mutually exclusive policies demand, not conciliation, but a clear-cut decision on one side or the other, that any attempt to weld the two into one leads straight to disaster, and that free and healthy development can only be secured after one or the other has come out victorious.

As if desirous of giving the completest proof of their naiveté, the men of St. Paul's came to Prussia and Austria with their gracious gift of a Constitution at the time when both these powers had finished dealing with the Revolution, and after Austria had already formally signified her disagreement. What possible purpose was served, in such circumstances, by offering the Imperial crown to the King of Prussia, as the National Assembly did on March 28, 1849 ? Did they expect him to declare war on Austria for the sake of a title which was devoid of any real executive power and pre-supposed the relinquishing of the throne of Prussia ? Frederick William declined the honour. Would any other man in his position have acted differently ? It is doubtful. At all events, no other response could be expected from him, and all concerned must have been aware of this. Thus the labours of the empire-builders of St. Paul's came to an end, a spectacle of tragi-comedy. They had attempted to construct a paper Empire, to erect castles in the air, to frame a fourth-dimensional Constitution. It was no use complaining when the soap-bubble burst.

THE STRUGGLE FOR UNITY

An attempt was then made by Prussia to adopt the nucleus of the scheme, after removing its democratic fangs, by suggesting a new voluntary "association" of the German states with herself in conjunction with Austria, without reviving the style of Emperor ; but this belated suggestion came to nothing. The secondary Powers in Germany were no longer enthusiastic for any closer union now that the danger of revolution had passed, while Austria showed determined opposition. The threatened intervention of Russia in support of Austria's standpoint settled the matter. But the flaccidity and clumsiness displayed by Prussia led to her abandonment of the scheme taking the form of a humiliating surrender to an Austrian ultimatum. The Convention of Olmütz, signed on November 29, 1850, put an end for a time to all hopes of a unified Germany under the leadership of Prussia. The old Federal Diet resumed its sittings under Austrian presidency as before. There was a complete reversion to pre-1848 conditions. The episode was over.

Was there still room for hope of better things ? To all appearances it had been demonstrated that Germany was unable to win her way to unity. Necessary as unity was to her, passionately as she desired it, it seemed impossible, impracticable. The rulers were unwilling, the people unable to bring it into being. The best minds in the nation relapsed into dull dejection, their sole remaining hope lying in a miracle, a hero who might make his appearance and unify Germany as if by magic. From many a heart all over the country during those gloomy years the cry went up for a Hero—a Great Man who would heal all divisions by the magic power of his genius and with a grip of iron would force all Germany—princes and people alike—to join together in unity. In tones of longing the Swabian poet Fischer thus apostrophized this saviour yet unknown :

> "Hero, if thou be living at this hour,
> Arise, we rest our hopes and faith in thee!
> What if it be Dictatorship thou bringest,
> Thrice welcome thou, Dictator of the Free!"

And he came, he arose and accomplished the task as the poets demanded. The strong wise dictator imposed his will on the whole world. In this one instance Fate smiled on the German nation, which had so often tasted the bitterness of her displeasure, seen so many buds crushed and so many blossoms broken before the fruit could form, been so often deprived of leadership. At this juncture the right man really did appear at the right moment.

The structure, the foundation of which was laid by the genius of Frederick the Great but which had been left untouched by his successors, and the completion of which was desired with ever increasing intensity by three generations of Germans, who yet could not discover the way to accomplish it, was brought to a triumphant finish by the genius of Bismarck in eight short years. The problem which seemed as baffling as the squaring of the circle was solved, and the solution was as simple, as unerring and as elegant as Columbus' famous trick with the egg.

Bismarck was no conjurer, no miracle-worker, but his mind was a magic mirror which showed him the reality of things as they were. He realized that German unity could only be attained if the duel which had started in 1740 were fought out to a decisive result. For three generations this awkward fact had been overlooked or burked, but Bismarck saw to it that the truth should prevail. He knew that only the old Prussian spirit, the Prussia of Frederick the Great, could solve the problem. His contemporaries imagined that force was no longer necessary, and that a general profession of faith in the new Liberal ideals must of itself lead to the unification of Germany under the Prussian banner. Bismarck dispelled this fog of well-meaning self-deception with word and deed. His new message rang out : Not by speeches or by passing resolutions, but by blood and iron ! He realized in addition what had been so entirely lost sight of in the Frankfurt deliberations, that the German Constitution was a matter of European importance, and that only by an extraordinarily favourable conjunction of circumstances could the German people hope to decide their own fate without foreign intervention. In 1848 the opportunity had been there, but it had been allowed to pass by unused. Bismarck watched for its recurrence, and the moment he saw the other European Powers at loggerheads and unable to take joint action, he struck.

He was the right man in the right place, equipped with every quality which his task required : an experienced Parliamentarian, a professional diplomatist, Conservative but without prejudices, German and Prussian combined, strong and subtle, bold and shrewd—a man to be trusted. And every possible obstacle was placed in his way. He was opposed, hated, despised and vilified, and only a merciful fate spared him from falling a victim to an assassin's bullet at the most critical moment. The nation did not recognize her saviour, would, in fact, willingly have crucified him or burned him alive. He had to save his country as he once saved a groom from drowning, by gripping it by the throat. When he had won and the work was practically over, then they cheered and lauded him to the skies. But what was the value of such belated converts? From the vast majority of the nation there never came a spark of understanding for the statesman who gave them what they wanted but had been incapable of obtaining themselves. As for learning from his wisdom, they obstinately refused to do anything of the sort.

This is not the place to dwell on his achievements. What is relevant to our discussion is common knowledge, and I am relieved not to have to enter into it in detail. For I must confess that I cannot utter the name of Bismarck without a sense of shame. I cannot help feeling how applicable to him are the lines in which a Swabian poet and patriot ninety years ago addressed the spirit of the national hero, Arminius :

> " Legend tells that fallen heroes wander
> Ghost-like till mankind their message heeds.
> Still must thou be restless, still rebellious,
> In a world which stultifies thy deeds."

The Bismarck celebrations which are constantly being held nowadays strike me as almost of the nature of blasphemy. What right have the men of this generation to celebrate Bismarck's glory, when they have done worse than kill him, have abandoned the structure he built to decay and ruin ?

When his work was completed the world imagined that Germany had turned her back on the past and begun a new and splendid page in her history—a period of fulfilment and happiness after such long years of waiting and suffering. Looking back as we are able to do now, we are constrained to say that that was a mistake. Bismarck's creation contained potentialities of a new era, but the generation that followed him was unable to turn these potentialities to account. Germany forgot all too quickly that what she had inherited from Bismarck was a sacred trust, a fiduciary legacy subject to the condition that the capital should be maintained intact and unhypothecated—in other words, that the price of security was eternal vigilance. Instead of proving worthy of this trust and expanding to the measure of his design, the nation clung to its old errors and closed its ears to the claims of loyalty and gratitude. The German Empire which Bismarck founded turned out to be a mere episode, a temporary break in the continuity of seven centuries in which the years 1648 and 1815 are the notable dates and 1918 their worthy congener.

One's reflections inevitably take this tinge in the atmosphere of to-day, and our study must end on a harsh discord; or, rather, it does not end, but merely points in dumb emotion to an unseen future.

We are all aware that Germany was never stricken so low as she is to-day. It is difficult not to despair and accept as the verdict of history the Biblical *Mene, Tekel, Upharsin*.

And yet something fundamental, a vital instinct, tells us that this verdict cannot be final, while our knowledge of the past history of the nation authorizes us to enter a *caveat* against the precipitate judgments of the passing hour. More than once in the past it has seemed as though Germany were lost beyond all human hope. Think of 1648, of 1808! But again and again the stubborn vitality and sterling qualities of her people have restored her, after painful exertion, to life and a more propitious future. Can this nation have lost its power of recovery? It is for the present generation to show that the same qualities are still at the nation's disposal, essentially unimpaired, and capable of renewed and vigorous effort. The fall may have been greater this time, but that was partly due to the fact that the height attained was also greater than ever before. Why should the nation not be able to cherish hopes of a fresh revival? History may demonstrate once more, as it did a century ago, that great events which seem at the time to have happened in vain bear fruit in later years. Then it was memories of the War of Liberation, now it may be the memory of the Bismarck era and the fleeting glories of the age he rendered possible that will fructify and bring forth a rich harvest at the appointed time. It will depend upon our own endeavours. If we Germans do our duty, we are justified in looking to the future with faith in our hearts. He who listens to the voice of history will hear the words of promise echoing down the centuries :

We bid you hope!

INDEX

Aachen, 5, 15
Adolf of Nassau, 58, 59, 68
Adolf von Holstein, 77-8
Aix-la-Chapelle, Treaty of, 161
Albert I, 58, 61, 66
Albert II, 61, 94
Albert Achilles, 93
Albert of Bremen, 79
Albert the Bear, 77-8
Alemanni, 3
Alexander I (of Russia), 180
Alexander III (Pope), 40
Alfonso of Castile, 55
Alsace, 12, 59, 89-90, 94-5, 132, 135, 141, 148-9, 151ff., 199
Ancona, 43
Anhalt, 51, 209
Ansbach, 92
Apulia, 33, 36
Aquileia, 26
Arabs, 18
Arles, 67
Armada, Spanish, 129
Armenia, 42
Arminius, 109, 186
Arndt, 202
Art, 108
Artois, 89, 97, 101
Auerstadt (battle), 180
Aufklärung, 216
Augsburg, 70, 72, 76
Augsburg (battle), 15
Augsburg, Bishop of, 12
Augsburg, Diet of, 119
Augsburg, Peace of, 123, 127
Augustus, 14
Austerlitz (battle), 179
Austria, 51, 56, 58-9, 63, 65, 90, 94-5, 98, 127, 132, 155, 161ff., 167, 171ff., 195, 198-9, 204ff., 224, 230, 232ff.
Austria, House of, 58
Austria, Lower, 15, 97
Austrian Succession, War of, 161

Babenberg, House of, 37, 50
Baden, 14, 63, 179, 195, 202, 211, 215, 222
Baden, Treaty of, 155
Balthasar of Dernbach, 129
Baltic, the, 78ff., 87, 138, 156-7, 208
Barbarossa, *see* Frederick I
Bärwalde, 138
Basle, 20, 70, 72, 89, 107, 142
Basle, Treaty of, 177-8
Bavaria, 16, 17, 51, 56, 63, 123, 131, 138, 169, 171, 177, 195, 202, 211, 215, 222
Bavarian Succession, War of, 169
Bavarians, 3, 6
Bayreuth, 92
Becker, 226
Beethoven, 190
Belgium, 151, 155, 161, 167, 171, 175, 177
Belgrade, 152-3
Benevento, 18, 33
Berengar II, 17, 24
Berg, 180
Berlin, 76, 230
Berne, 94
Bishops, 8-9, 18, 52-3
Bismarck, 135, 170, 172, 218, 235ff.
Bismarck, Duke of, 180
Black Forest, 89, 94-5
Blenheim (battle), 154
Blücher, 196-7, 225
Bohemia, 16, 56, 58-60, 65, 86-7, 90, 98, 102-3, 127, 132, 134-5, 173, 232
Boleslav the Brave, 16
Boniface, 11
Bornhövede (battle), 79
Bouvines, 45, 88
Brabant, 89
Brandenburg, 17, 27, 58, 60, 63, 77-8, 85, 91-2, 128, 137, 147, 152, 159ff.
Bräut, Sebastian, 109
Bremen, 141, 212
Brendel, Daniel, 129
Brenner (pass), 19, 25
Breslau, 76
Brunswick, 137, 209, 222
Brunswick-Lüneburg, 63
Buda, 151

241 R

INDEX

Buku, 78
Burgundians, 3
Burgundy, 5, 19-20, 31, 67, 88-90, 96-7, 100-1
Byelostok, 173

Calabria, 33
Calvinism, 129, 133
Cambrai, Peace of, 118
Campo Torino, Peace of, 178
Canossa, 35
Capua, 18
Carinthia, 51, 56, 65, 94-5
Carnot, 175
Carpathians, 83
Casimir the Great, 83
Catherine II, 168-9
Catholic League, 131, 136, 139
Cenis, Mont (pass), 19
Chambord, Treaty of, 122, 147
Charlemagne, 3, 11, 14, 23, 33, 149
Charles II (of Spain), 149, 154
Charles IV, 57-8, 61-2, 66-7, 76, 85, 88, 94, 108
Charles V, 100ff., 111. 114ff., 131, 143, 150
Charles VI, 154, 161
Charles VII (of France), 75
Charles VIII (of Bavaria), 161
Charles Augustus of Weimar, 172
Charles Eugene of Württemberg, 146
Charles Frederick of Baden, 215
Charles Martel, 3
Charles the Bold, 89-90, 95-6
Charles Theodore, 189
Chlodwig, 3
Christian of Anhalt, 133
Christian of Mainz, 38
Church, the, 8-12, 18, 23, 29ff., 112ff.
Civil Service, 215-6
Clausewitz, 197, 210
Cleves, 159
Cleves-Gueldres, 121
Coeur, Jacques, 75
Cologne, 5, 51, 61, 70, 72, 76, 107, 130
Cologne, Bishop of, 12
Cologne, Confederation of, 82
Condé, 140
Conrad I, 3, 6, 14-5
Conrad II, 16, 19, 20
Conrad III, 36-7, 39, 50, 52, 54
Conrad IV, 55
Conrad of Masuria, 79
Conservatives, 221
Constance, Treaty of, 40

Constantia of Sicily, 41
Constantinople, 17, 25, 40, 42, 168
Constitution of 1849, 233-4
Corvinus, see Matthias
Counter-Reformation, 129ff.
Courland, 143, 159
Cracow, 83
Crépy, Peace of, 121
Cruto, 78
Cyprus, 42

Dalberg, 189
Danton, 175
Danube, the, 14, 150, 168, 207
Danzig, 79, 83, 86, 141, 168, 173
Dauphiné, 88
Democrats, 221-2
Denmark, 79, 82, 141, 143, 233
Deutsches Reich, 4
Dinkelsbühl, 70
Dlugosz, John, 83
Döffingen (battle), 71
Donawoirth, 131
Duke (title), 6
Dürer, Albrecht, 109
Dutch, 87
Dvina, the, 143

Eberhard of Württemberg, 71, 92
Ecclesiastical Reservation, 128
Eck, Johann, 114
Eichhorn, 196
Eidgenossenschaft, 94
Elbe, the, 16, 27, 76, 82, 157, 180-1, 208
Electors, 60, 100, 104, 132-3, 149
Elizabeth of England, 143
England, 44, 72, 88, 129; see also Great Britain
Erfurt, 107
Esthonia, 79-80, 156
Etsch, the, 17
Eugene of Savoy, 153-4
Evangelical Union, 131, 133

Ferdinand II (of Bohemia), 119, 134-5, 136ff.
Ferdinand of Styria, 131-2
Ferdinand the Catholic, 100
Fichte, Johann Gottlieb, 183, 192-4
Fischer, 235
Flanders, 89, 97, 99
Florence, 73
Florentines, 68
Fordyce, Lord, 189
Four Cantons, Lake of the, 94

INDEX 243

France, 15, 28, 44-5, 72, 88, 97, 99ff., 138ff., 147ff., 161, 167ff., 174ff., 193-4, 206, 211, 220ff., 226
Franche-Comté, 88, 97
Francis I, 205
Francis II, 179
Francis Joseph, 232
Francis of Lorraine-Tuscany, 161
Franconia, 7
Frankfurt, 70, 72, 76, 232
Franks, 2-5, 13, 23
Frederick I, 37-41, 46-7, 49-50, 52-3, 62, 84
Frederick I (of Württemberg), 215
Frederick II, 42, 44-6, 48-9, 50, 52, 60, 79
Frederick III (Emperor), 90, 94-5, 97-8, 127
Frederick III (of Prussia), 160
Frederick (Elector Palatine) 133-5
Frederick the Great, 48, 55, 161ff., 169ff., 190, 210, 228
Frederick the Wise, 92, 101
Frederick William (Elector), 159-60, 184
Frederick William I, 146, 160, 165
Frederick William II, 170, 172-3, 176-7, 182
Frederick William III, 170, 180, 194, 196-7, 203, 205, 224-5
Frederick William IV, 227ff.
Freiburg, 107
French Revolution, 174ff.
Friedberg, 70
Frisians, 3
Fuggers, The, 74, 106
Fulda (abbey), 11-12

Galicia, 82-3, 98
Genèvre, Mont (pass), 19
Genoa, 101
Geography, its influence on history, 13, 47
George of Podiebrad, 87, 90
Gerhard of Jülich, 92
German Confederation, 200ff.
Germani, 1
Gersdorff, 210
Gervinus, 107
Gluck, 190
Gneisenau, 196-7, 199
Goethe, 187-8, 191-2, 194
Golden Bull of Eger, 52
Golden Bull of 1356, 61
Görres, 194
Gotha, 211
Gothic Art, 108

Gothland, 82
Goths, 3
Gottfried of Tuscany, 32, 33
Gotthard (pass), 19
Gottsched, 187
Graubünden, 94
Great Britain, 168, 198-9, 202, 209, 212, 222
Great St. Bernard (pass), 19
Gregory VII, 34-5, 39-40
Gregory X, 56
Greifswald, 107, 156
Grossbeeren (battle), 216
Grünewald, Matthias, 109
Guelph, House of, 37, 42, 50, 92
Gustavus Adolphus, 138-9
Gustavus Vasa, 143

Habsburgs, 56ff., 90, 92, 94ff., 127ff., 135, 143, 155
Hambach, 223
Hamburg, 76, 79, 141, 143, 212
Hanover, 63, 145, 209, 212, 222
Hansa Alliance, 81-2, 84, 87, 143
Hardenberg, 196, 203
Hartwin of Ivrea, 18
Havel, the, 16, 27, 77
Haydn, 190
Heidelberg, 107
Helmold of Bosau, 77-8
Hennegau, 88-9
Henry I, 7, 10, 15-6
Henry II, 16, 18
Henry III, 20, 30, 32-3
Henry IV, 31, 33-5, 49-62
Henry IV (of France), 131
Henry V, 36, 37
Henry VI, 41-2, 46-7, 50, 52, 54, 61
Henry VII, 57, 58, 67
Henry Raspe, 55
Henry the Lion, 78
Herder, 192
Hersfeld (abbey), 11
Hesse, 63, 92, 128, 211
Hesse-Cassel, 64, 209, 222
Hesse-Darmstadt, 64, 179, 195, 215, 222
Hettner, 185
Hildesheim, 129
Hohenlinden (battle), 178
Hohenzollerns, 91, 92, 159
Holbein, Hans, 109
Holland, 58, 89, 151
Holstein, 77-9, 141, 157
Hubertusburg, Treaty of, 162
Huguenots, Expulsion of, 152
Hundred Years' War, 88-9, 108
Hungarians, 15

Hungary, 17, 26, 84-5, 90, 96, 98, 102-3, 119, 127, 150, 152ff., 171
Huss, John, 86

Indulgences, 113
Ingolstadt, 107
Innocent III, 43, 52
Investitures, 33-4, 36
Italy, 17-20, 22, 24-8, 30ff., 38ff., 43ff., 57, 72-3, 99, 151

Jagellones, 98
Jagiel, 86
James I (of England), 134
Jena (battle), 180, 216
Jesuits, 130, 136
John George of Saxony, 133
John Sigismund of Brandenburg, 133
Joseph I, 154
Joseph II, 55, 163, 169, 171, 189
Jura, the, 94

Kahlenberg (battle), 152
Kalisch, Peace of, 83
Kalmar, Treaty of, 82
Kampfen, 81
Kant, 187, 194
Karlowitz, Treaty of, 153
Katzenelnbogen, 92
Kiev, Grand Duke of, 16
Kleist, 193
Klopstock, 185-8
Knights, 10
Königsberg, 168
Königsgut, 11
Körner, 193, 197
Kovno, 85
Kulmbach, 92
Kunersdorf, 48

Ladislaus, 95, 98
Landau, 155
Langobardi, 17, 18
Lausitz, 78, 90, 134
League of Princes, 171-2, 210
Legnano, 40
Leibnitz, 186-7
Leipzig, 107
Leipzig (battle), 138, 197, 216
Leitha, The, 16
Lemberg, 83
Lens (battle), 140
Leo IX, 32
Leopold I, 147, 149
Leopold of Austria, 66
Lessing, 187, 191, 194
Liberalism, 221

Liberation, War of, 195ff., 210, 217
Liechtenstein, 65
Liszt, Friedrich, 208
Literature, 107-8
Lithuania, 86, 98
Livonia, 79-80, 84, 143, 156, 202
Lombards, 3
Lombardy, 18, 24-6, 32, 38-9, 40-1, 45, 232
Lorraine, 15, 30, 31, 88-9, 142, 151ff.
Lorsch (abbey), 11, 12
Lothar of Saxony, 36-7, 39, 52
Lotharingia, 5, 7, 14-5
Louis XIV, 149ff., 154, 159, 174, 185
Louis XVIII, 222
Louis of Hesse-Darmstadt, 215
Louis of Hungary, 98, 119
Louis the Bavarian, 57-8, 67
Louis the Child, 3
Louis William of Baden-Baden, 153-4
Lübeck, 78-9, 143, 212
Lübeck, Peace of, 136
Luden, Heinrich, 192
Lunéville, Peace of, 178
Luther, Martin, 109, 113ff., 125, 186
Lützen (battle), 138
Luxemburg, 89
Lyons, 88

Machiavelli, 111
Magdeburg, Archbishop of, 77
Magyars, 16
Main, the, 207
Mainz, 60, 70, 92, 232
Mainz, Bishop of, 12, 147
Marchfeld (battle), 58
Marengo (battle), 178
Maria of Burgundy, 96
Maria Theresa, 161-2
Mark, 159
Matilda of Tuscany, 32, 35, 40
Matthias (emperor), 131-2
Matthias Corvinus, 90, 96-8
Maurice of Saxony, 122
Maximilian I, 96-100, 101, 109-10
Maximilian of Bavaria, 131-3
Mecklenburg, 17, 27, 77-9, 157
Medici, 106
Meissen, 56, 58-9, 78, 92
Meissen, Margrave of, 77
Memel, 79, 199
Mercenaries, 68, 106
Metternich, 205, 211-2, 230
Metz, 89, 122
Milan, 68, 73, 99, 101, 116, 155
Milan, Archbishop of, 20, 34

INDEX

Militarism, 166, 218-9
Military Service, Compulsory, 217
Mohacs (battle), 119
Mömpelgard, 64
Montgelas, Count, 215
Moravia, 90
Moscow, Tsar of, 143
Motz, 213
Mozart, 189-90
Mühlberg (battle), 122
Münster, Treaty of, 148

Nancy (battle), 89
Naples, 73, 99-101, 155
Napoleon, 175, 178-81, 193-4, 210
Narowa, the, 76, 80
Nassau, 179
National Assembly, 232
Neckar, the, 14
Netherlands, 100, 129, 142-3, 151, 199
Neuss, 89
Nibelungenlied, 106, 108
Nicholas II, 33
Nicolai, 183-4
Niebuhr, 196
Niemen, the, 206
Nördlingen (battle), 139
Normans, 32, 33, 35
Novgorod, 143
Nuremberg, 70, 72, 92
Nymwegen, Treaty of, 151

Oder, the, 76, 156, 208
Oldenburg, 222
Olmütz, Convention of, 235
Ostmark, 16
Otto I, 7, 9, 10, 15, 17, 18, 21, 23-7, 30, 33, 51, 57, 62
Otto II, 11, 26
Otto III, 18-9, 22-3, 26, 30
Otto IV, 21, 42-4, 48, 52
Ottokar II, 56, 58

Palatinate, the, 60, 64, 128-31, 135-6, 140, 148, 152
Palatinate, War of the, 152ff.
Papal State, the, 17, 26, 32, 39, 43-4
Paris, Treaty of, 200
Particularism, 7-8, 64, 70, 208-9, 211-2
Party Politics, 219-20
Peipus, Lake, 76, 80, 82
Peter the Great, 157
Pfizer, Paul, 210
Philip II of France, 45, 88
Philip III of Spain, 131-2

Philip of Burgundy, 96, 100
Philip of Heinsberg, 38
Philip of Hesse, 120-2
Philip of Swabia, 42-3, 48
Picardy, 89, 97, 101
Pilica, the, 173
Piedmont, 73
Poland, 16, 26, 79, 82-4, 86, 90, 98, 102-3, 143, 150, 156-7, 168, 172-4, 176, 199, 206, 222
Poltava (battle), 156
Pomerania, 78-9, 141, 156-7, 159-60, 164
Posen, 206
Pragmatic Sanction, 161
Prague, 132, 139-40
Prague, University of, 87, 107
Printing, 108
Promotion of Commerce, Society for the, 208-9
Protesters, 119
Provence, 67
Prussia, 79, 84, 86, 98, 157, 159ff., 191, 195ff., 204ff., 224ff.
Pufendorf, Samuel, 141
Pyrenees, Treaty of the, 148-9

Quinet, Edgar, 227

Railways, 213
Rastatt, Treaty of, 154
Ravenna, Archbishop of, 20
Ravensberg, 159, 166
Regensburg, 72
Regna, 6
Reichenau (abbey), 11-12
Reichenbach, Treaty of, 170, 173-4, 176, 178, 204
Reichskammergericht, 111
Reichsverweser, 232
Reinald of Dassel, 38
Restitution Edict, 137
Reuss, 65, 211
Reutlingen, 70
Reval, 79, 81
Revolution of 1848, 230-1
Rex Romanorum, 19
Rhenish League, 71, 147
Rhine, the, 14, 15, 59, 88, 148-50, 157, 174ff., 206-7, 226
Rhine, Confederation of the, 179
Richard of Capua, 33
Richard of Cornwall, 55
Richelieu, 138, 141
Riga, 79
Rittergüter, 10
Robert of Apulia, 33
Roman Empire, 19, 20, 23, 38

Rome, 17-19, 25-6, 35, 38, 40, 118
Rostock, 107
Rothenburg, 70
Roumania, 82, 85
Rückert, 193
Rudolf I of Habsburg, 56-8, 61-2, 94
Rudolf II, 129, 131
Rügen, 156
Rupert of the Palatinate, 67, 71
Russia, 156-7, 167ff., 171, 173, 179-80, 183, 198-9, 202, 206
Russia, White, 98

Saale, the, 16, 76
Sachs, Hans, 109
St Gallen (abbey), 11
Salerno, 18, 35
Samogitia, 85
Savoy, 88
Saxons, 3
Saxony, 6, 7, 51, 60, 63, 78, 128, 130, 134, 137, 139, 156-7, 167, 195, 211, 222
Scharnhorst, 196, 217
Schill, 193, 195
Schiller, 188, 191, 194
Schism, Great, 107
Schlegel, Friedrich, 192
Schleswig-Holstein, 233
Schmalkald Confederacy, 119ff., 133
Schmidt, Michael Ignatz, 190
Schneckenburger, 226
Schonen, 82
Schopenhauer, 191
Schwarzburg, 209
Schwarzenberg, Prince, 232
Sempach (battle), 66
Septimer (pass), 19, 25
Serbia, 85
Seven Years' War, 162, 166ff.
Sicily, 18, 33, 38-42, 43-48, 73
Siena, 68
Sigismund, 61, 68, 85, 89, 94
Sigismund of Tirol, 89, 95
Silesia, 78, 84, 90, 161ff.
Slavs, 16, 77-8
Spain, 100, 114, 122, 129, 131-2, 138-40, 143, 148-9
Spanish Succession, War of, 154ff.
Spires, Diet of, 118-9
Spoleto, 43
Staufen, House of, 47ff.
Stein, Baron, 194, 196, 202, 217
Stettin, 160
Stralsund, 138, 156
Stralsund, Peace of, 82
Strassburg, 70, 72, 89, 142, 151ff., 199, 211

Strassburg, Bishop of, 12
Styria, 51, 56, 58-9, 65, 94-5
Swabia, 6, 7, 51, 56, 71-2, 221
Swabian Union, 100
Swabians, 3
Sweden, 138ff., 150, 156-7, 159, 172
Switzerland, 94-5, 142, 202

Tannenberg (battle), 86
Tauroggen, Convention of, 196
Teschen, Treaty of, 169
Teutonic Order, 79, 83-6, 102, 159
Teutons, 1-2
Theutonicum (regnum), 4
Thirty Years' War, 67, 134ff., 156, 184, 203
Thorn, 173
Thorn, Peace of, 86, 102
Thuringia, 56, 58-9, 64, 92
Thuringians, 3
Tilly, 136
Tilsit, Treaty of, 180, 183
Tirol, 58, 94, 99
Toul, 88, 122
Towns, 69ff.
Trade Routes, 25, 70, 80
Transylvania, 202
Trent, Council of, 130
Trier, 5, 61
Trieste, 66
Truchsess, Gebhard, 130
Tübingen, 107
Turenne, 140
Turks, 119, 127, 150ff., 156-7, 171
Tuscany, 32, 40-2, 43, 99

Ukraine, 82, 98
Ulm, 70, 72
Ulrich of Württemberg, 101
United Diet, 229
Urban II, 35, 39

Venice, 25-6, 40, 73, 99, 103
Verden, 141
Verdun, 88, 122
Verona, 19, 26
Vienna, 97, 119, 149, 151-2
Vienna, Congress of, 199, 200, 206, 210-1, 216
Vienna, University of, 107
Vistula, the, 79, 83, 168, 173, 199, 206, 208
Völkerwanderung, 1
von Arnim, Achim, 191-2
von Dornberg, Baron, 195
von Eues, Nicolas, 110
von Falersleben, Hoffmann, 226
von Humboldt, Wilhelm, 199

INDEX

von Hutten, Ulrich, 109, 113
von Schön, Heinrich, 201-2
von Steinbach, Erwin, 188
von Sybel, Heinrich, 21
Vosges, the, 14

Wagrians, 77
Waldeck, 65
Waldemar IV (of Denmark), 82
Waldemar the Victorious, 79
Wallenstein, 136-8
Warsaw, 173
Waterloo (battle), 197, 216
Weimar, 222
Weissenburg, 211
Weissenburg (abbey), 11, 12
Welsers, the, 74
Wenceslaus of Bohemia, 61
Wends, 16, 17, 27, 76-7, 78
Weser, the, 141, 156, 208
Westphalia, 130-1, 179-80
Westphalia, Treaty of, 140-3, 145, 147-8, 159
Wetterau, 72
Wettin, House of, 92

Wetzlar, 70
White Mountain (battle), 134-5
Wichmann of Magdeburg, 38
William of Holland, 55
Wimpfeling, Jacob, 109
Winckelmann, 187
Wittelsbach, House of, 85, 92
Wittenberg, 107
Worms (battle), 71
Worms, Concordat of, 36, 37
Worms, Diet of, 116
Worms, Edict of, 118-9
Worms, Synod of, 34
Wrangel, 140
Württemberg, 14, 63-4, 92, 101, 120, 140, 145, 179, 195, 202, 211, 215, 222

Yorck, General, 196

Zenta (battle), 153
Ziegenhain, 92
Zollverein, 212-4, 227
Zürich, 94

For Product Safety Concerns and Information please contact our EU
representative GPSR@taylorandfrancis.com
Taylor & Francis Verlag GmbH, Kaufingerstraße 24, 80331 München, Germany

www.ingramcontent.com/pod-product-compliance
Lightning Source LLC
Chambersburg PA
CBHW071820300426
44116CB00009B/1383